# CHANNEL CATFISH FEVER

### An In-Fisherman® Handbook of Strategies

# CHANNEL CATFISH FEVER

## An In-Fisherman®
## Handbook of Strategies

Doug Stange
Steve Quinn
Toad Smith

*Published by*
In-Fisherman® Inc.

# In-Fisherman® Corporate Educational Publications
## Book Division

Director *Al Lindner*
Publisher *Ron Lindner*
General Manager *Dan Sura*

Executive Editor *Doug Stange*
Editor *Steve Quinn*
Managing Editor *Joann Phipps*
Editorial Assistant *Rose Baldwin*
Production Manager *Bob Ripley*

## CHANNEL CATFISH FEVER

Compiled by *Steve Grooms*
Cover Art by *Larry Tople*
Edited by *Doug Stange, Joann Phipps, Steve Quinn*
Layout and Design by *Ted Tollefson*
Typesetting by *Nelson Graphic Design*
Litho Prep by *Quality Graphics*
Printed by *Bang Printing*


ISBN 0-780929 384047 (Volume 6)

## God, Country, Family,
## Friends, Apple Pie, Baseball, Blue Cheese . . .
## and Catfish.

ONE CRISP AUTUMN MORNING, A GRASSHOPPER WAS SITTING AT A ROADSIDE, SNIFFING THE LAST ROSE OF SUMMER, WHEN AN ANT CAME BY CARRYING A KERNEL OF CORN.

"I'LL LET YOU SMELL THIS ROSE IF YOU'LL GIVE ME A BITE OF THAT CORN", SAID THE GRASSHOPPER.

"WHAT WERE YOU DOING LAST SUMMER WHILE I WAS BUSY HARVESTING?", INQUIRED THE ANT.

"CHIRPING AND SINGING", SAID THE GRASSHOPPER.

"YOU SHOULD HAVE PREPARED YESTERDAY FOR THE WANTS OF TODAY", SAID THE ANT, AS HE STARTED ACROSS THE ROAD.

"AND YOU SHOULD HAVE STOPPED AND SMELLED THE ROSES", SAID THE GRASSHOPPER, AS A PASSING AUTOMOBILE SQUASHED THE ANT AND GROUND THE CORN TO A FINE, PALATABLE MASH WHICH SUSTAINED THE GRASSHOPPER THROUGH ANOTHER DAY OF CHIRPING AND SINGING.

*A true conservationist is a man who knows that the world is not given by his fathers, but borrowed from his children.*

John Madson

# TABLE OF CONTENTS

For three decades we've been privileged to fish with most of the best fishermen in the world—experts on bass, experts on walleye, experts on trout, muskie, and pike.

Doug Stange, Toad Smith, and Steve Quinn rank among that select group of fishermen, as experts on channel catfish.

The best catfishermen in the world? Perhaps. Certainly the unique perspective offered by the three will push catfishing into a new era, changing fishermen and how they fish, manufacturers and the products they offer, and fishing educators and how they teach catfishing.

This is a salute to the three men who made this book possible. Good reading, good fishing, and God bless.

*Al Lindner, Director*
*Ron Lindner, Publisher*

## Chapter 1

# THE CHANNEL CATFISH

### America's Favorite Mystery Fish

Let's talk catfish. It's about time somebody did.

The channel cat is one of the most fascinating and exciting gamefish in North America. It's also our most overlooked and misunderstood gamefish, a fish of mystery and contradiction.

For starters, consider that cats are at once one of North America's most popular fish and our most neglected fish. How can that be? How can a fish be both ignored and extremely popular?

We know the channel catfish is enormously popular. The 1985 survey of fishing-, hunting-, and wildlife-associated recreation by the U.S. Fish and Wildlife Service reported that catfish and bullheads were the second most pursued fish group in this country, following the far more highly publicized black bass. Surprised? Many people were.

The survey shows there were approximately 13 to 15 million catfishermen in 1985. Catfish came in a close third in that rating, with black bass first and pan-

# National Fishing Surveys

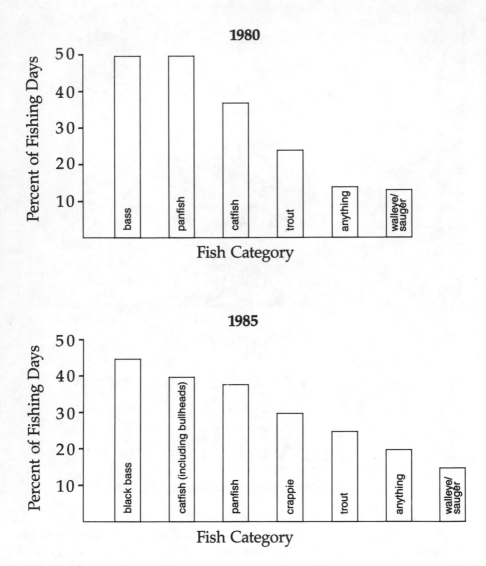

The U.S. Fish and Wildlife Service, in conjunction with the Bureau of the Census, conducts a national survey of fishing-, hunting-, and wildlife-associated recreation every five years. Results show trends in economic, sociological and angling characteristics of American fishermen.

These bar graphs illustrate data from 1980 and 1985. In 1985 the catfish category included bullheads, while they were in "panfish" in 1980. Similarly, crappie were apparently included in "panfish" in 1980.

Catfish popularity remains high. Since "panfish," even excluding crappie and bullheads, comprises many locally popular species, it's likely that channel catfish trail only largemouth bass in nationwide species popularity.

## Catfish Statewide Popularity

*Peak catfish popularity occurs in the Mid-South and Midwest. Their popularity in Utah, Arizona, and Colorado, where their original distribution was limited, is noteworthy. They're moderately popular in the Southeast and localized states in the Midwest, Mid-South and Northeast. In other areas, they're not so popular, although they don't occur in Rhode Island or Maine. And they're not present in most drainages of New England or the Mid-Atlantic states.*

*Channel cats occur in parts of Manitoba, Ontario, and Quebec, but Canadian surveys indicate they don't rank high in province-wide popularity.*

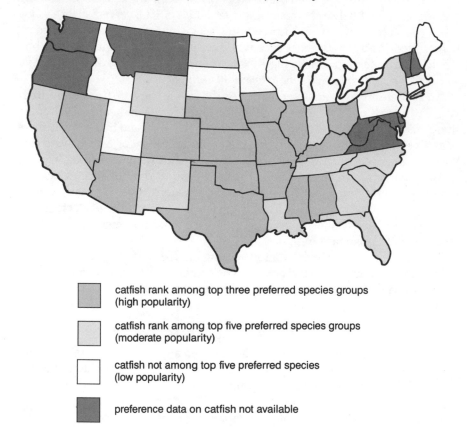

catfish rank among top three preferred species groups (high popularity)

catfish rank among top five preferred species groups (moderate popularity)

catfish not among top five preferred species (low popularity)

preference data on catfish not available

fish second. Obviously, catfish in general and channel cats in particular are near the top of the chart with U.S. anglers.

A case can be made for ranking the channel cat America's number-one fish. Largemouth bass receive a tremendous amount of promotion. Catfish don't. Sometimes people answer what they think they're supposed to in surveys. Bass may be "the" answer in those cases. Catfish are also considered panfish in some regions, another reason they may not get a fair showing in the ratings.

Certainly, in some midwestern states (Iowa, Kansas, Nebraska, and parts of Illinois), catfish are the top choice of anglers. And in Mississippi, for example, a larger percentage of anglers caught catfish than any other fish group, an example that probably applies to many other states, even though surveys don't exist to prove it.

In other words, if the channel cat isn't "America's favorite fish," it's certainly second-favorite.

Yet somehow catfishing has a curious status as an almost invisible activity. Look at outdoor magazines to see how many catfish articles they run. You'll have a tough time finding *any*. It's almost as if catfishing doesn't exist.

Check the library for books on catfish. Or check a book like *McClane's Game Fish Of North America* for its coverage of catfish (one of our most popular fish, remember). Authors A. J. McClane and Keith Gardner include a chapter on landlocked salmon (less than 5% of North America's anglers fish for salmon) and even cover whitefish (probably less than 1/10th of 1%), yet catfish (at a whopping 36%) aren't in the book! Until recently, television fishing shows ignored catfishing, too. And frankly, bass pros who toss in a token cat show or two have a hard time appearing convincing—"*Well, gol-ley, it's a, well, uh, catfish! Pass those fancy fish grippers so I don't have to touch this thing!*"

And where are the catfish seminars? And who are the "pro fishermen" in the world of catfishing? And how many catfish clubs have you heard of? Although there are instructional videos about muskies, a fish pursued by a small number of anglers, we haven't seen even one instructional video for catfish. And have you ever seen a "catfish rod" or a reel sold specifically for catfishing?

Trout, largemouth bass, walleyes, striped bass, and other species have entire magazines devoted to them, whereas catfish aren't covered by even one decent article in most magazines. Even the scientific community neglects catfish, conducting relatively little research on them except in the context of aquaculture (commercial catfish farming).

Strange. Make that tragic! Millions of anglers fish catfish, yet catfishing remains almost an underground activity. The catfish is a mystery wrapped in contradiction, a well-known secret, our best-loved invisible fish.

It's time to change that, and we mean to try.

## *CATFISH MYTHS*

Unless you are an exceptionally well-informed angler, many of the things you know about catfish are wrong. The list of catfish myths is almost identical to the list of common knowledge about catfish.

*Myth: Catfish are slow, sluggish fish.*

Catfish, including channel cats, are impressive predators that can capture prey with quickness and precision, much like bass, trout, or walleyes. Like other gamefish, catfish also routinely move slowly and take food cautiously, but move with great speed when it's the most effective way to feed. Cats have sleek bodies built for speed; they're more streamlined than largemouth bass, for example. A crankbait can't be retrieved too fast for a catfish to overtake it. That hardly sounds like a "slow" fish.

*Myth: Catfish are stupid.*

Fish intelligence is difficult to measure, but catfish certainly do not have second-rate brains. In fact, in one test of catfish learning ability, in a master's thesis by Gordon Farabee, catfish rated higher than other fish in learning ability. Farabee rated fish in three categories of learning ability. The slowest and poorest performers were famous sportfish: rainbow trout and pike. The middle category (fish of average ability to learn) included bass, fish famous for

*Where are the catfish seminars? Who are the pro catfishermen? How many catfish clubs have you heard of?*

In-Fisherman staff members annually speak to thousands of people at seminars across North America. The fish topics have always been bass, walleyes, pike, muskies, and crappies, in part because show organizers have assumed that's what folks were interested in—the "popular" "glamor" species, you know. But during 1989, Doug Stange hit the trail to talk catfishing in Cincinnati, Kansas City, and Minneapolis. In each case, crowds enthusiastically greeted some of the same information offered in this book. In Minneapolis, the heart of bass-walleye-pike-muskie country, show officials were amazed to have at least 1,000 catfishermen attend.

Presently we know of no "pro catfishermen" unless Toad counts, but catfish clubs exist in many areas where catfishing is popular. The Ocheydan Catfish Club, of Ocheydan, Iowa, for example, meets monthly to talk catfishing and conservation and plan club outings. They make sure that area kids have a chance to (cat)fish by funding fishing days and stocking ponds.

The fishing world hasn't been completely without fishermen willing to serve as ambassadors for catfish. Texan Russell Tinsley has written his fair share on catfishing. And well-known writer and fisherman, Dan Gapen (pictured here), has done his part by lecturing about catfish at seminars and sportshows, and by writing a book, How To Fish Catfish.

# Head of the Class

*Gordon Farabee, a fisheries biologist with the Missouri Department of Conservation, studied the comparative learning ability of fish species as part of his master's thesis at the University of Missouri. Fish in test tanks were trained to avoid a light source by administering a mild electric shock to them.*

*After a training period, groups of fish of each species were scored for correct responses. Farabee grouped the species into high, intermediate, and low categories according to their average scores.*

| High | Intermediate | Low |
| --- | --- | --- |
| channel catfish 90%<br>bigmouth buffalo 78%<br>carp 67% | spotted bass 51%<br>smallmouth bass 44%<br>bullhead 42%<br>largemouth bass 41% | rainbow trout 30%<br>northern pike 30%<br>bluegill 26% |

*Channel cats also demonstrated greater memory than other species. Farabee noted that the trout score might not be comparable because rainbows appeared unsettled in test tanks. Because of their need for cold water, they were kept in a different facility.*

learning to avoid anglers. Catfish, bigmouth buffalo and carp learned the quickest and achieved the highest overall scores. And what fish ranked at the top? The channel cat!

*Myth: Catfish are primitive.*

What's primitive? This fuzzy value judgement has little scientific basis. Catfish include slightly more than 2,000 of the more than 20,000 fish species known to science. Catfish inhabit six continents and many marine environments. Their diversity of size, form, and behavior are equalled by no other fish group. In terms of having a highly developed sensory system, catfish are the most advanced gamefish in North America. The catfish is one huge swimming sensory organ, amazingly in tune with its habitat. It can sense the presence of prey or predators not detected by other species. Primitive hardly fits an animal so intelligent, versatile, and sensitive to its surroundings.

*Myth: Catfish are bottom feeders that exist mainly on carrion.*

Catfish are omnivores, meaning they eat just about anything. They often feed on the bottom, as lake trout and pike do, but also attack prey at mid-depths and even feed on the surface. Cats in most reservoirs primarily feed on shad. They eat dead shad off the bottom when dead shad are available, but at other times will stalk and prey on free-swimming shad. Commercial catfish "farmers" often feed floating pellets to catfish, which wouldn't make sense if cats fed only on the bottom. In areas of the country where mulberry trees lean over rivers, catfish hang below the surface to snack on drifting berries, just as rising trout might. Opportunist, thy name is catfish.

*Myth: Catfish are crude creatures capable of living in the poorest water.*

Like most gamefish, catfish require adequate water quality. True, they can feed in turbid, flooded rivers where other fish can't. And cats can tolerate lower dissolved oxygen levels as well as an unusually wide range of temperatures. Those facts are misleading about the quality of water catfish need to thrive.

## A Catfish's Revenge

*Catfish and bullheads are famous for their sharp dorsal and pectoral spines, spikes, horns, or whatever you prefer to call them. The spines become somewhat blunted as fish age.*

*How dangerous is a "spining"? Bullheads and catfish do not have venom or poison glands associated with their spines. Close relatives, madtoms, do.*

*A spining causes infection that means redness, swelling, and pain. Shallow puncture wounds heal quickly if they are kept clean and exposed to air. No Band-Aids please. Deeper puncture wounds require medical attention if infection sets in.*

Cats do best in clean water. Since bullheads, close relatives of channel catfish, are amazingly tolerant of marginal water, people mistakenly assume catfish also thrive in foul water.

*Myth: The best catfishing occurs during the heat of summer.*

Catfish bite well in hot weather, especially at night or early morning, yet that's not always the best time to catch them. Peak fishing times often are associated with cool water. North-country anglers occasionally catch catfish through the ice.

*Myth: The best bait for catfish is the ripest, smelliest stinkbait.*

Rank, rotten baits catch catfish, but they usually aren't best. Our favorite bait is no stinkier than the baits commonly used for walleyes or pike. Anglers mistakenly assume that a bait foul smelling to humans is attractive to catfish. The chemistry of the human sense of smell, however, is different from the chemistry that allows a catfish to taste or smell a bait underwater.

*Myth: Catfish have poison that moves through their spines and infects careless fishermen.*

No poison gland or other source of poison exists in channel catfish, though a few related fish possess them. A small catfish, the madtom or "willow cat," has venom that can be painful. Bullheads and catfish have stiff, sharp pectoral and dorsal spines with no venom. Get stabbed by these spines and the wound is painful for the same reason any puncture wound hurts—puncture wounds often become infected. Venom isn't involved.

Myths, myths, myths!

Get the picture? We could go on and on about catfish myths. Catfish are badly misunderstood.

Keep in mind that largemouth bass were badly misunderstood 25 years ago. Only when bass tournaments focussed attention on bass were old myths placed under intense scrutiny. Modern bass fishing was born when the best bass anglers began to rethink the sport.

That's just beginning to happen with catfish. Catfishing stands today where bass fishing was 20 years ago. We think it's time to look at this fascinating gamefish with the sophistication and appreciation it deserves.

## THE UNIQUE CATFISH

Some gamefish are easy to admire, and some are not. Salmon amaze us with acrobatic leaps and ability to migrate thousands of miles across oceans.

If channel catfish jumped, perhaps they'd be as famous as other gamefish. Catfish rarely are used on the covers of magazines, yet if catfish leaped when hooked, they would more likely appear on covers. Catfish pull far harder than fish that leap, but pulling doesn't make a sensational photo.

Catfish also suffer from the unfair notion that they are ugly and potbellied. Cats are sleek, muscular, and well-proportioned. But many fishermen draw impressions from pictures of exceptionally large catfish. Hung from a rope, a big catfish's belly droops. But cats in water are streamlined and powerful. And about those barbels or "whiskers." Gee, Ron and Al Lindner have whiskers, too, and we don't think those guys look *too* ugly.

Catfish aren't as easy for some folks to admire as today's more glamorous fish. But get past stereotypes and catfish are amazing. They are the fish of the masses today, the glamor fish of tomorrow, as North America begins to understand them.

Catfish, far from being sluggish and crude, are extremely sensitive to their surroundings. The total of their sensory systems is *the most impressive* in the North American world of freshwater fish. Compared to cats, fish such as bass and trout are limited and...well, a bit primitive!

Every gamefish is adapted in special ways to function in certain environments. Basically, catfish are adapted to rivers, and river water can be murky for weeks on end. For catfish to function in such surroundings, they need information from many senses.

Logically, the sense of sight would not be important to fish adapted to a turbid environment. We do not think catfish have especially well-developed sight. But they have eyes and use them as a critical part of their feeding strategy whenever water's clear enough. In clear water, they probably are capable of seeing color.

The catfish's sense of hearing is highly developed. Cats are sensitive to sounds

# CHANNEL CATFISH

*World record channel catfish: 58 pounds.*

IGFA photo

## State Records

| State | Weight | Angler | Water | Year |
|---|---|---|---|---|
| Alabama | 42 lbs. 8 oz. | Fred M. Gay | Finks Lake | 1986 |
| Alaska | None | | | |
| Arizona | 35 lbs. 4 oz. | Wando L. Tull | Topock Marsh | 1952 |
| Arkansas | 31 lbs. 4 oz. | James D. Stiles | James McKeown Pond | 1987 |
| California | 48 lbs. 8 oz. | Bobby Caihoun | Irvin Lake | 1984 |
| Colorado | 33 lbs. 4 oz. | Russell Good | Nee Noshe Reservoir | 1973 |
| Connecticut | 11 lbs. 4 oz. | Henry C. Barber | Cedar Lake | 1988 |
| Delaware | None | | | |
| Florida | 44 lbs. 8 oz. | Joe Purvis | Lake Bluff | 1985 |
| Georgia | 44 lbs. 12 oz. | Bobby M. Smithwick | Altamaha River | 1972 |
| Hawaii | 43 lbs. 13 oz. | Dennis Miyamura | Lake Wilson | 1974 |
| Idaho | 31 lbs. | Lorraine Ravary | Snake River | 1975 |
| Illinois | 45 lbs. 4 oz. | Todd Baumeyer | Baldwin Lake | 1987 |
| Indiana | 37 lbs. 8 oz. | Randy Eugene Jones | Vanderburg City Lake | 1980 |
| Iowa | 31 lbs. | Kyle Gettschalk | Gravel Pit | 1986 |
| Kansas | 33 lbs. 12 oz. | Larry L. Wright | Kaw River | 1980 |
| Kentucky | 22 lbs. 5 oz. | Wallace Carter | Farm Pond | 1978 |
| Louisiana | None | | | |
| Maine | None | | | |
| Maryland | None | | | |
| Massachusetts | 26 lbs. 8 oz. | Dana R. Dodge | Ashfield Lake | 1989 |
| Michigan | 47 lbs. 8 oz. | Elmer Rayner | Maple River | 1937 |
| Minnesota | 38 lbs. | Terrence Fussy | Mississippi River | 1975 |
| Mississippi | 43.94 lbs. | Lester L. Gammill | Lake Tom Bailey | 1988 |
| Missouri | 34 lbs. 10 oz. | Gerald Siebenmorgen | Lake Jacomo | 1976 |
| Montana | 25.89 lbs. | Gordon Wentworth | Fort Peck Reservoir | 1984 |
| | 25.89 lbs. | Tom Hilderman | Fort Peck Reservoir | 1988 |
| Nebraska | 41 lbs. 8 oz. | John Cunning | Merritt Reservoir | 1985 |
| Nevada | 31 lbs. 1 oz. | Harry Stephens | Lahontan Reservoir | 1980 |
| New Hampshire | None | | | |
| New Jersey | 33 lbs. 3 oz. | Howard Hudson | Lake Hopatcong | 1978 |
| New Mexico | 28 lbs. | John H. Montgomery | Cochiti Lake | 1978 |
| New York | 28 lbs. | Richard L. Robertson | Allegeny River | 1984 |
| N. Carolina | 40 lbs. 8 oz. | P. P. Paine | Fontana Reservoir | 1971 |
| N. Dakota | 28 lbs. 3½ oz. | Duane Widme | Red River | 1987 |
| Ohio | 30 lbs. | Kenny Mauk | Ferguson Reservoir | 1987 |
| Oklahoma | 30 lbs. | Richard Sirmons | Washita River | 1974 |
| Oregon | 36 lbs. 8 oz. | Boone Haddock | McKay Reservoir | 1980 |
| Pennsylvania | 35 lbs. | Jim Rogers | Allegheny River | 1970 |
| Rhode Island | None | | | |
| *S. Carolina | 58 lbs. | W. H. Whaley | Lake Moultrie | 1964 |
| S. Dakota | 55 lbs. | Roy Groves | James River | 1949 |
| Tennessee | 41 lbs. | Clint Walters Jr. | Fall Creek Falls Lake | 1982 |
| Texas | 36 lbs. 8 oz. | Mrs. Joe L. Cockrell | Pedernales River | 1965 |
| Utah | 32 lbs. 5 oz. | LeRoy E. Mortenson | Utah Lake | 1978 |
| Vermont | 32 lbs. 4 oz. | S. Warren Kluger | Lake Champlain | 1974 |
| Virginia | 32 lbs. | Hugh Wyatt | Lake Chesdin | 1980 |
| Washington | 32 lbs. 8 oz. | Tom Peterman | Aspen Lake | 1987 |
| W. Virginia | 22.75 lbs. | Lester F. Hough | Farm Pond | 1975 |
| Wisconsin | 44 lbs. | Larry Volenec | Wisconsin River | 1962 |
| Wyoming | 23.17 lbs. | Alan Williams | Keyhole Reservoir | 1986 |

*Hook-and-line world record
State record list from Fresh Water Fishing Hall of Fame

# FLATHEAD CATFISH

*World record flathead catfish: 98 pounds.*

## State Records

| State | Weight | Angler | Water | Year |
|---|---|---|---|---|
| Alabama | 80 lbs. | Rick Conner Sr. | Alabama River | 1986 |
| Alaska | None | | | |
| Arizona | 65 lbs. | Pat Coleman | San Carlos Lake | 1951 |
| Arkansas | 67 lbs. | Ernie Merrill | Lake Millwood Dam | 1980 |
| California | 55 lbs. | Herbert Caldwell | Imperial Reservoir | 1980 |
| Colorado | None | | | |
| Connecticut | None | | | |
| Delaware | None | | | |
| Florida | None | | | |
| Georgia | 53 lbs. | Larry S. Smith | High Falls Lake | 1987 |
| Hawaii | None | | | |
| Idaho | 36 lbs. 4 oz. | R.L. (Bob) Zeller | Snake River | 1979 |
| Illinois | 60 lbs. 8 oz. | Roy Schwass | Lake Warren | 1980 |
| Indiana | 79 lbs. 8 oz. | Glen T. Simpson | White River | 1966 |
| Iowa | 62 lbs. | Roger Fairchild | Iowa River | 1965 |
| Kansas | 86 lbs. 3 oz. | Ray Wiechert | Neosho River | 1966 |
| Kentucky | 97 lbs. | Esker Carroll | Green River | 1956 |
| Louisiana | None | | | |
| Maine | None | | | |
| Maryland | None | | | |
| Massachusetts | None | | | |
| Michigan | 38 lbs. 2 oz. | John Kamyszek | Grand River | 1974 |
| Minnesota | 70 lbs. | John L. Robert | St. Croix River | 1970 |
| Mississippi | 65 lbs. 08 oz. | Wade Arnold | Pickwick Lake | 1987 |
| Missouri | 66 lbs. | Howard Brownfield | Truman Dam | 1987 |
| Montana | None | | | |
| Nebraska | 76 lbs. | Orville Sudbeck | Missouri River (snagging) | 1971 |
| Nebraska | 80 lbs. | William Swanson | Silver Creek (set line) | 1988 |
| Nevada | None | | | |
| New Hampshire | None | | | |
| New Jersey | None | | | |
| New Mexico | 78 lbs. | Jim Wilson | Ash Canyon | 1979 |
| New York | None | | | |
| N. Carolina | 62 lbs. 07 oz. | Royce Flippin | Yadkin River | 1987 |
| North Dakota | 29 lbs. 6 oz. | Kenneth Klein | Heart River | 1985 |
| Ohio | 76 lbs. 8 oz. | Richard Affolter | Glendening Lake | 1979 |
| Oklahoma | 66 lbs. | Nick Freling | Lake Spavinaw | 1970 |
| Oregon | 41 lbs. | Edward F. Moyer | Snake River | 1988 |
| Pennsylvania | 43 lbs. 9 oz. | Symour Albramovitz | Allegheny River | 1985 |
| Rhode Island | None | | | |
| S. Carolina | 61 lbs. 15 oz. | Cathy Shannon | Lake Marion | 1987 |
| S. Dakota | 54 lbs. | Harlin K. Horsley | Lake Francis Case | 1986 |
| Tennessee | 65 lbs. 8 oz. | Rickey D. Groce | Barkley Reservoir | 1982 |
| *Texas | 98 lbs. | William Stephens | Lewisville Floodgate | 1986 |
| Utah | None | | | |
| Vermont | None | | | |
| Virginia | 57 lbs. | Allan Robinette | South Holston | 1972 |
| Washington | None | | | |
| W. Virginia | 70 lbs. | L. L. McClung | Little Kanawha River | 1956 |
| Wisconsin | 65 lbs. | Michael J. Bellemore | Fox River | 1987 |
| Wyoming | None | | | |

*Hook-and-line world record
State record list from Fresh Water Fishing Hall of Fame

# BLUE CATFISH

*World record blue catfish: 97 pounds.*

IGFA photo

## State Records

| State | Weight | Angler | Water | Year |
|---|---|---|---|---|
| Alabama | 84 lbs. 12 oz. | Dennis Irvin Johnson | Wheeler Reservoir | 1988 |
| Alaska | None | | | |
| Arizona | 31 lbs. | Richard Lujan | Randolph Park. | 1970 |
| Arkansas | 86 lbs. 15 oz. | Kyle B. Searcy | Arkansas River | 1983 |
| California | 59.4 lbs. | H. Pravongviengkham | Irvine Lake | 1987 |
| Colorado | 20 lbs. 1 oz. | Joe Poss | Private Lake | 1976 |
| Connecticut | None | | | |
| Delaware | None | | | |
| Florida | None | | | |
| Georgia | 62 lbs. | Ralph H. Barbee Jr. | Clark Hill Lake | 1979 |
| Hawaii | None | | | |
| Idaho | None | | | |
| Illinois | 65 lbs. (Tie) | Ernest Webb | Alton Lake | 1956 |
| | 65 lbs. | Andrew Coats Jr. | Alton Lake | 1956 |
| Indiana | 65 lbs. 10 oz. | Ed Ravellette | White River | 1988 |
| Iowa | 30 lbs. 11 oz. | Steve Proper | Des Moines River | 1986 |
| Kansas | 82 lbs. | Preston Stubbs Jr. | Kansas River | 1988 |
| Kentucky | 100 lbs. | J. E. Copeland | Tennessee River | 1970 |
| Louisiana | None | | | |
| Maine | None | | | |
| Maryland | None | | | |
| Massachusetts | None | | | |
| Michigan | None | | | |
| Minnesota | None | | | |
| Mississippi | 53 lbs. 04 oz. | Robert Pharr | Mississippi River | 1988 |
| Missouri | 68 lbs. | Ralph Greenstreet | Missouri River | 1983 |
| Montana | None | | | |
| Nebraska | 100 lbs. 8 oz. | Raynold Promes | Missouri River (snagging) | 1970 |
| Nevada | None | | | |
| New Hampshire | None | | | |
| New Jersey | None | | | |
| New Mexico | 19 lbs. 2 oz. | Jimmy York | Elephant Butte | 1988 |
| New York | None | | | |
| N. Carolina | 69 lbs. 4 oz. | Randy Marion | Badin Lake | 1988 |
| N. Dakota | None | | | |
| Ohio | None | | | |
| Oklahoma | 80 lbs. | Ron Smith | Lake Texoma | 1980 |
| Oregon | None | | | |
| Pennsylvania | None | | | |
| Rhode Island | None | | | |
| S. Carolina | 86 lbs. 4 oz. | Ivan Earl Gaston | Cooper River | 1988 |
| *S. Dakota | 97 lbs. | Edward B. Elliott | Missouri River | 1959 |
| Tennessee | 68 lbs. | Homer Parton | French Broad River | 1983 |
| Texas | 71 lbs. | Sammie Roberson | Livingston Lake | 1986 |
| Utah | None | | | |
| Vermont | None | | | |
| Virginia | 45 lbs. 8 oz. | Frank Beavers Jr. | Rappahannock River | 1989 |
| Washington | 17 lbs. 12 oz. | Rangle Hawthorne | Columbia River | 1975 |
| W. Virginia | None | | | |
| Wisconsin | None | | | |
| Wyoming | None | | | |

*Hook-and-line world record
State record list from Fresh Water Fishing Hall of Fame

in their environment—more so, in fact, than trout, bass, pike, or walleye. Wade into a catfish's pool and he likely knows you're there; he probably heard you when you were several pools away. He may still bite, but he's aware of you. Many a heavy footed catfisherman has unknowingly spooked his prey before wetting a line.

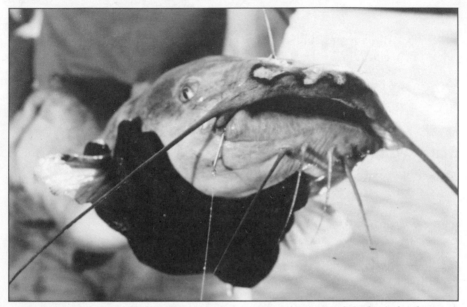

*Barbels. Eight total. Fine taste- and touch-sensing devices and the basis for the name ''catfish.''*

The sense of touch is highly developed in catfish, too, which makes sense for a fish that often lives around snags. Because cats have no scales, their entire bodies are soft and sensitive. In addition, they have barbels: eight whiskers of varying length—the basis for the name *cat*fish. Catfish investigate their surroundings with the help of their whiskers, though their entire bodies are sensitive.

Additionally, catfish have a more highly developed sense of taste and smell than other inland gamefish. You'll learn more about these remarkable abilities in another chapter.

Add it up, and you have a fish more impressive by far in its acute awareness of its surroundings than glamorous species like bass and muskies. Again, a catfish is like a big, swimming sensory organ, keenly sensitive to its environment.

No wonder the catfish is such an amazingly successful predator and potentially the most formidable

Personally, the catfish has always been a favorite of mine.

opponent swimming. And—can you believe it?—this is a fish scorned by some as sluggish, crude, and dumb! Some fish don't get respect, no matter how much they deserve it.

## THE IMPORTANCE OF CATFISH

The distribution map of channel catfish in North America (see Chapter 2) shows them widespread. Catfish originally occurred east of the Rocky Mountains, but now they're established through stocking in most western states.

But maps don't tell an important part of the story. To see that, you need to study maps of individual states to see where catfish can be found. Better yet, focus on the county level. An enormous number of counties have almost no fishing opportunities—except for channel cats!

Most of the glamorous species have more restrictive habitat requirements than catfish. Even though largemouth bass became widespread, thanks to the creation of impoundments and farm ponds, they can't live in nearly as many places as catfish. Walleyes, now being stocked in many new waters, are even more fussy about habitat. Even most panfish species, by their requirements for water and habitat, are more limited in distribution than catfish.

*Channel cats! Widely distributed, especially on a county by county level across North America, and a tough, determined battler that grows very large and is delicious fried, baked, broiled, chowdered, or casseroled.*

Some anglers can afford to travel hundreds of miles to impoundments or lakes where glamor fish occur in good numbers. Many more cannot. For millions of North American anglers, the only fishing they can enjoy must be reached on foot, by bicycle, or with a short drive.

Fact: In many areas of the country, catfish are the *only* sizable predator fish available to many anglers. If millions of factory workers, kids, farmers, ranchers, doctors, lawyers, school teachers, and accountants didn't have catfish to fish for, they wouldn't fish at all or would be limited to fishing much less often.

We've experienced this. As we grew up, we read about muskies, dreamed about arctic char, and made occasional trips to fish for walleyes and largemouth bass. But the fish we fished for, the only sporting gamefish readily available was catfish.

When we were kids learning to fish, we appreciated catfishing as a fairly simple act that didn't require expensive gear. A kid with little change in his jeans from lawn-mowing jobs could afford a rod and reel, and a few sinkers and hooks. Catfish were close at hand and affordable.

And what sort of experience did we have trying to catch catfish on our little creeks and weedy ponds? It was *fishing*—the mystery of luring a canny creature into making a mistake. We looked at a river's surface and tried to guess what existed below. We probed the bottom with sinkers, trying to understand it's shape. We learned about current and how it affects fish behavior. We experimented with baits and learned to set hooks. And then, when it went well, we thrilled at fighting a fish that pulls as hard as any fish in North America.

> *Some men fish all their lives without knowing it isn't really the fish they are after.*
> Henry David Thoreau

It wasn't *just catfishing*, it was *fishing*. We might have been influenced by the prejudices of the outdoor press into wishing we were on other waters fishing for other fish, but when we forgot those prejudices we experienced the joys of one of fishing's purest, most potent forms. Today, we realize how vital and influential those early experiences were and how important they remain today.

Why are catfish so important? They provide fishing—excellent fishing if you remove biases—for millions of anglers who have no other access to fishing. In particular, catfish often serve as "entry" fish for millions of kids. Thanks to the ubiquitous catfish, those kids have the opportunity to know and love fishing, a source of healthy fun for a lifetime.

Through fishing, kids learn to care about the natural world, the world that sustains us. Yet modern society hides that fact from us, communicating instead the idea that we can endlessly pollute and alter the environment without suffering consequences. Increasingly, too, we live in a society with unrealistic views of animals and how they depend upon their environment. Can we help but forget that we are animals too, with our own inescapable habitat requirements that differ little in final analysis from needs of other animals?

> *When man's aware of beauty and the worth of his resources, he will naturally work to keep up what he has and improve what is damaged. Then conservation becomes a way of life.*
> Gerald Lyons

We need a connection to nature's world. For many, the most available way to make that connection is by fishing for catfish. We need recreation, too, a chance to exchange the hustle and bustle of the work-a-day world for the peace and quiet solitude of a lake, river, or stream. Finally, catfish are nutritious, delicious, and renewable, too, if harvested wisely.

Today, more than ever, this world needs catfish.

## CAT MEN

Catfishermen, like catfish, often are ignored, even mocked by fishing snobs. Cat men are often characterized as low-class folks fishing with crude tackle and techniques for low-class fish. That stereotype of catfishermen isn't flattering.

One reason few books and articles are written about catfishing may be that big-city editors of fishing magazines think "catfishermen don't read." Why should catfishermen read outdoor magazines that don't include articles that talk to them? Catfish get two kinds of press: no press and bad press.

By now, we hope you understand that the catfish stereotype is just as wrong as it could be. If you are a dedicated cat man, you either didn't believe catfish were crude or you didn't care. Most likely, you didn't care. You knew you liked catfish and catfishing, and to heck with snobs who thought you shouldn't! We hope, though, that you'll discover you've been pursuing one of the most remarkable predator fish in the world. Hold your head high!

And what about the stereotype of catfishermen? Are they simple, crude folks?

Based on years of contact with them, we think catfishermen are unique. They aren't simple people, but people who know how to enjoy simple pleasures. They're catfishermen, in spite of prevailing prejudices against cats. Some get angry when catfish are scorned. Others don't understand why they enjoy a fish that's supposed to be second-rate. But they're mature enough to accept that they enjoy catfish.

Catfishermen don't worry about commanding the prestige of corporate moguls, at least not while they're catfishing. Perhaps that's why it's natural for them to enjoy a fish that people with supposedly more conventional tastes can't respect. Cat men tend to be straightforward folks with a sense of "what it's all about." You don't have to be a country boy to fall into that category. It's a matter of attitude. When cat men look at more "glamorous" forms of fishing—today's frenetic, high-tech bass fishing—they can't help feeling it's a little abnormal, too far removed from the pure pleasure of fishing.

THE TROUTIN' MAN    THE BASSIN' MAN    THE CATFISHIN' MAN

Cat men as a group aren't hooked on doing what they're "supposed" to do. They may or may not own $15,000 bass boats, but they usually don't fish contest style. And when they do, it's because they want to: it feels right; it's not because the world demands it. All they ask is a river, a rod and a few quiet hours of trying to catch catfish.

Catfishermen love catfishing. That's the basic truth, and cat men respect basic truths.

The only part of the stereotype about catfishermen that seems true is the claim they fish in simple, even crude ways.

Careful. Here again, the stereotype isn't altogether fair. Many crafty catfishermen really know their fish. Almost every town has an old river rat, the local champion cat man, the guy who takes big-old boss cats nobody else catches. He probably fishes with simple sophistication in tackle and technique.

Yet many catfish anglers *are* working with myths, crude tackle, and limited tactics that limit success. It's a shortcoming, the result of the way anglers, manufacturers, and the outdoor press ignore catfish. Basically, however, it isn't the fault of catfishermen that catfishing is stuck in stagnant backwater.

## WHAT THIS BOOK WILL DO

Catfishing needs attention! If we can sweep away myths surrounding catfish and how to catch them, we've accomplished an important task.

We want to do more. We want to make *you* a better catfisherman.

First, we'll introduce you to common-sense principles to help you understand this fish, his world and how to find him. All sorts of catfish holes exist, from mediocre to prime holes. We'll show how to identify the best ones. We'll tell you when catfish are most active and catchable.

*Bigger catfish, more of them, and more fun catching them!*

These principles aren't complicated. But neither are they understood by many catfish anglers.

We'll also cut through the confusion about catfish baits and rigs. Much of what we have to say about baits is common sense—plain talk. We'll offer proven rigs, plus a few you probably haven't seen. They work. We'll tell you which ones work best in which situations.

We'll explain effective stream tactics, too. For example, there are times to move and times to stick with a hole, times to drift a bait and times to let it sit in a prime location. We'll explain the differences.

We'll offer advanced tips on fishing for cats in many waters under many conditions.

The concepts and techniques here can improve your catfishing. We want you to catch more cats. But we want you to enjoy catfishing more, too—something more ambitious. We also want you to have a feeling for the future of catfishing, which sometimes means knowing when to gently release a catfish in healthy condition, and almost always means telling politicians who risk our natural resources and our fishing heritage to get their priorities in order.

We do *not* want to make catfishing complicated or convince you to buy a lot of expensive equipment. Catfishing is beautifully simple. We never want to lose sight of that. You wouldn't let us, anyway. Catfishermen have a sharp eye for the difference between fancy "bs" and useful wisdom. Let's talk plainly then, opening the sport to fresh approaches.

No radically different approach to your sport is required. Do no more than pay attention to the information about baits and you'll be a better angler. Do no more than learn to use one new rig and your catch rates can soar. Take what you want and stick with as many of your traditional approaches as you want. We believe, though, that you'll find tactics and tips to excite you and mark a turning point in your fishing.

A high goal? Sure. We hope, though, to generate new thinking and new respect for catfish and the anglers who love fishing for them.

Catfish and catfishermen deserve no less.

Zacker, arthritic and 80, a short, thin, almost frail man, gnarled as an old oak limb, speaks with a voice like rusty barbed wire. Doug Stange and Toad Smith know Zacker, an old-timer big-cat man, self-described as one of the crookedest ol' polecats you could ever meet.

Those were different times. Illegal trotline sets. Snagging. Netting. Anything to catch a cat. Beat the fish. Win. Income and family depended on it. High water, low water, good weather or bad. No matter. Catch fish. Catch catfish.

Yet old Zacker, who prefers to remain nameless for obvious reasons, tempered the catching with his brand of conservation. Never take every big cat from a hole; never waste a fish, the rules went. And when the market for cats was bad, he fished anyway and kept only enough for the family: trotline catch and release. He lived many a man's dream.

Zacker's reformed, more due to old age and changing times than guilt. But then "guilt" is a paradox, isn't it, for guilty by today's standards wasn't necessarily so by yesterday's. The letter of the law and certainly the spirit of it changes with the times, the people and the part of the country. We want to offer a bit of Zacker's perspective as we move through the book, just to stay in touch with the way things were, just to highlight our observations with the observations of a man who spent more time on good cat water and caught more catfish than perhaps any man alive.

Zacker rambling about catfishing today and heaven knows what else with Doug Stange in 1986:

"Crap," Zacker growls occasionally as he sits smoking a Camel on a bench on a porch overlooking a tiny creek and cows in a meadow behind his small home. Mostly he misses the way things were, or dislikes the way things are.

"Crap!" Mostly he hates being 80-something and not being on the river.

"Times ain't good," he'll say. "Dang 'em for changin' the river. No sand bars to hunt geese. No holes to corner big cats. Rivers run like plastic plumbing."

"No big cats left?" I asked.

"Course there are," he scowled as he turned toward me. He wanted to be heard. "Maybe more. But 'less you got a free runnin' river—not like these flowing reservoir pieces of crap—they're tougher to find. Course you can still catch 'em, but I'd as soon fish a smaller river now. You can see the holes, you know."

"Sport fishing!" he snorted to another question. "Times sure change. Now some folks say our fishing with set lines wasn't right. Now, you gotta race around in a fast boat and catch fish no bigger 'an we used for bait and win money. That's sport. Don't make sense. But that's fine. Seems to me that folks should just let other folks be, long as there's fish and game.

" 'Nother thing about set lines," he continued. "Big cats need quiet. Set lines work because some dink fisherman isn't standing around pawing the ground like some dumb jackass, or tossing his bait in 50 times an hour like some TV fisherman in women's pants.

"You don't wear those pants, do you?" he asked as he squinted at me.

"You mean shorts—cutoffs?" I asked. "Me?"

"Good for you!" he said. "Toss the dang bait in, let 'er set and shut up."

Jan Eggers

Chapter 2

# CATFISH HERE AND ELSEWHERE

## Fascinating Catfish Worldwide

The Good Lord must have loved catfish, or he wouldn't have made so many of them. Worldwide, there are over 2,000 species, not counting saltwater catfish, making catfish the most diverse group of fish in the world. Most places with rivers and reasonably warm weather have catfish. They're found on every continent except Antarctica—too cold. You'll find them in unlikely places: blind catfish living in cave springs; Himalayan catfish clinging to sheer rock walls in torrential mountain streams.

Without doubt, some catfish species—maybe some large or unusual ones—haven't been scientifically documented. Most likely, parts of Africa and South America have catfish that scientists haven't discovered.

North America has a meager collection of catfish, compared to other continents. Of 31 families of catfish in the world, we have only one family (Ictaluridae). Perhaps, though, we make up in quality what we lack in quantity. The three primary North American catfish species—blue, flathead, and channel—are among the world's largest.

Anyone planning to become a catfish biologist will not lack for important work. Most American catfish research has been limited to aquaculture and the investigation of multispecies commercial fisheries. More questions than answers remain about catfish in North America and worldwide.

## FASCINATING CATFISH AROUND THE WORLD

There's something intriguing and spooky about huge catfish lying in their holes in rivers. In many areas of the world, catfish are the biggest fish. In North America, blue and flathead catfish are exceeded in size only by sturgeon and alligator gar. Huge catfish aren't seen often, which adds excitement. Although catfish usually are nonviolent creatures of no threat to man, there are a few genuinely scary catfish you wouldn't want to meet under the wrong circumstances.

Catfish probably were abundant in Europe at one time. In particular, the Rhine and Danube Rivers were reputed to hold fantastic catfish. Now many portions of Europe's rivers are tragically polluted, and Europe's catfish population is a remnant.

The wels is the giant catfish of Europe. English angling author Stephen Downes described wels as "among the ugliest of fishes, and the most sinister. Pike are merely predatory; a wels rising from dark waters has a look of alien, powerful, profound malevolence. The great thick-lipped mouth gapes across the dark leathery face, the small wide-set eyes glitter in the flattened head; an Idi Amin among fishes."

The wels inspires such emotions partly because it can be huge. Wels 12 feet long weighing over 220 pounds have been caught in recent times, and there are reliable accounts of wels reaching 14 feet in length. Unverifiable historical accounts speak of far larger wels. Imagine a 16-foot-long 650-pound wels. Some scientists take these reports seriously.

The wels is part of the mythology of Europe. One story tells of an angler forced to run three miles along the treeless banks of the Rhone fighting a wels. Wels have been accused of eating dogs, small children, and even horses. You've heard of giant pike and muskies snatching swimming ducks; German waterfowlers have reported losing their retrievers to wels! The ancient author Aelian describes giant fish in the Danube taken on lines attached to teams of oxen. They probably were wels.

Southeast Asia has giant catfish, too. Most impressive is the Chinese plant-eating whale catfish of the Mekong River basin, which grows to at least 10 feet and 500 pounds. This inland giant has a huge broad head and a sharklike body. By some reports, the whale catfish is vulnerable to fishing pressure when it migrates upstream to spawn. Once widespread, whale catfish may now be endangered.

Another giant Asian catfish, the goonch of India is also found in Borneo and Sumatra. A predator, it reaches 6 feet and 200 pounds.

Africa has vast numbers of catfish, and few have been well researched. The

*A recent-day 200-pound-plus wels catfish.*

Jan Eggers

*Anglers of yesteryear display a wels weighing 280 pounds.*

most feared is the electric catfish, a sausage-shaped fish that can reach 4 feet and 50 pounds.

Electric catfish produce up to 500 volts in a sudden discharge, dangerous in a fish described as pugnacious. The electric catfish uses this jolt to stun prey.

Although these shocks are hazardous to humans, with the protection of insulated gloves and boots, some African fishermen catch electric catfish.

Electric catfish use their special ability in several ways. They emit charges of 5 to 10 volts to orient within their environment, sense the presence of prey, and communicate with other electric catfish. Perhaps North American catfish also emit very low-voltage electrical charges to communicate or sense their surroundings. Salmon use the earth's magnetic field to navigate. Sharks sense the electrical fields produced by prey. If any North American freshwater fish has this ability, we would bet catfish.

Africa is also home to the upside-down catfish, who swim with their ventral surface up. Some upside-down catfish have reversed shading—belly dark, back light. As is the case with smaller channel catfish, some emit a grunting noise audible in and out of water.

The labyrinth catfishes of Asia and Africa can live on atmospheric air for many hours, if they remain moist. Walking catfish prop themselves on their pectoral fins and move overland by wriggling their tails. This lets them leave stagnant pools during the dry season to seek water with oxygen. A predator, walking catfish capture frogs and other food during their walks. Some species of walking catfish reach 4 feet.

Steve Quinn and his brother Tom kept a few walking catfish in tanks, but not for long! They squirmed from the water, hooked their pectoral spines onto the tank top and walked off.

Asian walking catfish were introduced into Florida waters apparently by aquarium owners. They reproduced and threatened to expand their range, but currently do not seem to have adapted to many American waters.

South America has the world's largest collection of catfish. The Amazon River basin, with ten times the discharge of the Mississippi River, remains largely unexplored. The Amazon and its tributaries have large and intriguing catfish— armored catfish, for example. The armor is needed in jungle rivers where someone is always biting someone else.

The king catfish of the Amazon basin is the mighty *azulejo*, first written about less than 20 years ago. They have a massive yet sleek almost sharklike body with

*A Siamese fisheman with a whale catfish weighing about 250 pounds.*

the power to force their way up swift rapids. *Azujelos* of 250 pounds have been documented, but they grow much larger. The bigger ones simply aren't caught.

Another giant Amazon catfish is the *jau*, a stout fish that can weigh more than 200 pounds. Amazon natives describe its flesh as *remoso* (poisonous) and won't eat it. Yet the residents of southern Brazil have no such qualms; they import and eat *jau* from the Amazon.

The tiger shovelnose or *caparari* is a beautifully marked catfish that reaches a modest size of 5 feet and 90 pounds. Small *capararis* are sometimes imported as aquarium pets, though they have the bad habit of outgrowing tanks and eating tank mates.

The redtailed catfish, another Amazonian giant, also grows to nearly 200 pounds. Their bright red tails may be used to lure crabs from burrows. The omnivorous redtails eat fruits while swimming through the flooded forests during seasons when fruit is abundant.

*The half-inch long candiru catfish. Most feared fish in South America?*

The most feared fish in South America and perhaps the world? The piranha you say? Did you know that many piranha species eat fruit, not flesh? South American natives dread the infamous *candiru*, a small parasitic catfish that enters the urinary tract of men or women who urinate while bathing. Once inside, the *candiru* erects spines to prevent removal. The effect is every bit as painful as you'd expect. If the fish is not removed before it gets to the bladder, a *candiru* invasion can be fatal. Surgery is usually called for, which is difficult deep in the jungle, though there are reports that eating the fruit of a certain tree will purge a victim of the parasite.

# TOAD SMITH TALKS SOUTH AMERICAN CATFISH

*Toad with a 60-pound Azulejo.*

*Toad Smith:* "I don't know how to tell you what it's like. One minute it's civilization and the next minute you're there—a jungle river—and it hits you—this is it, the Beni, a tributary to the Amazon, a river so immense, so wild, so remote, so unexplored, that less is known about it and the fish that swim there than is know about the oceans.

" 'Aqui! Aqui!' the Indians say as the boat stops. *'Fish here!'*

*A bit of bait.*

*"Fish?* you ask yourself as you look at 3 pounds of jagged flesh hanging on a hand-forged shark hook connected to your 50-pound-test line. Geez! And the bait, that's another thing. We get our bait when a guide nonchalantly tosses a cotton-pickin' stick of dynamite into the river. One minute we got no bait; the next minute we got lots. And you realize this *is* how they sometimes get bait.

"And then you look around again, at the jungle, the river, and it hits you what the Indians keep saying: Fishermen come here to fish for namby-pamby stuff like piranha and dorado. The Indians do not understand this—the little rods or the fishermen who use them. Why would someone fish like that for those little fish?

"But you are here to fish for *their* fish—giant catfish. There has never been a fisherman here to fish for them. They tell you a giant cat has never been landed on sportfishing tackle. Furthermore, they tell you there never will be one landed—at least not a good one—a 200- or 300-pounder—and you know they are amused that you think you can do it. They will gladly watch, for it will make good stories.

"They are very curious though. And respectful. After all, someone should come from America to fish for these fish—should have come long ago. Piranha? Again, they do not understand the American fascination with piranha. What is the big deal? Respect their teeth when you lop their heads off before you eat them, sure, but you're more likely to be hit by a Coke can tossed from a UFO than be bitten by a piranha. Cripes, most piranhas eat fruit, for heaven sake.

"And so you have a generation of Bolivian Indians who think America means fishermen with fly-rods and fancy clothes—the *lovely* American. It hasn't occurred to them that there are Americans who spend as much time in the woods as they do. That there are

*The Caparari.*

Americans who wear $15 blue jeans until they get holes in them. That there are Americans who would rather spend 12 hours fishing than be in a bar telling stories by noon. That there are Americans who can shoot a bow, skin an alligator, or rig a set line just as slick as they can.

"And so I show them. And I tell them about hunting for bear and elk and moose, about guiding in Alaska and Montana, about fishing for muskies, salmon, American catfish, and about trapping. And suddenly I can tell they feel better about America.

"But just imagine you are there like I am there, ready to cast this side of fish flesh into this jungle river in Bolivia. The stories are there with you too: Stories of humans eaten by giant catfish. Stories of Indians drowned when the rope they use to fish for the cats tangles around a leg and they are torn from the boat. Stories of fingers lost to loops in line, and stories of trees uprooted when trot lines are tied to them at night.

"Suddenly my bait has settled *but it hasn't settled* and I instinctively set the hook and it's impossible, incredible, I just have time to realize that in 30 seconds I won't have any 50-pound-test line left on my Garcia 7000.

"Miscalculation: Twenty-two seconds later, minus 150 yards of line, I am relieved to still have a rod and a reel with a functioning drag. I count my fingers and other appendages. Next time we'll start the boat to follow the fish.

"The Indians have a way of fishing for the cats. They take a 2 X 4 and wrap a heavy cord around it. Don't ask me what the cord tests at. All I can tell you is that we tried to break it from a snag by wrapping it around the front of our 40-foot dugout canoe and running away from it with the 40 hp motor. Usually we pulled the snag out. I'd guess 3, maybe 400-pound test.

"They get the bait down, a cat grabs it, and they grab the board with two hands and set like they're curling a dumbbell. Cripes it's something. The board goes into the river, hopefully without a finger or leg tangled in the line. The board hits the water, spinning furiously and spraying water as cord peels off. Suddenly, Booosh! the board gets ripped under just like that barrel in the movie *Jaws*.

"Sometimes the board comes back up, sometimes not. If it's a 50-, maybe a 100-pound cat, they'll chase him and pull him in unless he gets into a snag. The big ones, well, you just never see the board again. Case closed.

"My biggest cat that first day is a 50 or so. Of course, most of the fish just *leave* when I set. Pretty soon I don't have any tackle left.

"About the cats. We're not talking channel cats, blues or flatheads like we have in America. I only know what the Indians called the cats. The big guy, biggest of the big is the *azulejo*. But there are these other critters, too. Big fish. Beautiful fish. Incredibly tough. I don't know how to tell you what it's like."

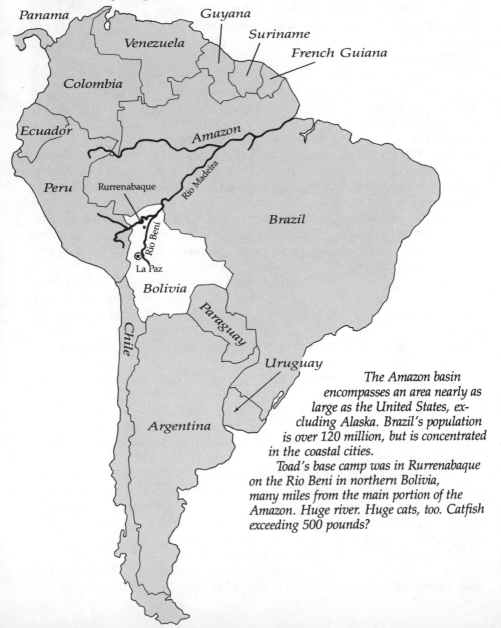

The Amazon basin encompasses an area nearly as large as the United States, excluding Alaska. Brazil's population is over 120 million, but is concentrated in the coastal cities.

Toad's base camp was in Rurrenabaque on the Rio Beni in northern Bolivia, many miles from the main portion of the Amazon. Huge river. Huge cats, too. Catfish exceeding 500 pounds?

## NORTH AMERICA'S CATFISH

North American catfish belong to the family Ictaluridae. Ictalurids have four pairs of barbels, smooth skin, an adipose fin and spines in front of short dorsal and pectoral fins. There are 37 species of ictalurids, ranging from the giant blue catfish to tiny madtoms and two species of blind catfish living in artesian wells near San Antonio, Texas.

## MADTOM

Joseph R. Tomelleri

Madtoms are the smallest ictalurids. These 2- to 4-inch-long fish have a very long attached adipose fin and a rounded tail. They resemble small bullheads. Being nocturnal, madtoms hide in rocks and crevices by day, then forage at night. They can be trapped in empty cans lowered into the water during the day, when they look for shady caves to hide in. Madtoms (sometimes called

## MADTOM DISTRIBUTION

Adapted from the *Atlas of North American Freshwater Fishes.* N. Carolina State Mus. Nat. Hist.

*Madtoms include 23 species distributed throughout most of the eastern United States, extending into the Red and St. Lawrence river drainages in Canada. The most common is the tadpole madtom. Another common madtom, the slender madtom is illustrated above.*

*The freckled, brindled, and speckled, named for their mottled coloration, are common in localized areas of the Southeast and Midwest. Many species occur in only a few river drainages and seventeen are legally protected or are species of special concern in states or provinces due to their threatened or endangered status.*

*Madtoms are small (maximum size 4 inches) and primarily nocturnal. Most are stream dwellers, but some species occupy ponds, lakes, and reservoirs. They feed primarily on aquatic insects in shallow riffles or other shallow habitat.*

"willow cats") are prized by some river fishermen as an attractive and durable bait, especially for walleyes.

Handle madtoms with care because they have venom sacs and grooved spines that inject venom into the hands or feet of the unwary. According to writer John Madson, "It is at least a hard bee sting; at worst, it's an almost electric jolt that produces a dull, throbbing ache that may persist for several hours." The madtom's spines and venom seem to give little protection against hungry predators, including its cousin, the channel cat. We've often found madtoms in the bellies of big channel cats.

## STONECAT

Stonecats are small, slender 6- to 8-inch catfish. Like madtoms, they have long attached adipose fins, but are shaped more uniform and streamlined. Also like madtoms, they are nocturnal.

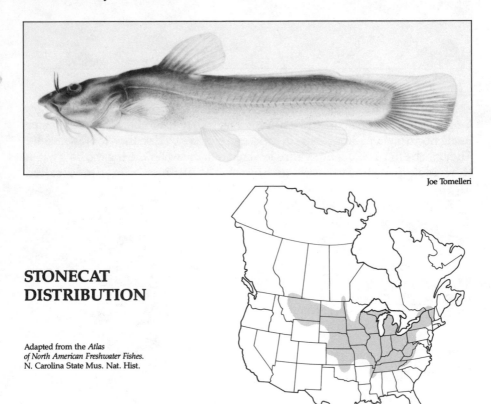

Joe Tomelleri

**STONECAT DISTRIBUTION**

Adapted from the *Atlas of North American Freshwater Fishes.* N. Carolina State Mus. Nat. Hist.

*The stonecat Noturus flavus is a small catfish (maximum size 12 inches), common in streams and rivers of the central United States north into southern Canada. They're also found in lakes including Lake Erie. They feed primarily on larval mayflies and other immature insects, and are in turn eaten by channel cats and other predators.*

*Stonecats are uniformly dark on the back; fins often are lightly colored at their margins. They spawn in rocky crevices in summer. Males guard clutches of 500 to 1,000 eggs.*

*Stonecats can inflict a painful, but not dangerous wound with their pectoral spines and associated poison glands.*

Bullheads are described in a separate section in this chapter. Briefly, there are three common species, yellow, brown, and black. Snail, flat, and spotted bullheads have limited distribution in the Southeast. All are chubby, square-tailed catfish rarely exceeding 3 pounds. Bullheads are widespread and common because they tolerate warm, poorly oxygenated water. They are active at night, among the easiest fish to catch, and delicious tasting when taken from cool, clean water.

How can you identify bullhead species? First, any catfish with a round or square tail—not forked—and the upper jaw equal or longer than the lower jaw is a bullhead. If the chin whiskers are cream colored, it's a yellow bullhead. If the chin whiskers are dark, look at the meaty part of the tail just before the fin begins. A light crescent mark at the base of the tail and uniformly dark coloration on the back means a black bullhead. Brown bullheads are mottled with dark blotches on a lighter background.

## Identifying American Catfish

The four large American catfish are the white, blue, flathead, and channel. To tell them apart, look at the tail, the head, and the anal fin (the fin just in front of the tail on the lower surface of the fish).

*Tail*: If the tail is not forked, it's a bullhead or flathead catfish. You'll probably know which on the basis of size alone, but there are better ways. If the lower jaw juts past the upper jaw, it's a flathead. If not, it's a bullhead. Flatheads have extremely wide, flattened heads; broad mouths; and a mottled brown skin.

If the tail is forked, it's a white, blue, or channel cat.

White catfish look much like channel cats. Both are streamlined, light-colored, and fork-tailed. But whites have a less deeply forked tail and a broader head and wider mouth.

There is a precise way to tell them apart.

*Anal fin*: If the anal fin of a fork-tailed catfish has less than 26 little bones (scientists call them rays), it's a white catfish. If the anal fin has a nearly straight outer edge and 30 or more rays, it's a blue catfish. If the anal fin has between 24 and 29 rays and is rounded on its outer edge, it's a channel catfish.

Large male channel cats and blues are often confused. Both are unspotted, with dark backs and lighter bellies; and both have deeply forked tails. The most obvious difference is the blue's anal fin, which is perfectly straight on the lower edge. Also, a side view of the head of a blue is more blunt and full than the head of the male channel cat. Blues are usually pewter color, sometimes with a bluish cast. Male channel cats are almost always slate-blue on top, with a cream-colored stomach that may be mottled with dark splotches.

The channel is a very streamlined catfish with a deeply forked tail and an anal fin with a rounded outer edge. Small channel cats usually are spotted. Larger channel cats lack spots, and the two sexes look distinctly different, as you'll see in a moment.

*Big blues and channel cats look a lot alike. Note, however, that the anal fin of the blue catfish (left) is longer and the outside edge straighter than the anal fin of the channel catfish, which is shorter and more rounded.*

## Bullheads

Horned pout, pout, chucklehead, butterball, yellow belly, wogger, paper skin, polly, wally, wooly willow cat, mud cat. A bullhead by any other name is still a bullhead, a close channel catfish relative. You'll certainly know a bullhead when you catch one, but you may have trouble distinguishing the three common species: brown, black, or yellow. Their ranges overlap, there may be several stocks or genetic variations of each species, and they produce hybrids. In short, brown bullheads may look like blacks or yellows, and so on. Never mind; in spring and early summer they all taste fine.

The following range maps were drawn from information from W.B. Scott and E.J. Crossman's *Freshwater Fishes of Canada*, and Milton Trautman's *The Fishes of Ohio*. These indicate basic ranges that have been widely extended by stocking.

### BLACK BULLHEAD

Probably the most commonly caught bullhead is the black bullhead, called "brown" bullhead by many fishermen because its coloration often is more olive-

Joe Tomelleri

green, brown or yellow than black. Scientific sources often use the pectoral spine to distinguish the bullhead species. Blacks have a smooth back edge on the pectoral spine, although hybrids (brown x black) may have a slight serration that catches the finger.

Sources confirm that blacks are the smallest bullheads, yet both the International Game Fish Association and the National Freshwater Fishing Hall of Fame list a mammoth 8-pound black caught in 1951 from Lake Waccabuc in New York as the all-tackle world record. Of thousands of Iowa specimens sampled, the largest black was a 15-incher that weighed almost 2 pounds. Of thousands of Ohio specimens, the largest black was a 16.8-incher that weighed 2 pounds 12 ounces.

Black bullheads generally prefer shallower, softer bottom areas than yellow or brown bullheads, although in spring their habitats may overlap. Black bullheads may live 8 or 9 years, although 3 or 4 years is more typical. Blacks usually are 8 to 11 inches long and weigh less than a pound.

World Record: 8 pounds — Kani Evans, Lake Waccabuc, New York, 8/1/51.

## BLACK BULLHEAD DISTRIBUTION

## BROWN BULLHEAD

The brown bullhead has different habitat requirements than the black bullhead, although during spring, the two species often inhabit the same backwater areas. Brown bullheads dominate in bigger, deeper, clearer bodies of water with harder bottom. Blacks dominate in shallower, more turbid waters with soft bottom. Hybrids (black x brown) bullheads are common, and popula-

Joe Tomelleri

tions may be almost entirely composed of hybrids.

Pure-strain brown bullheads are easy to distinguish when they are distinctly mottled—dark blotches on a light background. The spotted bullhead, found only in parts of Florida, Georgia, and Alabama, has light blotches on a dark background. Browns average slightly larger than black bullheads and, sources agree, generally reach larger maximum size. Of thousands of specimens sampled in Ohio, the largest was 18.8 inches long and weighed 3 pounds 14 ounces. Twenty-one-inch blacks have been reported from Florida, and anglers occasionally report 6- to 8-pound fish.

Like the black bullhead, the typical brown bullhead lives 3 or 4 years, measures 8 to 11 inches, and weighs less than a pound. The 8-pound world-record black bullhead may have been a brown bullhead or a hybrid.

World Record: 5 pounds 8 ounces—Jimmy Andrews, Veal Pond, Georgia, 5/22/75.

**BROWN BULLHEAD DISTRIBUTION**

## YELLOW BULLHEAD

The yellow bullhead is less common than either the brown or black bullhead and appears to do well only where it doesn't compete with them. Yellow bullheads prefer clearer water than black bullheads and more vegetated water than brown bullheads.

Joe Tomelleri

Yellow bullheads are distinguished by a long anal fin and chin whiskers that are yellow or white, never spotted or pigmented. Their coloration is much like the black bullhead, but generally more yellow.

Yellow bullheads average slightly larger than blacks and slightly smaller than browns. The largest Ohio specimen was 18.3 inches long and 3 pounds 10 ounces.

World Record: 4 pounds 4 ounces—Emily Williams, Mormon Lake, Arizona, 5/11/84.

**YELLOW BULLHEAD DISTRIBUTION**

## *AMERICA'S LARGE CATFISH*

### White Catfish

White cats are sometimes categorized as intermediate between catfish and bullheads. A big white weighs 8 pounds. The world-record white is 17 pounds 7 ounces. Whites not only look like channel cats, but they often live in the same rivers, although often in different sections.

Whites originally occurred in rivers along the Atlantic coast and the Florida Gulf Coast. Tolerant of somewhat salty water, whites often exist in lower stretches of rivers that hold channel cats in upper stretches. They've been stocked in western ponds and reservoirs. Whites are aggressive biters, which makes them popular in commercial "catch-out" or "pay" ponds.

## WHITE CATFISH DISTRIBUTION

## NORTH AMERICAN DISTRIBUTION OF RARE AND EXOTIC CATFISH

*Several species of* armored catfish *have been discovered in Florida, Texas, and Nevada. These Amazonian natives were imported as aquarium pets and illegally liberated. Populations are reproducing in some areas. The* walking catfish *is now common in parts of southern Florida, also the result of careless or malicious releases. This pugnacious cat grows to several pounds and preys on many fish species.*

*Two native cats, both similar to channel cats, are endangered or threatened because of habitat destruction and competition with other species. The* yaqui catfish *may have disappeared from American waters, but still exists in the Rio Yaqui drainage in Mexico.* Headwater cats *reportedly still occur in the Pecos River system of the Rio Grande drainage. They've disappeared from the Colorado River drainage.*

*The* toothless blindcat *and* widemouth blindcat *exist only in five artesian wells near San Antonio, more than 1/4 mile below the earth's surface. Larger widemouths eat the toothless species, along with subterranean shrimp and other invertebrates.*

 Distribution of armored catfish, *Hypostomus* spp.

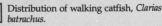 Distribution of headwater catfish, *Ictalurus lupus.*

Distribution of walking catfish, *Clarias batrachus.*

 Distribution of yaqui catfish, *Ictalurus pricei.*

Distribution of toothless blindcat, *Trogloglanis pattersoni* and widemouth blindcat, *Satan eurystomus.*

# Blue Catfish

Native distribution of blue catfish includes the major river basins of the Mississippi, Missouri, and Ohio in the central and southern United States, south into Mexico and Guatamala. Blues have been introduced into a few rivers and reservoirs, but their present range has shrunk, due to dam construction, pollution, and commercial fishing. They are the least common of large North American cats.

Blue catfish are the fish of legends. Nobody knows how big blue cats get. The official world record is 97 pounds, but catfish records probably don't reflect the

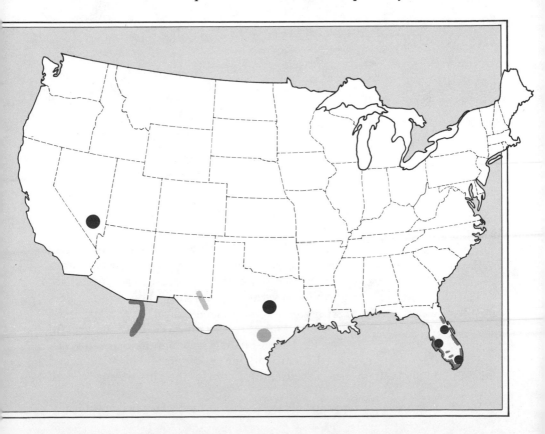

ultimate size of this fish, particularly in the past. Nineteenth-century reports of tremendous catfish in the Mississippi and Missouri rivers were probably blues.

Before 1900, blues over 100 pounds seem to have been common. A naturalist traveling Missouri in 1854 reported that "A lad caught on hook and line to-day a catfish weighing 136 pounds." When the U.S. Commissioner of Fish and Fisheries requested a large catfish from the Mississippi, the chairman of the Missouri Fish Commission went to the local fish market. He wrote: "Upon visiting the market this P.M. I luckily found two—one of 144 lbs., the other 150 lbs. The latter I ship to you by express." In spite of the "express" shipment, we wonder how a 150-pound blue smelled after being shipped from St. Louis to the East Coast in those early days of travel.

Other fabulous reports exist. Captain William L. Heckman reported a 315-pound blue catfish, caught from the Missouri near Morrison shortly after the Civil War. He wrote that it was common to catch catfish weighing from 125 to 200 pounds. Recently, 89-, 90-, and 117-pound blues have been taken from the Missouri River, where 40-pound blues are common.

Blue catfish favor big rivers and open, moving water. They use river areas with more current than other catfish. Blues also are reportedly more migratory than other catfish.

## BLUE CATFISH DISTRIBUTION

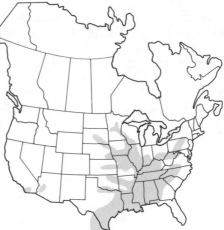

Blues, planted in many large reservoirs, grow, but probably don't reproduce. Most large hook-and-line blue catches in recent years have come from southeastern reservoirs.

Small blue catfish feed on fish, crayfish, clams, mussels, and immature aquatic insects. Larger blues forage on other fish—carp, sheephead, bullheads, and shad.

The In-Fisherman Master Angler Awards program shows how often anglers misidentify catfish. When an angler submits a "channel cat" over 30 pounds, we automatically suspect it's a blue. Many are, as a photo check of the anal fin proves. Of course, we also see large male channel cats identified as blue cats. Their anal fins make it easy to tell them apart, but people are fooled by the forked tails common to both species. The scientific name for the blue means "forked (tail) catfish."

Because big blues are rare and solitary, few fishermen today fish specifically for them. Some are taken on trotlines and jug lines baited with small fish, especially oily fish such as shad and skipjack herring. A few are taken by "noodling," which involves wading a river and groping for fish in holes in riverbanks. If a 315-pound blue still exists in American rivers, beware the noodler who grabs it.

Blues and channel cats are similar in their habits, so learning to fish channel cats enables you to catch blues. You have to be willing to put in more time to fish for blues, however.

## Flathead Catfish

Flatheads are more predatory than blues and more abundant, their range expanded by stocking. Flathead native distribution includes the Ohio, Mississippi, Missouri, and Rio Grande river systems. Flatheads have adapted better to impoundments than blues, and thus have been stocked far more widely. As a result, they are common in the southeast and southwest, including California. They can reproduce successfully in impoundments. Other common flathead names are shovelhead, mudcat, yellow cat, appaloosa and Johnny cat. Their scientific name translates "olive-colored mudfish."

Flatheads are associated with big rivers, though not as much as blues, and they like slower water than blues. While blue cats are associated with the lower and middle stretches of big rivers, flatheads are the big catfish of the middle and upper reaches.

John Madson's fascinating book, *Up On the River*, tells a story of the upper Mississippi River valley travels of an 18th century fur trader named Peter Pond. Pond's party set lines overnight, then in the morning hauled in catfish of 104, 100, and 75 pounds. One measured 16 inches between the eyes. Probably flatheads.

Historical accounts of pioneers also refer to spearing flatheads as they moved through riffles at night. Some fish, larger than a man, reportedly were taken this way.

Flatheads do well in rivers with heavy current or great current fluctuation. Flatheads usually spend the day in the deepest spots of long, sluggish pools. Even more than other catfish, flatheads hold in or near snags and debris. Flatheads are very solitary; find one under a snag and there might be another, but probably not. In some cases, flatheads are known to choose specific resting spots to spend their daytime hours.

# FLATHEAD CATFISH DISTRIBUTION

Flatheads are nocturnal feeders that move from deep snags or holes to roam shallow flats and riffles. Their prey is similar to blues: insects and small fish when young, crustaceans and fish when larger. Flatheads are aggressive predators that usually shun rotting meat. The stinkbaits and deadbaits that catch channel cats and blues usually aren't effective on flatheads.

Flatheads probably don't reach the fabulous sizes of blues, though again we don't have adequate records. The world-record flathead is a 98-pounder from Texas. But there are reports of larger flatheads. The present record will fall, probably to a reservoir fish.

*Zacker:* "Take a big mud cat (flathead). He's a mean sucker, the meanest fish swimmin' for my money. Danged right! He's the toughest, orneriest, meanest customer that swims in any natural (fresh) water. He won't likely pick up a dead bait, much less a ball of stinky crap. He wants somethin' live and big, like a big sucker or, better yet, one-, two-, or three-pound carp. Mud cats eat carp like peanuts: crack, and a head shake and then the carp's gone. Only time a big mud cat takes dead bait is spring. They take cut (filleted slabs) carp or sucker, then."

Flatheads don't get big overnight. A 10-pound fish may be over 7 years old. A 30-pounder is likely in its late teens or even 20s, and 60- to 70- pounders are perhaps 30 to 40 years old. One obvious conclusion: Remove a huge flathead (or other catfish) from a river, and it might be as old as you. It won't be replaced in your lifetime.

Because flatheads get so big and are so mysterious, they also inspire myths and legends. Or are they more than myths—fishermen who have arms broken while noodling for flatheads; noodlers pulled into muddy pools and drowned by their intended prey? John Madson repeats the story of a man gigging fish in a Kansas reservoir who was foolish enough to rope his spear to his waist. According to the story, he was found dead, still attached to a large dead flathead.

# Channel Catfish

Channel cats are the topic of the rest of this book. The channel cat can lay fair claim to being "America's fish," the most widespread and popular of our large catfish. It certainly is America's favorite catfish. In John Madson's opinion, the channel cat is "that trim, sagacious, freckle-flanked, clean-lined, fork-tailed, bighearted wonder of a fish—one of the best of all reasons for being a corn-country boy in early summer, or for going down to the River in any summer of one's life."

Apparently, channel cats were important to early Americans long before Christ was born. The spines of channel cats have been found in archeological explorations of early Indian sites. Channel cat spines were adapted by Indians for use as awls and needles.

Channel cats are sleeker, less pot-bellied than the flathead and blue. Many fishermen think of channel cats as the "trout" of farm-country rivers. Like trout,

*"...That trim, sagacious, freckle-flanked, clean-lined, fork-tailed, big-hearted wonder of a fish..."*

John Madson

they are streamlined fish living in or near current, often using it to facilitate feeding. Like trout, they feed on a wide range of food. Channel cats even have the trout's adipose fin. Or should we say that trout have the catfish's adipose fin?

Compared to the plug-ugly flathead, the channel cat is a beauty queen with a sleek shape designed to cut current. Channel cats, to repeat, are fork-tailed fish. While flatheads have a protruding lower jaw, channel cats have a longer upper jaw.

They usually have dark backs and lighter sides, although considerable color variation exists. At times, females are very light, and albinos occur. More often, channel cats are pale blue to pale olive with a silvery overcast. Small fish are lighter colored than large ones. Channel cats darken as they age, and this obscures spots. The channel cat's scientific name translates "spotted catfish." Big male channel cats usually are slate blue, with splotches of color on the lighter stomach that look as if they slid off the fish's back and stuck there.

Channel cats occur in many types of water. They are not so much a big river fish as blues and flatheads, though North America's biggest rivers have large channel cat populations. While channel cats are present almost everywhere, they do better in northern waters than flatheads and blues. A few of the best channel cat waters are in Ontario and Manitoba.

You'll find channel cats in impoundments, ponds, lakes, and rivers of every size, including little farmland "cricks." But best populations usually occur in moderate-size rivers.

In terms of growth, channel cats rank between whites and flatheads or blues. The world record is 58 pounds, but we think larger ones have been caught and misidentified or not registered.

D oug Stange recalling a conversation with Zacker concerning the size of the fish he caught in "those days":

"How big were the fish in those days?" I'd asked.

"Didn't weigh 'em much. Got paid for bulk weight," he'd answered. "Big cats are big cats. But we had lots of fish that weighed 75 pounds. Some maybe 100."

"Mostly flatheads?" I'd asked.

"Mostly," he'd answered. "But plenty of forks (channel cats) weighed 60 pounds and blues, too."

I'd told him that the world-record channel catfish was a 58-pounder. He'd shrugged. "So what? We've caught hook-and-line forks that easy weighed 60. Records ain't worth squat on the river. The fish ain't impressed 'till you catch 'em. And the only man I ever wanted to impress with fish was the bill collector. 'Sides, if you'd a put your name in some fancy-assed record book for something that was no big deal, well, you'd a been a laughing stock."

Joe Tomelleri

## Chapter 3

# MEET THE CHANNEL CATFISH

## A Unique Package of Abilities

Every fish was sent into this world with a survival kit, a package of abilities and weaknesses, a unique set of characteristics.

Muskies and pike have impressive teeth and short-range burst speed. But they can't turn instantly. Largemouth bass have a big mouth and wonderful ability to maneuver in the confined environment of aquatic vegetation. But they aren't good at chasing prey over longer distances. Walleyes and saugers can see to feed where other fish are almost blind. But they aren't fast.

When the packages were handed out, catfish were given a strange deal. They didn't get exceptional speed or vision, sharp teeth, or turn-on-a-dime agility. They didn't even get scales. Cats go through life naked, their soft skin offering meager protection against injuries.

Sound like channel catfish got a raw deal? No. In comparison, channel catfish received an extraordinary set of sensory systems that provide an

*Adult Male Channel Catfish*

Joe Tomelleri

*Juvenile Channel Catfish*

Joe Tomelleri

unparalleled awareness of the environment. We've described cats as "big swimming sensory organs." Cats were also given great power, so they're also big swimming muscles.

Catfish received something else that scientists can't measure, but which anglers appreciate. Cats have a temperament allowing them to be calm when other fish panic and behave erratically. Cats have a remarkable ability to "keep their cool." It's one reason they fight so hard and long and probably why they score well in laboratory intelligence tests. That's why, unlike many other fish, the catfish we've kept in tanks at In-Fisherman adapted and began feeding quickly. Cats cope.

## CHANNEL CATFISH DISTRIBUTION

*The channel catfish is the most widely distributed gamefish in the United States.*

So cats didn't get the short end when survival abilities were passed out. On the contrary, cats have a controlled temperament, terrific power and an astonishing awareness of their surroundings. No wonder they thrive in so many different waters.

## Sexing Catfish

You can determine male from female channel catfish. Male cats are very dark blue, especially during the spawn. Males also have broad, flattened heads with conspicuous bulging muscles in back of the eyes and flowing toward the top of the head.

Female channel cats are lighter colored than males. Females also appear less bulldoglike, with smaller, rounder, less muscular heads and rounder, more robust bodies. Females and males are equally likely to attain large size.

But there's a more exact way to sex cats. Turn a catfish over and inspect its "private parts," just in front of the anal fin. You'll see two openings. The one closest to the head is the anus.

*The broader more muscular head and dark-slate color of the male channel cat (left) in comparison to the narrow head, lighter color, and more rotund body of the female channel cat.*

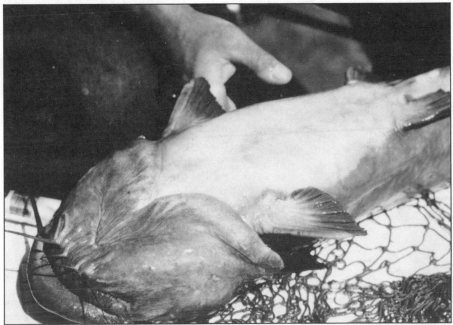

*The broad head and slate color of the male channel cat is still obvious when the cat's turned over. Note the slate mottle marks on the margins of the stomach, absent on the stomachs of lighter-colored females.*

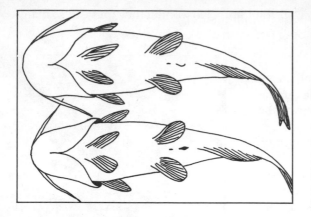

The opening closer to the tail is the genital opening. The male has a small protuberance here, the genital papilla. The female has a slit tapering toward the anus. The female genital opening is separate from the urinary opening and has small flaps covering both orifices. Near spawning time, female genitalia become swollen and reddish.

## The Swimming Muscle

The pulling power of catfish is legendary.

When Steve Grooms was growing up in Iowa, he heard of a famous catfish fight that took place in a little lake near his grandmother's home in the northwestern part of the state. Two anglers were in a small boat when one hooked a large catfish that began to tow their boat around. After several hours, a crowd gathered on shore. Once or twice, people rowed out to offer food and drink to the guys in the boat. The fish would come in close enough to be seen, then move off again, dragging the boat and the two anglers as if they were a bobber. Finally, as night fell, the fellow with the rod gave up. His back and arm muscles burned as if they were on fire, and he seemed no closer to landing the catfish. He cut the line. Similar stories abound in catfish country.

The pulling power of catfish isn't strictly a matter of muscle. Catfish have flattened heads, unlike fish like bluegills that have thin, flattened bodies. Bluegills spin crazy circles when hooked, while catfish are built for keeping their heads down. Cats, in fact, are shaped much like the fish-shaped downrigger weights designed to plane downward when pulled.

Nevertheless, catfish have "big shoulders." The muscles in the forward and middle of their bodies are highly developed. Fish famous for pulling hard—tuna, for example—have beefy shoulders and midsections. That's where the power lies.

This muscular development indicates how healthy a cat is. In prime condition, a channel cat is thickly muscled from the head down. A catfish that isn't healthy will be noticeably less muscled.

The body of a catfish tapers to a slender caudal peduncle—that wristlike area of a fish just ahead of its tail. You can pick them up by the tail like a salmon.

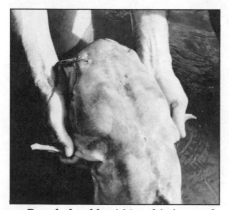

*Broad shoulders! Yes, this is a male channel cat.*

Cats also have extraordinary crushing power in their jaws. They use that power to smash food, including large fish and crustaceans.

Put your hand in the mouth of a 20-pound channel cat and he could break a bone. Toad Smith knows. He once caught a channel cat of about 25 pounds. Toad, being Toad, had to fool around. He stuck his hand in the fish's mouth. Toad, by the way, is built like a grizzly bear, has "paws" to match, and one of his amusements is giving handshakes that leave people temporarily unable to use their hand. This time Toad got a big dose of his own medicine. That cat crunched down on Toad and left him begging "Uncle!"

Catfish have white flesh. Fish such as salmon that travel long distances have oily, dark flesh because it better distributes oxygen for sustained swimming. Fish like catfish and walleyes that usually expend energy in shorter bursts have white flesh.

## The Swimming Sensory Organ

Humans have five senses used to get information about our environment. The water environment of fish is very different and their senses obtain information in different ways. In this section, we'll describe the senses of catfish in terms familiar to us. Remember, though, that a fish's senses function differently from ours and synthesize sensory input in ways we don't understand.

### Sight

Channel catfish have small eyes for their body size. Bullheads have smaller ones and the toothless blindcat and widemouth blindcat (subterranean species from Texas) have none.

Since the senses of smell, taste, and touch in catfish are excellent, some anglers wrongly assume that catfish hardly see. On the contrary, catfish in clear water use vision to find and capture food.

Catfish are adapted to life in rivers, where turbidity sometimes makes vision useless. Their other powerful senses take over, making it possible for them to function almost sightless. But whenever vision is possible, catfish use their eyes.

*Channel catfish may not see as well as clear-water inhabiting predators such as pike, walleyes, and bass, but they see well and use vision when they can as an important element in their feeding strategy.*

If you walk into a room containing catfish in tanks, you may see the fish lying still except for their eyes, which follow your every move. Catfish eyes, similar to other fish's eyes, have 6 sets of muscles to shift eye position. They lack choroid glands, however, which increase oxygen concentration in the retina. Perhaps they didn't develop this organ because of the typically high oxygen levels in rivers.

Channel catfish possess a tapetum lucidum, the reflective aspect of the retina so distinct in walleyes. This structure increases eye sensitivity in low light by reflecting light back over the rods like a mirror.

Rods and cones are present in catfish eyes in approximately equal numbers. Rods allow vision in dim light, while cones primarily discriminate color in daylight. Experiments on a channel catfish's ability to see color haven't been done, but they're physiologically able to detect it, so they probably do. Our fishing experience also suggests that cats see colors.

## Hearing/Lateral Line

To understand fish's hearing and the unique, related lateral-line sense, visualize sound as waves. Different sounds consist of varying wave frequencies. Fish hear with two inner ears, similar in many ways to our own. They lack our fluid-filled inner ear because their watery environment functions as our inner ear.

Three semicircular canals are used for balance, and three fluid-filled saclike structures are used for hearing. These sacs, lined by cells covered with fine hairlike projections, contain calcium carbonate earbones, called otoliths.

A sound wave passing through water, enters the body of the fish as if it weren't there—a fish's body has a density similar to water and is acoustically transparent to sound—until it hits the earbones, which are about 3 times denser than fish flesh. The earbones vibrate at a rate different from the tissue surrounding them. Hairlike projections on the cells under the earbones bend and a sound message is sent to the brain.

Catfish can hear sounds of much higher frequency (up to about 13,000 cycles per second) than other species. Catfish and minnows have better hearing because of a bony structure (Weberian ossicles) that connects the swim bladder and inner ear. The bladder acts as a resonating chamber (like a guitar body) to amplify vibrations, improving the sensitivity and range of hearing. Lacking Weberian ossicles, bass, pike, and other gamefish detect sounds from about 20 to 1,000 cycles per second.

Fish, however, are unable to *hear* low-frequency sounds. But because predators, prey, and school mates create low-frequency waves in water, catfish have developed a lateral-line system to detect them.

The lateral line is a series of tiny pores running in a line along each side of the fish. Each pore contains cells with hairlike processes. These hair cells respond to low-frequency waves by firing the nerve that runs along the lateral line. Lateral-line nerves also send messages to the part of the brain associated with hearing. Low-frequency vibrations from 1 to about 200 cycles per second are received—felt—by the lateral line.

Note the overlap between feeling and hearing. Some vibrations are probably felt as well as heard. These senses are closely related in fish. Hearing dominates when objects are far from the catfish. The lateral line becomes increasingly important for vibration detection at closer distances.

In both the lateral line and the inner ear, some sensory cells are oriented in one direction, others in the opposite direction. This helps fish pinpoint the source of sound. While we have no basis for saying that catfish's lateral-line sense is more sensitive than other sportfish, certainly in conjunction with its hearing sense, catfish stand above other sportfish in hearing sensitivity.

To the angler, this hearing ability means catfish are more aware of activities in their environment. If a wounded sucker is struggling on the other side of the pool, a catfish probably senses its presence and predicament as its brain translates waves passing through water into a mental image of prey. Tromp up to a pool, and cats are aware of your footsteps long before you're within casting range.

Some catfish are known to be electrically sensitive. African electric catfish communicate with low-voltage electrical discharges. They also detect prey from the

## Hearing and Lateral Line in Fish

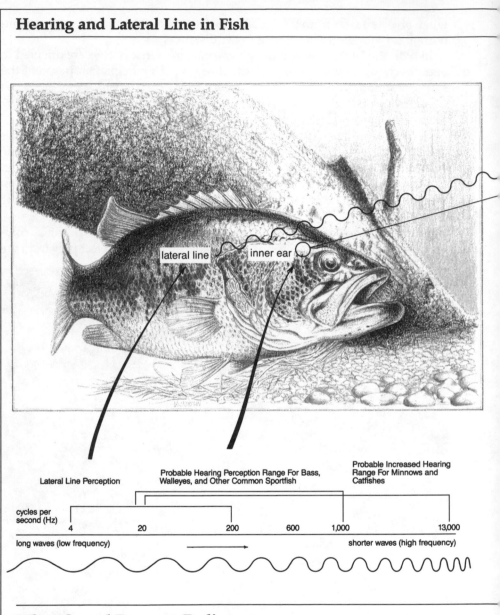

lateral line

inner ear

Lateral Line Perception

Probable Hearing Perception Range For Bass, Walleyes, and Other Common Sportfish

Probable Increased Hearing Range For Minnows and Catfishes

cycles per second (Hz)

4        20        200      600    1,000                  13,000

long waves (low frequency)                    shorter waves (high frequency)

## When Sound Becomes Feeling

Some vibrations can only be *felt* (lower pitches or frequencies within about the 1 to 200 cycle per second [Hz] range), while other vibrations can only be heard (higher pitches within about the 100-600 to 3,000-13,000 Hz range, depending on the fish species). There apparently is an area of overlap where a fish can hear and feel vibrations (about 20 to 200 Hz).

A bait moves toward a fish. At 50 feet, higher-frequency sound waves from the rattling shot and the hooks tinkling on the body of the bait reach the fish's inner ear, and low-frequency vibrations from the plug's wobble reach its lateral

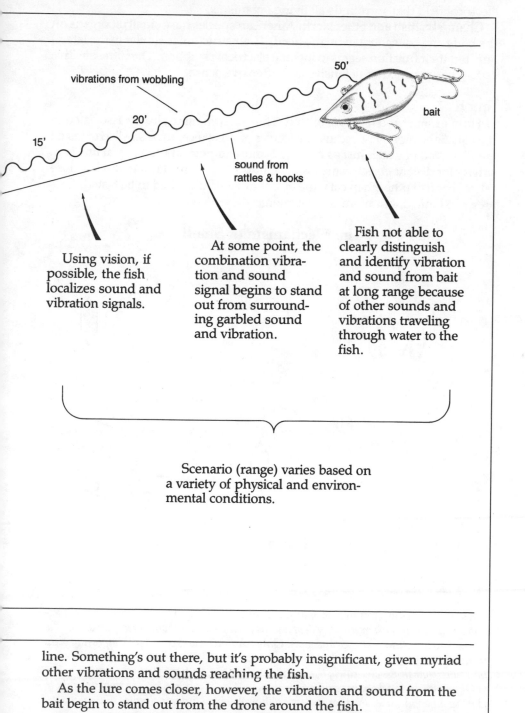

vibrations from wobbling

50'

20'

15'

bait

sound from
rattles & hooks

Using vision, if possible, the fish localizes sound and vibration signals.

At some point, the combination vibration and sound signal begins to stand out from surrounding garbled sound and vibration.

Fish not able to clearly distinguish and identify vibration and sound from bait at long range because of other sounds and vibrations traveling through water to the fish.

Scenario (range) varies based on a variety of physical and environmental conditions.

line. Something's out there, but it's probably insignificant, given myriad other vibrations and sounds reaching the fish.

As the lure comes closer, however, the vibration and sound from the bait begin to stand out from the drone around the fish.

Using vision in combination with hearing and feeling, the fish tries to localize where and what the thing (lure) is. The closer it comes, the more distinguishable it becomes.

electrical field that surrounds all living organisms.

Channel catfish and other North American species have small pit organs on the body and concentrated on the head. Their structure is similar to the lateral line, but their function seems to include electrical reception. The ultrasensitive catfish has yet another defensive and offensive sense.

## Smell

Human smell and taste are related. They're even more closely associated in the aquatic environment because molecules of substances to be smelled or tasted are dissolved in water. Just as hearing is more important than lateral line sensitivity for distant objects, smell is most important from afar and taste at close range. For fish other than cats, the object must be mouthed to be tasted. Cats aren't so limited, but more on that later.

### The Mechanism of Smell

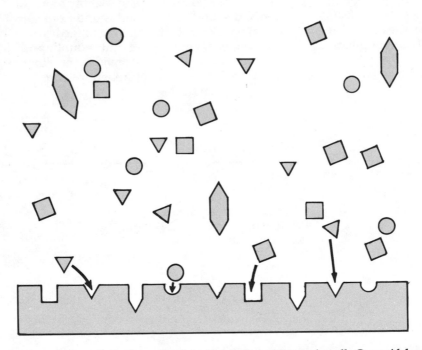

*Many theories explain the mechanism (detailed workings) of smell. One widely accepted theory is that there are tiny depressions on the surface of smell receptor cells. The depressions are various shapes and sizes. Only odor molecules of certain shapes and sizes fit into these specially shaped depressions. It's a sort of "lock and key" setup, and only molecules that fit exactly cause the receptor cell to fire an impulse to the brain.*

*Different species likely have different "lock and key" mechanisms so they respond to odors in different ways. Further research will probably identify molecules that excite certain fish the most.*

# Olfactory Folds and Smell

| Species | Weight | Number of Olfactory Folds |
|---------|--------|---------------------------|
| Channel Catfish | 2.5 lbs. | 142 |
| Channel Catfish | 1.5 lbs. | 110 |
| Flathead Catfish | 1.5 lbs. | 126 |
| Flathead Catfish | 0.5 lbs. | 92 |
| Striped Mullet | 1.0 lb. | 52 |
| Striped Bass | 1.25 lbs. | 34 |
| Black Bullhead | 1.0 lb. | 32 |
| Freshwater Drum | 0.5 lb. | 32 |
| Walleye | 1.7 lbs. | 29 |
| White Bass | 1.0 lb. | 24 |
| Sauger | 0.5 lb. | 22 |
| Gizzard Shad | 0.3 lb. | 20 |
| Rainbow Trout | 1.2 lbs. | 18 |
| Spotted Bass | 3.5 lbs. | 17 |
| Spotted Bass | 0.8 lb. | 11 |
| Yellow Perch | 0.4 lb. | 15 |
| Brook Trout | 1.0 lb. | 14 |
| Smallmouth Bass | 1.2 lbs. | 14 |
| Largemouth Bass | 7.0 lbs. | 13 |
| Largemouth Bass | 0.6 lb. | 8 |
| White Crappie | 0.8 lb. | 13 |
| Bluegill | 0.3 lb. | 12 |
| Redbreast Sunfish | 0.3 lb. | 10 |

*This table summarizes the number of olfactory folds found in 17 fish species dissected by Dr. W. Mike Howell, Samford University. If the number of folds is related to function, and it appears to be, then the top-listed fish should have the best developed sense of smell.*

*But Dr. Howell cautions about making such an assumption. What may be important is the number and sensitivity of smell receptor cells present on olfactory folds. This cannot be determined without intricate microscopic examination.*

*The surface area of an olfactory organ may be greatly increased by increasing the number of olfactory folds and packaging them as in the channel catfish. Thus, the surface area available to odor molecules could be increased several thousandfold.*

Most fish can smell very dilute concentrations of substances in water, but cats are unusually sensitive to smells. Molecules enter the fish's nostrils (nares) and pass through an olfactory sac. The shape and sensitivity of the olfactory sac varies among species and groups of fish. The number of folds on the inside of the olfactory sac seems related to sharpness of smell. Channel catfish have more than 140 folds; rainbow trout, which have a good sense of smell, have only 1 to 2 dozen; some fish that rely little on smell have none. The mechanism for detecting and identifying particular odors remains a mystery in the fish world.

Catfish recognize and respond to amino acids in extremely dilute concentrations (less than one part per million, which is approximately a teaspoon of substance in a railroad tank car). Blinded catfish easily follow a scent trail from a food item.

So not only are catfish very aware of vibrations in water caused by predators or prey, but they're more aware than other gamefish of scents, too.

Studies of captive bullheads have demonstrated that the sense of smell is also very important in establishing and maintaining social hierarchy. Bullheads identify individual fish by their unique chemical scent. Similar behavioral tests have apparently not been conducted on channel catfish, but the capabilities of their sense of smell certainly allows the possibility of chemical communication.

## Taste

Taste in the aquatic environment is closely linked to smell, but is more important at close range. But the nares can be experimentally blocked to eliminate strictly olfactory cues. Again, taste buds in catfish are much more abundant and

## Anatomy of Taste

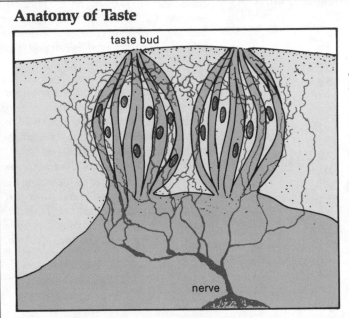

taste bud

nerve

Fish can taste chemical substances because they have receptor cells located in bundles called "taste buds." Unlike humans, however, whose taste buds are restricted to the tongue and palate, fish may have widely scattered buds, depending upon the species. Sharks have taste buds scattered mainly within their mouth and throat. Catfish, on the other hand, have thousands of taste buds scattered over their whiskers, inside the mouth and throat, over the head, body, and even on the fins. Each cell within a taste bud can be stimulated by a chemical substance dissolved in water. When stimulated, taste receptor cells fire impulses to taste centers in the brain, where the taste sensation is interpreted as either a "food" or "non-food" taste.

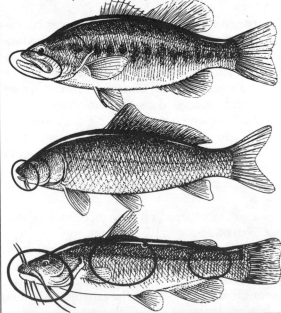

Bass, Walleye, Pike: Taste buds centered around mouth and lips.

Carp: Taste buds centered around mouth, lips, and especially barbels.

Catfish: Taste buds centered around mouth, lips, and especially barbels, but taste buds also distributed over body.

sensitive than in scaled species. Organs of taste are located over the catfish's entire body, with concentrations in the mouth, barbels, and gill arches.

Catfish need not bite an item to determine what it tastes like. Brushing it with the body is sufficient. Tests on bullheads, however, indicate that through taste alone they can locate distant food. Searching fish move in an S-shaped pattern and apparently taste the difference in dissolved materials on each side of the barbels and body. If the left side senses a stronger taste than the right, the bullhead veers left while continuing comparative taste tests. Bullheads are extremely taste sensitive. Channel catfish probably have similar ability.

## Feel

Channel catfish lack scales, a defense of most fish against predators and skin injuries. The body is very sensitive without the thousands of tiny plates that act as armor on other fish. But without that line of defense, catfish are subject to many infections.

Catfish skin is composed of epidermis and dermis below it, generally similar to most vertebrates. The epidermis, in addition to mucous cells, taste buds, and pit organs contains club cells which emit an alarm substance when the skin is injured. Club cells in catfish are larger than most fish, suggesting that this form of communication is highly developed. Simply, when an injured fish emits the alarm substance, other members of the species are immediately aware of its plight through their sense of smell. Predators may also detect alarm substances of prey and orient toward them.

Cells that change color (melanophores) are present in the skin, enabling catfish to rapidly become darker or lighter. Catfish seem to be aware of and protect their delicate skin. We once kept a large flathead catfish in a tank full of sharp rocks. The cat appeared to want to lie on the bottom, but found the rocks uncomfortable. So it propped itself up in the corner with its head straight up and its tail on a small flat piece of wood.

Clearly, the sum of the sensory capabilities of channel catfish surpasses any other fish we're aware of. Catfish aren't as fast or as toothy or as agile as some fish, but they have adapted remarkably well to their native habitats. They have also thrived in diverse waters they've been stocked into, thanks in great part to their sensory systems.

## CATFISH AS PREDATORS

Channel cats are omnivores, meaning they'll eat almost anything. They're opportunists, not specialists. If carrion is available, they feed on carrion. If living fish are the best available food source, they prey on them. When cottonwood trees release their fluff, channel cats may feed on that. They even eat plants and fruits, and feed day or night on the surface, on the bottom, or in-between.

This is where the cat's extraordinary awareness of its surroundings pays off. If crayfish are moving in a river, catfish know and can take advantage. If a large number of dead fish are on the bottom at ice-out, cats know.

Channel cats switch diets as they grow. Young cats rely on insect larvae. Later, they feed mostly on small fish. Although channel cats eat many things, most large ones depend on fish available throughout the season, unlike other food sources that come and go. Channel cats in impoundments rely heavily on shad, the most available protein source.

The list of what channel cats eat reflects their opportunistic nature: mayflies, caddis flies, midges, snails, crayfish, algae, grasshoppers, tree seeds, clams, small water plants, and fish of many sorts, not to mention more exotic things, like cotton rats and watersnakes. Anything of reasonable size may be eaten.

Specific insects important to catfish are much the same as insects important to trout. Larval dobson flies, mayflies, and dragonfly nymphs are particularly important. Their main fish targets depend on what's swimming in their environ-

## COMMON CATFISH FORAGE

Newly hatched catfish subsist for several days on nutrients stored in the yolk sac. After it's absorbed, cats must hunt, generally finding abundant zooplankton such as *Daphnia* (water fleas) and copepods. Many tiny invertebrates must be consumed to provide energy for growth. Cats soon switch to meatier fare like larval insects. Tiny fish may be eaten, but cats rely primarily on invertebrates until they're at least 8 inches long, when fish and large invertebrates like crayfish become important.

Large cats prey mostly on fish, but remain opportunistic. Unusual food items include birds, snakes, and mice. Cats often consume vegetable matter, too, although its nutritional value is unknown. Large numbers of seeds, algae, and small fruits sometimes are found in cat guts.

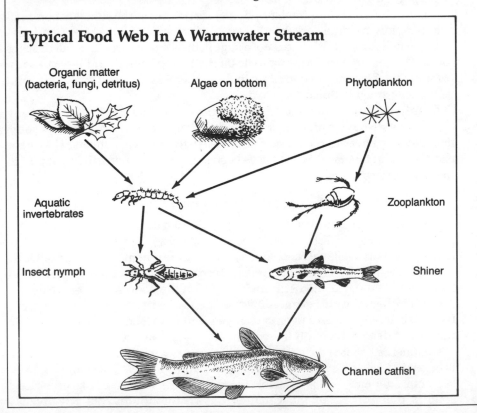

### Typical Food Web In A Warmwater Stream

Organic matter (bacteria, fungi, detritus)

Algae on bottom

Phytoplankton

Aquatic invertebrates

Zooplankton

Insect nymph

Shiner

Channel catfish

ment. Most rivers offer various species of sunfish, darters, dace, shiners, and other river minnows, suckers, bullheads, shad, mooneyes, goldeyes, and small gamefish.

At least one Cincinnati, Ohio riverboat serves a particular brand of French fries. Some fries end up in the water, where they're eaten by channel cats. You guessed it. In that stretch of river, French fries ar a great bait for cats. For similar reasons, we believe chicken liver is a good bait for channel cats in areas where people often fish with chicken liver. Catfish may be ominivores, but that doesn't

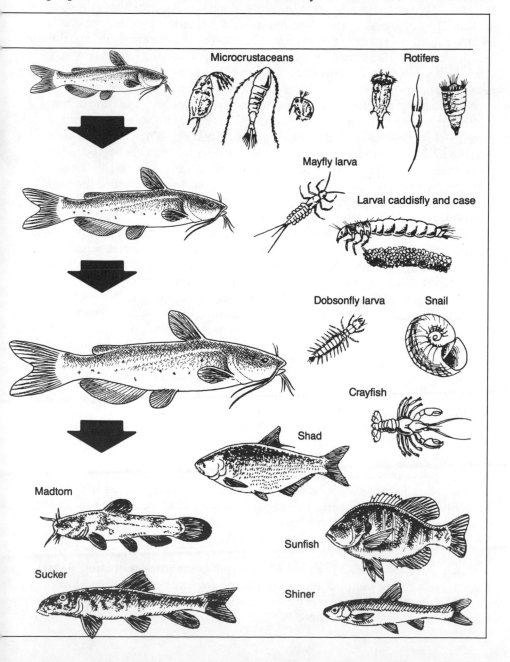

Microcrustaceans

Rotifers

Mayfly larva

Larval caddisfly and case

Dobsonfly larva

Snail

Crayfish

Shad

Madtom

Sunfish

Sucker

Shiner

mean they're incautious feeders. They bite best on foods they recognize from past experience.

## How Channel Cats Feed

We know how channel cats feed from having fished for them and by observing them in tanks.

When they want to move quickly and attack an object, they can. During one experiment, we occasionally threw a live waterdog (salamander) into the catfish tank. The results usually were the same. A cat would attack the waterdog, shake it like a dog shakes a rat, then spit it. We're not sure why this happened. Did the cat see the waterdog as a threat to be killed, but not eaten? Perhaps the catfish would have fed if we'd left the dead waterdog in the tank longer. Anyway, when a cat wants to grab something, it can do so quickly and aggressively. They never missed the waterdog on the first pass when they had a good shot.

More typically, a cat feeds by first swimming to a stationary object and tasting without touching it. The catfish cruises from 3 to 6 inches above the bottom, a distance that might be related to the length of its barbels. It may position itself over the food item with its longest upper barbels extended straight down toward (but usually not touching) the food. Those two barbels can be pointed like fingers and apparently are used by catfish to check food items. The cat is tasting the food from a slight distance, probably checking the taste against the memory of foods previously eaten.

When the cat decides this is something it wants, it bites it from above, pinching the bait against the bottom. Channel cats have a slight overbite, which affects their eating strategy. They come down on food from above, snapping and pinching the food, not sliding belly-flat to the bottom and scooping it.

Cats have some trouble nailing a bait lying flat on the bottom. Their overbite makes them a little clumsy when feeding this way. But what they particularly missed in our tank tests were little balls of commercial dough bait. The catfish "dinked around" with these baits. This apparent feeding difficulty might have been due to feeding on an unfamiliar bait.

Limited tank observations suggest two conclusions. First, if a catfish wants a bait, he's going to get it, positively and quickly. Second, foods lying flat on the bottom are hardest for them to take.

That conforms to fishing experience. Catfish rarely fool with a bait they want. If they want it, they take it, and they have it, and they have it *right now*. Larger catfish are aggressive, positive biters.

Do they ever play with a bait? It sometimes seems so, but that impression is usually false. If you feel fish messing with your bait but not taking it, they're probably little fish—bullheads, madtoms, or small catfish—that just can't take a large bait. Catfish may have trouble nailing a bait in heavy current. Otherwise, if fish are playing with your bait, but not taking it, they're telling you to switch baits or move.

Other fish may peck and sample a bait before committing, but rarely a cat. The cat has already sampled and committed to the bait before biting. Most of the big channel cats we've caught have taken the bait positively. Big channel catfish don't nibble. They don't need to.

# Tank Feeding Strategy

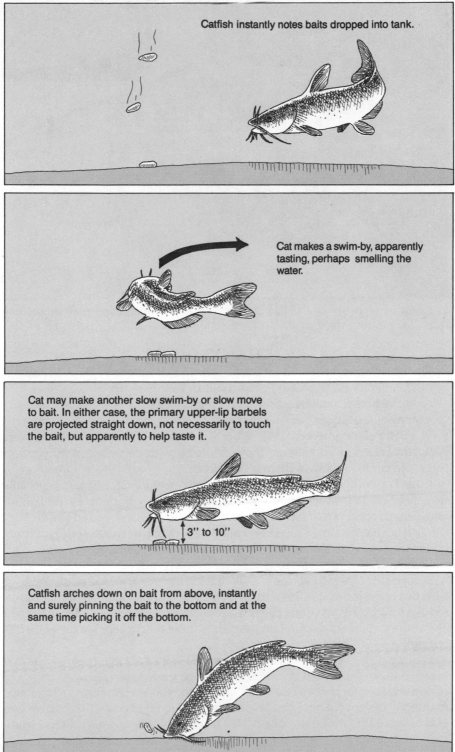

Catfish instantly notes baits dropped into tank.

Cat makes a swim-by, apparently tasting, perhaps smelling the water.

Cat may make another slow swim-by or slow move to bait. In either case, the primary upper-lip barbels are projected straight down, not necessarily to touch the bait, but apparently to help taste it.

3" to 10"

Catfish arches down on bait from above, instantly and surely pinning the bait to the bottom and at the same time picking it off the bottom.

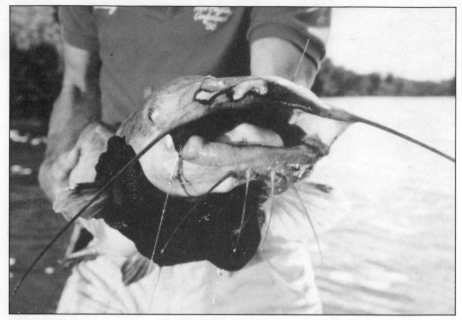

*The plenty-big maw of a 15-pound male channel cat—margin for error in grabbing baits. They want it, they got it.*

## BIG CHANNEL CATS

The world-record channel cat is a 58-pound fish caught by W. B. Whaley in South Carolina's Santee-Cooper Reservoir in July 1964.

As we've noted, catfish records aren't characteristic of how big catfish really get. Many of the biggest catfish ever caught were taken in the 19th Century for food, not for glory or records. When the Mississippi, Ohio, and Missouri rivers were first fished by white men, those rivers gave up tremendous numbers of huge, old catfish, many of them channel cats.

What kept the biggest fish from being recognized? First, catmen, especially in times past, just weren't into winning ribbons the way people who fish for bonefish or salmon are. If somebody catches a new line-class-record tarpon, they contact the International Game Fish Association to initiate the records procedure before they call their friends to tell the story. But we're sure many channel cats over 60 pounds went right from the river to the frying pan, no photos please.

Second, big channel cats are mistaken for blue cats, and vice versa. We have seen this many times at In-Fisherman. A big channel cat looks dark and unspotted like a big blue if you don't check the anal fin to see it's rounded, not straight like a blue's. A record channel cat weighs no more than a big blue cat—nice fish but nothing exceptional.

In our travels, we have heard many credible stories of large channel cats that failed to make the record books. Doug Stange grew up in northwest Iowa, a region with decent channel cat water. One man who lived in Rock Valley, Iowa, frequently caught channel cats ranging from 40 to 60 pounds. His biggest was said to be a 62-pounder, one of perhaps hundreds of world-record-class channel cats that went to the family table instead of to the record books.

*Doug Stange and Toad Smith discussing coffee, catfishing, politics, this year's corn crop, and reorganization of world monetary systems.*

Z acker considering forks—channel cats: "A real crackerjack, those forks. Not the biggest river cat, but the baddest for his size for sure— quickest runners, sure enough. Evil tempered suckers, too. A big fork will kill a baiter (bait-size fish) just for sport. Seen it plenty of times. OK, so they come back later to eat those kills. It's the reason we rigged fresh (live) baiters on sets."

kohlsaat

I've been fighting this catfish all day -
I think it's a special breed of catfish... a Tomcatfish.

Chapter 4

# THE WORLD OF THE CHANNEL CAT

## Habitat Hideaways

The range of channel catfish is best described as "nearly everywhere" in the lower 48 states, plus portions of Mexico and Canada. Originally, channel cats were most common in the rivers and extended drainage systems of the Missouri, Mississippi, Ohio, Rio Grande, and St. Lawrence, plus many lesser rivers in the southeast. That's a lot of country, ranging from the western slope of the Appalachian Mountains westward to the Rocky Mountains, from Canada to the Gulf of Mexico.

So popular and adaptable is the channel cat, however, that its range has been extended east and west by stocking. Particularly in the west, channel cats were stocked in newly built reservoirs. They now inhabit reservoirs in California, Nevada, Utah, and Idaho. The only states without channel catfish are Alaska, Maine, Delaware, and Rhode Island.

Additionally, channel cats have been stocked in many of America's farm ponds. Responding to the water problems of the 1930s, the U.S. Department of Agriculture encouraged farmers to create ponds for soil and water conservation. The program began in 1937, and by 1970 about 3.5 million ponds had been built.

Originally, most ponds were stocked with bass and bluegills. Then researchers found that channel cats were compatible with those species and that the presence or absence of bass and bluegills had little impact on numbers and growth of catfish. Catfish may help control sunfish numbers, probably because small channel cats compete with sunfish for insects, and omnivorous adults eat small sunfish. Today, many ponds, particularly in the Southeast, are stocked with bass, bluegills, and channel cats, which have surprised some pond owners by occasionally spawning successfully in farm ponds with no running water.

Advances in fish culture opened the way to a thriving catfish industry. "Fish farming" or aquaculture for channel cats is a multimillion-dollar industry.

## BASIC REQUIREMENTS

Although channel catfish do well in ponds, lakes, and reservoirs, the species is originally and most typically a fish of rivers. Channel cats are best suited for life in large streams or large rivers having a low to moderate gradient. Channel cats live mainly in moderately cool, clear water over bottoms of sand, rubble, or gravel. They are generally intolerant of salt water.

Catfish are similar to largemouth bass in oxygen requirements. They can survive oxygen levels as low as 2 ppm (parts per million), but to support a successful population of catfish, a body of water must sustain a level of at least 5 ppm dissolved oxygen. Catfish don't thrive when oxygen levels fall below 3 ppm. Below 2 ppm, they gulp oxygen at the surface. In shallow lakes that winterkill (lose their oxygen), catfish last longer than walleyes, but not as long as bullheads.

Effects of turbidity or murkiness of water on catfish isn't clear. Certainly cats with their highly developed senses of taste, smell, touch, and hearing are well adapted to turbid water. This puts them at an advantage over less well-equipped species in murky rivers, reservoirs, and ponds. Studies of reservoirs by Dr. Homer Buck, then with the Oklahoma Fisheries Research Lab, indicated that cats thrived in murkier Oklahoma impoundments. Sunfish and

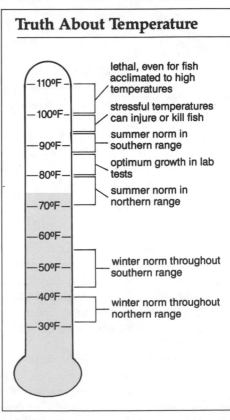

**Truth About Temperature**

- 110°F — lethal, even for fish acclimated to high temperatures
- 100°F — stressful temperatures can injure or kill fish
- 90°F — summer norm in southern range
- 80°F — optimum growth in lab tests
- 70°F — summer norm in northern range
- 60°F —
- 50°F — winter norm throughout southern range
- 40°F — winter norm throughout northern range
- 30°F —

bass were relatively more abundant in clearer waters. In addition to their sensory capabilities, Buck hypothesized that turbidity provided protection for young catfish, which hatch later than other species and are often selectively preyed upon.

Yet in Kansas streams, channel catfish biomass (pounds per acre) tended to be higher in clearer streams. Clearly, habitat type and presence of other species as competitors, predators or prey interact with turbidity and its effect on catfish populations.

Few fish can match channel cats for tolerating a broad range of temperatures. Catfish survive extended temperatures in the low 30s during winter. They aren't active and they don't gain weight at such low temperatures, but channel cats survive long periods of extremely cold water by reducing activity. On the other end of the scale, channel cats survive temperatures over 95°F in south Georgia and Florida. That doesn't mean you can take a channel cat from a tank at 33°F and plunge it into a pot of water at 95°F.

Two factors affect how fish respond to temperature. Many fish, possibly including channel cats, have genetic sub-types (such as Florida and northern largemouth bass) adapted to different environmental variables such as temperature. In other words, we suspect that Manitoba cats are genetically different than Alabama cats. Fish also acclimate (get used to) certain water temperatures. When a fish acclimated to one temperature is suddenly

---

Fish are poikilotherms, meaning cold-blooded or unable to regulate body temperature. Basically, their body temperature is determined by their surroundings.

Laboratories allow controlled testing of temperatures that fish choose to stay in. Lab tests of young channel catfish generally show excellent survival and growth at 82°F to 87°F as long as sufficient food is provided. Temperatures of 92°F to 94°F can cause damage that belatedly kills fish used to temperatures in the mid-80°F range. Yet for young cats used to the low 90°F range, it may take 100°F to cause large-scale mortality.

In North America, channel catfish are found from southern Canada to southern Florida, a longitudinal range of about 1,900 miles. The Red River population, near the northern edge of catfish range, grows very fast and individuals achieve huge size. Yet water temperatures remain in the 30°F range for five to six months. At the southern edge of their range, summer surface water temperatures reach the low 90°F range and rarely drop below 50°F for extended periods in winter. Yet growth in many cases isn't faster than in Manitoba.

Channel catfish are highly adaptable and most waters across the United States can support healthy populations. Yet it's likely that Florida cats brought to Manitoba wouldn't thrive. Future stockings should be considered carefully so the best-adapted genetic stocks are used.

# Catfish Water Quality Needs

## Dissolved Oxygen

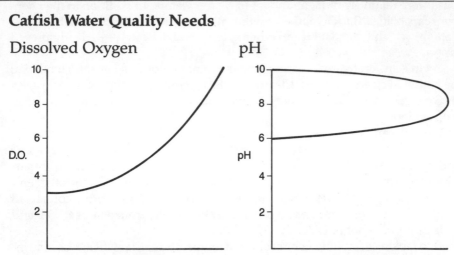

Catfish Production

## pH

Catfish Production

*Dissolved oxygen probably is the most widely studied environmental parameter except temperature. Catfish do best when dissolved oxygen contrations are over 7 mg/l (parts per million). When dissolved oxygen drops to 3 mg/l, cats are stressed, growth slows and fish are more likely to contract diseases. Below 2 mg/l, catfish and other species often rise to the surface to breathe air. In lab studies, cats have survived dissolved oxygen levels slightly below 1 mg/l for short periods of time.*

*pH, a measure of hydrogen ion concentration, is critical for maintaining the chemical balance within a catfish's body. Negative effects of low pH (acidic water), from acid rain and other causes, on fish populations have been documented. High altitude, northern ponds and rocky streams are most susceptible to acidification. Such waters aren't catfish habitat. Normal pH ranges of 6.5 to 8.5 seem best for catfish production. Populations suffer as alkalinity increases above 9.5 or acidity increases—drops below 5.5.*

## Salinity

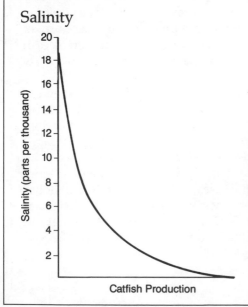

Catfish Production

*Channel cats are typically freshwater fish. In Eastern catfish rivers like the Connecticut and Hudson, channel catfish populations dwindle and white cats, known to be more tolerant of a broad range of salinity, dominate brackish downstream reaches. Yet in the St. Lawrence River, channel cats have been collected in salinities as high as 20 parts per thousand, more than half-strength seawater. In Louisiana bayous, channel cats also occur in brackish areas. In these situations, however, growth is slow, even stunted. Lab studies have also shown detrimental effects of salt.*

introduced to much hotter or colder water, it is stressed and may die.

Channel cats, remember, are temperature tolerant, but more active and healthy at certain temperatures. The temperature preference for channel catfish (temperature they grow best at) is from 75⁰F to 80⁰F, similar to the preferred range of sunfish and largemouth bass. Don't be too impressed with numbers, though. Channel cats can be caught in water much colder than 75⁰F. And we've had wonderful August and September fishing in water 85⁰F.

Think of channel cats as being much like brown trout, only adapted to slower and warmer water. Current affects where cats hold and how they feed, just as it does trout. Like trout, little cats are insect eaters and bigger ones feed heavily on fish. Trout and catfish organize their lives around the typical riffle-hole-run structure of streams and rivers. More about that in a moment.

*Famous English carp fisherman and bait manufacturer Duncan A. Kay with a channel catfish taken during the August dog days, when water temperature reached 87°F. Fishing "before breakfast" was the key to catching big fish.*

## HOLES, SNAGS, AND STREAM STRUCTURE

The center of a river catfish's life is a hole. But holes don't just happen. They are created by moving water.

*Riffles* are shallow spots in streams where water constricts and rushes quickly over a firm bottom. The top of the water is frisky, and canoeists know these areas as rapids. They can be short or long, intense or mild. The quickened current flow then strikes an area of softer bottom and scours a hole.

*Holes* lie below riffles because the current flowing from the riffle creates a hole. Holes are the deepest spots in a river. The flow of current will be brisk toward the upstream end of the hole; but as the stream gets wider and deepens, current loses force. Suspended particles drop to the bottom, causing the back of the hole to fill in and gradually become shallower.

At that point, the river moves along with no significant change in depth. We call such stretches *runs*. The current is fairly slow here and the bottom is uniform. Some anglers accustomed to fishing lakes might naturally call these areas "flats." They're mostly dead water, though cats occasionally feed in runs, especially the portion of a run preceding a riffle that precedes a deep cover-laden hole.

Most catfish rivers consist of a continuous series: riffle-hole-run, riffle-hole-run. That's one of the most important factors in the world of the catfish, so we'll treat the idea at length in Chapter 7.

Holes are the heart of the catfish world. While cats use runs and riffles, holes

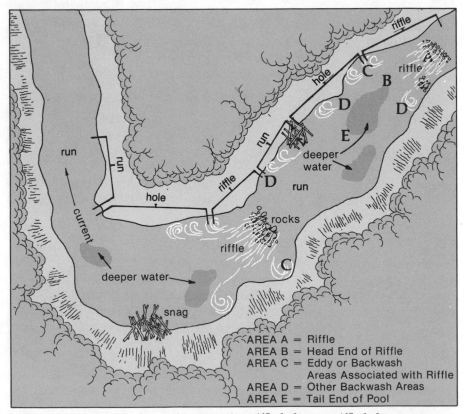

*Most rivers consist of a continuous series: riffle-hole-run, riffle-hole-run.*

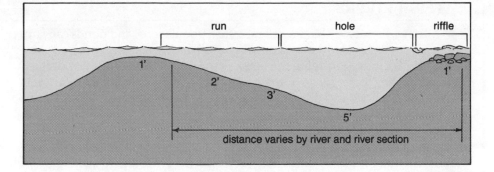

are where they spend most of their time. Once a cat settles in a hole, it gets to know that hole and perhaps those above and below it, if conditions favor such exploration. A catfish probably is a more successful predator when it becomes familiar with a hole, knowing which areas produce which food under which circumstances.

How about the stories your Uncle Louie used to tell about the huge old cat that defeated his efforts to catch it for six years running? That same catfish sat in its hole by the same snag for years. Every time Uncle Louie hooked that old brute, he got his line busted, or worse.

Tales like that make good stories, but they arise from common misunderstandings. A big channel cat that resides in a pool might stay there for many weeks at a time, especially if the water level is low and stable. Then the water level goes up or down and—*zoom!*—he's gone. If the same catfish spends the summer in the same river another year, he may or may not again reside in the same hole. A prime location in a prime hole will, however, always hold the biggest cat, which gives Uncle Louie the idea that one fish remains in that location season after season, year after year.

There's logic to where catfish hold in a hole. Remember, the catfish family is social. Fish learn to recognize each other and seem to organize according to a pecking order.

Key locations within a hole offer the most security or best feeding opportunities. At various times, different fish use those locations, but first rights to the best spots eventually belong to dominant fish.

Doug Stange observed catfish in a little stream north of his boyhood home. Often that stream became clear enough in June for Doug to see each catfish as it held by day in different locations around a snag in one hole. The biggest fish was a 6-pounder, not a monster, but a big fish for a small farmland creek. That cat spent most of its time in the prime lie under a snag, a spot that offered protection and access to food. Though the cats would often move around and switch positions, the prime lie was claimed by the biggest catfish when he wanted it.

## RIVER HABITAT

What characterizes a good catfish river?

*Size* is important. Little creeks don't have the carrying capacity for as many catfish or catfish as big as you find in bigger rivers. There's a limit to the size of catfish produced in small streams, though small feeder creeks sometimes get runs

# CATFISH RIVERS

While many reservoirs have excellent catfish populations, and ponds can support almost unbelievable densities of whiskered denizens, catfish evolved as inhabitants of current. Rivers are the home of the catfish. Rivers, loosely defined as freely flowing water, range from high-gradient, high-elevation rocky torrents to vast low-gradient, low-elevation tidal waters. Yet this great diversity can be represented in a single river.

Steve Quinn grew up near the banks of the Hudson River in Manhattan where incoming tides pushed water upstream and international vessels plied the waters. Summer trips 350 miles north revealed the Hudson's headwaters as a rocky brook in the Adirondack Mountains. Channel cats aren't native to the Hudson or any other Atlantic Coast drainages north of Georgia, but the river typifies the progression in habitat from source to the sea. Fish species communities shift with habitat.

Within the native range of channel cats, or where they've been introduced, ideal cat habitat is in the middle of this river-type continuum. They're not suited to fast, rocky trout streams and generally disappear before the beginning of tidal influence. In the midsection of America, where catfish is king, many rivers pro-

## River Type Continuum

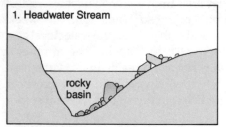

*Bottom rocky; water cool and clear; depth shallow; width narrow; gradient steep; current fast; no aquatic vegetation. Madtoms may be present but no other catfish species.*

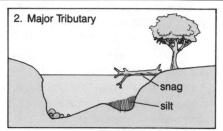

*Bottom variable; deeper pools common; water warmer and more turbid, especially after rain; gradient and flow rate reduced; typical riffle-pool-run sequence. Excellent channel catfish habitat.*

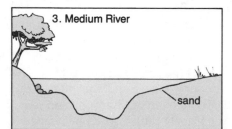

*Bottom variable; riffle-pool-run sequence occurs, but not as well defined; water usually murky and warm; aquatic vegetation may be present on shallow banks; tributaries common. Excellent habitat for channels and other catfish species.*

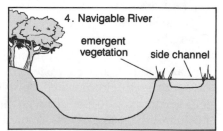

*Current moderate; channel complex, possibly dredged; aquatic vegetation locally abundant; bottom soft; water murky and warm. Channel cats often abundant; other catfish species also occur.*

vide cat habitat from their beginning, where smaller tributaries combine their flows, to their mouth at the edge of a larger river.

Catfish rivers are sometimes called "mature." They're slowing down and growing in width and complexity, as many living creatures do with age. Gradient is usually less than a drop of two feet per river mile. Depth is moderate in upstream sections, averaging 3 to 5 feet. Depth increases downstream.

Flow rates drop and rivers meander. Oxbows, islands, and sloughs may form. Silt is deposited by reduced flow and shifted by currents. Deep pools and shallow flats are sculpted. Rocky outcroppings remain as riffles. Softer substrate allows aquatic plant growth along banks or below the surface. Trees grow along banks but may be toppled by undercutting current. Water temperatures rise with more water exposed to sunlight and typically warmer climate.

Sandy flats foster shiners and young suckers, while riffles and snags produce invertebrates and preyfish. Backwaters provide a steady supply of sunfish, frogs, and other flatwater species. Tributaries are areas for spawning and other migrations. Downstream, deeper holes, manmade cover, and an expanded forage base beckon. Channel catfish thrive in such diverse river environments.

**5. Tidal River**

soft bottom

*Water subject to tidal influence; salinity varies with location, tide, and rainfall. White catfish are dominant catfish species.*

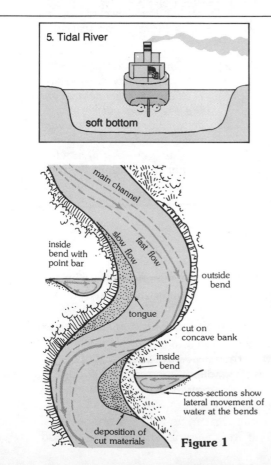

*The force of water is constantly remodeling the riverscape. Over time, rivers change their course. It is this change that constructs adjacent flood plains. If a river stretch does not have an extensive adjoining flood plain, it means that its bed is very stable or the river is geologically very young. Water is a universal solvent; given time, it can chew away granite, dissolve iron, and move mountains!*

*In streams, the action of water along with the meandering effect cuts materials on the outside bend where there is high current flow and deposits other materials on the inside bend where there is reduced current speed and force. Notice how the current has created a tongue-like structure. The deepest part of any river stretch is always on the outside bend.*

main channel

inside bend with point bar

slow flow

fast flow

outside bend

tongue

cut on concave bank

inside bend

cross-sections show lateral movement of water at the bends

deposition of cut materials

**Figure 1**

## Coriolis Effect

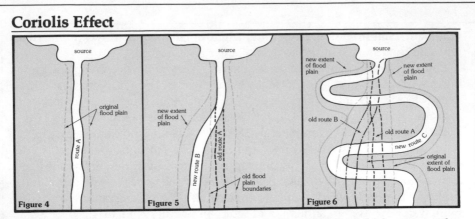

Figure 4

Figure 5

Figure 6

The earth's rotation creates a force known as the Coriolis Effect which, among other things, causes water to flow clockwise and rebound counterclockwise in the northern hemisphere (reverse in the southern hemisphere.) The flow and counterflow of Coriolis Effect causes rivers to loop or meander, eroding and depositing their way down the flood plain to the sea. An example of the Coriolis Effect can be observed as water flows down the drain from a sink or toilet.

Figure 1 shows a very young river with a straight course and a small undeveloped flood plain. In time, because of the Coriolis Effect, the stream meanders clockwise and begins to gradually erode the outside bend (Figure 2). Eventually, the stream will evolve into a shape similar to Figure 3.

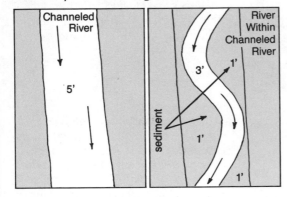

Coriolis Effect also creates rivers within rivers. Say a river is channeled (channelized) and the flow moves quickly straight ahead. Eventually, rebounding water meandering from bank to bank will create a deeper flow within the banks of the channeled river.

of bigger fish. Big waters produce big cats, apparently a matter of holding area and the amount of available forage. Big rivers more often provide a steady supply of food.

*Proximity to other branches of water* may be important. A little creek associated with a bigger river can at times yield bigger channel cats. A stretch of big river fed by several tributaries is usually better than a stretch lacking tributaries.

*Gradient* is important. Streams with steep gradients and resulting strong current are not suitable for catfish. Oppositely, streams with extremely low gradient and sluggish current aren't good catfish habitat.

*Temperature* makes a difference. Channel cats can do well in warm water, so more rivers would produce more cats if they weren't so cool. Take a good smallmouth-walleye river and decrease the gradient while increasing the temperature a little, and it becomes a good channel cat river.

*Current stability* promotes food production. Rivers with excessive water level fluctuation are not as hospitable to catfish as rivers with more stable flows. Of course, rivers always fluctuate seasonally, but some more than others. Erratic flows resulting from the opening and shutting of dam gates can also hurt. When river levels jump too much, food production drops, and fish suffer.

*Water quality* matters. Though channel cats can feed in silty water, rivers or streams with serious soil erosion are not as good as cleaner streams. Pollution hurts catfish production, and so does erosion caused by poor land-use practices.

*Soil fertility* determines how much food a stream will produce. Rivers washing over sterile soil or rock won't produce as much food or as many catfish as streams draining fertile watersheds. Streams with many riffles are better, though, given the general fertility of the surrounding area. Riffles are natural food-producing areas. Broken rock creates a wealth of places for insects to grow and small fish to hide.

All those factors help create a good catfish stream or river. But *the riffle-hole-run structure of a catfish river is the key* to understanding where to fish. This is so important that we'll focus on it in a later chapter.

A good catfish river has basic water-quality requirements. Yet finding a catfish river, or even a good catfish river, is just one step to good fishing. In every catfish river, there are good stretches and stretches to avoid. In·every stretch, there are good holes and holes to skip.

## Distribution of Species by In-Fisherman River Category Stretch

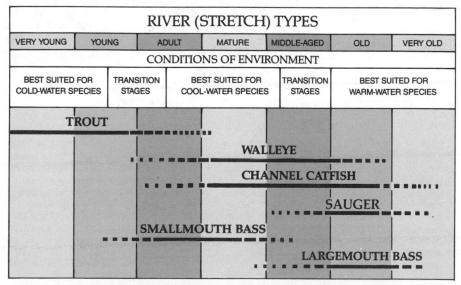

*This chart shows the species present in each In-Fisherman river category. A fish's numbers peak and then gradually decrease based on the environmental conditions offered by the river section.*

# Major River Drainages

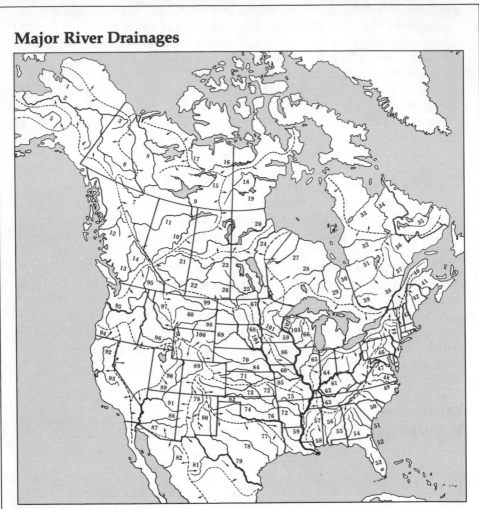

Match numbers on the map with the river names below
*Denotes channel catfish in river drainage.

Watershed boundary of drainage basins. ------------------    Direction of flow. ———→

## RIVERS

| | | | | | | |
|---|---|---|---|---|---|---|
| 1. Kobuk | 16. Black | 31. Rupert | *45. Delaware | *60. Missouri | *75. White | *91. Little Colorado |
| 2. Yukon | 17. Coppermine | 32. Fort George | *46. Susquehanna | *61. Ohio | *76. Red | *92. Sacramento |
| 3. Porcupine | 18. Thelon | 33. Leaf | *47. Potomac | *62. Cumberland | *78. Colorado | *93. San Joaquin |
| 4. Tanana | 19. Kazan | 34. Koksoak | *48. James | *63. Tennessee | *79. Rio Grande | 94. Klamath |
| 5. Kuskokwim | 20. Churchill | 35. Winston | *49. Roanoke | *64. Wabash | *80. Pecos | *95. Columbia |
| 6. Pelly | 21. N. Saskatch. | Churchill | *50. Savannah | *65. Illinois | *81. Rio Conchos | 96. Snake |
| 7. Liard | 22. S. Saskatch. | 36. Manicouagan | *51. Altamaha | *66. Wisconsin | *82. Rio Yaqui | *97. Clark Fork |
| 8. Mackenzie | 23. Saskatch. | *37. Saguenay | *52. St. Johns | *67. Red | *83. Cimarron | *98. Yellowstone |
| 9. Slave | 24. Nelson | *38. St. Lawrence | *53. Peace | *68. James | *84. Republican | *99. Milk |
| 10. Athabasca | *25. Assiniboine | *39. Ottawa | *54. Flint | *69. Cheyenne | *85. Kansas | *100. Big Horn |
| 11. Peace | *26. Qu'Appelle | 40. Rimouski | *55. Chattahoochee | *70. Platte | *86. Des Moines | *101 Minnesota |
| 12. Skeena | 27. Severn | 41. St. John | *56. Alabama | *71. Smoky Hill | *87. Gila | *102. St. Croix |
| 13. Fraser | 28. Albany | 42. Kennebec | *57. Tombigbee | *72. Neosho | *88. Salt | *103. Chippewa |
| 14. Kamloops | 29. Missinaibi | *43. Connecticut | *58. Pearl | *73. Arkansas | *89. Colorado | *104. Big Sioux |
| 15. McLeod | 30. Abitibi | *44. Hudson | *59. Mississippi | *74. Canadian | *90. Green | |

# PONDS

In most farm ponds, catfish usually hold near the deepest holes, just as they do in rivers. And just as in rivers, a deep hole with a snag is better than a deep hole with no cover.

Where are the deep spots in ponds? Depends on how the pond was made. When a creek is dammed to make a pond, the deep water will usually be near the dam. But on "borrow" ponds, there usually won't be much depth variation. Borrow ponds are made by a bulldozer shoving earth from the center of the intended pond and scooping out a broad low spot surrounded by the displaced fill.

It doesn't take a deep pond to hold catfish. Unless the pond is far enough north so winterkill is a problem, channel cats can live in ponds as shallow as 3 feet. But most ponds have a limited food base, so cats don't grow large unless they receive supplemental feeding.

In ponds without definite holes, catfish roam. Three types of cover concentrate them: Brush piles, stumps, or snags. Sometimes snags or brush piles are sunk to concentrate fish.

Corners of a pond concentrate catfish, too. Good corners often occur by the edges of a dam. A borrow pond might have a rectangular shape, with four good corners.

Finally, feeder creeks often attract channel cats. An incoming creek with a brush pile in slightly deeper water with current flow would be a good spot. Shade produced by shoreline trees or aquatic weeds attracts catfish, too. In large ponds built by damming creeks, standing timber, creek channel ledges, and schools of baitfish mean nearby cats.

*Pond corners often concentrate catfish.*

## TYPES OF CATFISH PONDS

Pond structure and function (morphometry) are important in determining fish population characteristics and behavior. The size and type of watershed (the area around a pond that brings runoff to it) determine water level, water clarity, productivity, flow-through, and water-quality characteristics like pH and dissolved oxygen.

Pond management (fertilization, stocking, feeding, weed control, drawdowns) affects the number and size of fish and the way they use structural elements in ponds.

Most ponds are one of 3 basic types:

## DUG POND

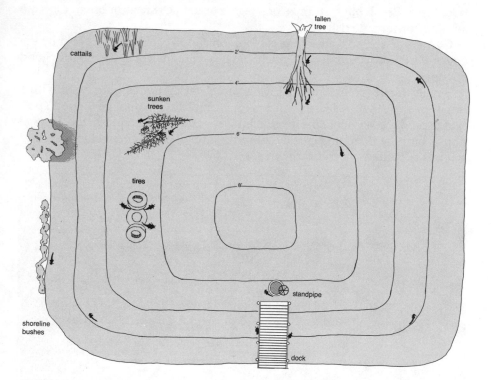

*Farm ponds with shallow, featureless basins are often dug with earth-moving equipment. Water runs off adjacent land to keep them full, but supplemental pumping from wells may be necessary in dry periods.*

*Dug ponds are generally less than 5 acres, but management can make them very productive for channel catfish.*

*Active cats roam shallow banks. They hold near structural elements like fallen trees, docks, and weedbeds, or in shade produced by shoreline trees and bushes.*

*Corners and depth breaks attract cats when better cover is scarce. During summer, the deepest areas lack oxygen. Fish avoid them despite the cooler water. When water is pumped into a pond, cats often are attracted to the flow.*

# BUILT POND

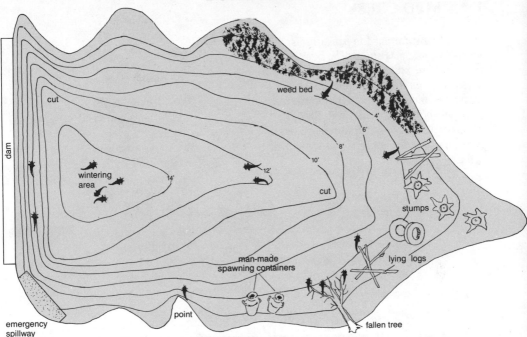

Building a dam across a low area will create a pond if the watershed and soil type have been accurately surveyed. The dam backs up runoff. Ponds of up to 100 acres can form.

The area near the dam is deepest. Cats winter there and move toward shallow areas in spring. Cuts, points, and flats with wood hold spring cats. As the spawn approaches, cats search shallow areas for hollow logs, natural crevices, and manmade structure like tires, drums, or cans in which to lay eggs.

Pond types range from simple dug ponds of less than an acre, to small reservoirs that may span 500 acres.

## DAMMED CREEK

Creeks are dammed to power mills, for irrigation, and for fishing. The creek channel is a focal point for catfish during all seasons. Standing or submerged timber along channels is particularly attractive.

Creeks often keep ponds from stratifying so some cats move deep in summer. Species diversity usually is high, and structural elements are diverse.

Low fishing pressure can mean superb catfishing.

Final tip for ponds: The biggest cats tend to suspend during summer. Fish baits halfway down in the column of water.

## Chapter 5

# THE YEAR OF THE CHANNEL CATFISH

### Calendar Of The Seasons

Channel catfish like all fish have an annual cycle of activities. Understanding this cycle helps to catch them consistently. Use Calendar Periods to categorize catfish behavior, location, activity, and catchability throughout a year. It's the basis for comparison that helps you plan fishing strategy.

In-Fisherman divides the fishing year into 10 basic Calendar Periods of fish response. A general characterization of each period includes:

*Winter:* Coldest water of the year. Frozen water occurs in northern regions. River catfish reside in deep holes away from heavy current.

*Cold Water:* Occurs during late fall and very early spring. Fish are grouped in or near winter holding areas.

*Prespawn:* Fish are on the way to or in the vicinity of spawning areas. Fish often feed and group heavily. Fishing can be very good.

*Spawn:* A brief, variable period linked to the range of preferred spawning temperatures for each fish species. Feeding activity usually slows when fish are spawning, although fish of the same species don't always spawn at the same time.

## The Ten In-Fisherman Calendar Periods

| 1 | 2 | 3 | 4 | 5 | 6 | 7 | 8 | 9 | 10 |
|---|---|---|---|---|---|---|---|---|---|
| Prespawn | Spawn | Postspawn | Presummer | Summer Peak | Summer | Postsummer | Turnover | Cold Water | Winter |

*Postspawn:* A brief transition period with length depending on water and weather conditions. Fish begin feeding strategies and move toward areas they'll use for much of the rest of the year.

*Presummer:* A continuing transition period. Fish search for areas to spend the summer and begin to establish summer patterns.

*Summer Peak:* Fish establish a pattern in a habitat that can sustain them for summer. The sudden presence of other fish usually spurs competitive feeding and good fishing.

*Summer:* Usually a long period when fish remain in habitat areas established during the Summer Peak. Fish activity and location are predictable.

*Postsummer:* Cooler weather lowers water temperatures, and fish move toward areas where they'll spend winter. Cooler water often spurs feeding.

*Fall Turnover:* Occurs in lakes, ponds, and reservoirs that stratify into 3 distinct water-temperature layers during summer. As fall progresses, colder weather lowers surface water temperatures, the colder water sinks, and stratification breaks down, allowing fish to use the entire column of water. Usually a time of poor fishing. Rarely affects rivers—Postsummer slides into the fall Cold Water, then Winter Periods.

Calendar Periods are at the mercy of Mother Nature. They don't last a certain number of days, nor do they occur on specific dates each year. Their length varies yearly, depending on weather trends and water conditions. Calendar Periods that last a few days one year may last several weeks the next year.

Of course, the annual rhythm of rivers differs from the rhythm of lakes, and the rhythm of annual channel catfish activity differs from other species. For example, the growth and death of a yearly crop of aquatic vegetation is a major influence in lakes. Weeds don't have this impact on catfish in rivers. Rivers, on the other hand, go through turbulent runoff periods; most lakes don't. Most importantly, though, catfish spawn much later than most other North American fish species. A long Prespawn Period produces an extended period of good fishing.

On a simpler note, catfishing begins after rivers stabilize during spring and catfish move into a long Prespawn Period. After spawning, cats settle into holding areas for summer. Fall weather cools water and generally moves cats downriver to seek large, deep holes in which to spend winter. Winter, which may include ice cover, reduces catfish activity, except during periods of extended warm weather, which may produce very good fishing.

The catfish calendar presented here includes the 10 In-Fisherman Calendar Periods grouped to capture the special flavor of the channel catfish year in rivers. Begin with the Winter Period moving into spring. Our "Spring Period" includes the end of the spring Cold Water Period as well as the Prespawn, Postspawn, and Presummer Periods—periods that last well into June and July in many regions.

Our "Summer Period" includes the Summer Peak, Summer and Postsummer Periods. The "Fall Period" or "Cooling Period" includes the Cold Water Period preceding winter.

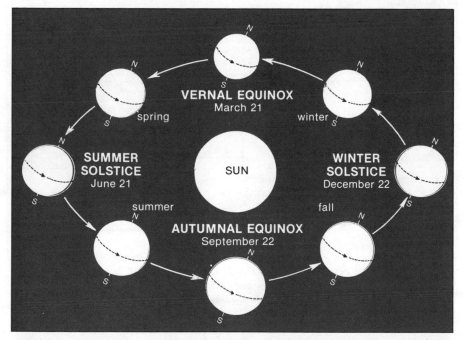

*Spring, summer, fall, winter. The pendulum swings between seasons, bringing obvious changes on land, but more difficult-to-define changes underwater. Photoperiod (length of daylight) influences the tempo of the environment, from microorganisms to top-of-the-line predators. The intensity and duration of light in a yearly cycle influences catfish migrations, spawning, and feeding.*

## WINTER PERIOD
*Water Temperature: A Body of Water*
*at its Coldest for an Extended Period*
*General Fish Mood: Negative*

This is an extended period that can't be defined by precise environmental markers since catfish live in a variety of geographic areas. The Winter Period includes two In-Fisherman Calendar Periods: Cold Water and Ice Water or Winter. In the southern half of the catfish range, ice-up doesn't occur.

The Winter Period is characterized by almost constant cold temperatures. How cold depends on geographic location and winter's severity. In Minnesota and Manitoba, water on lakes and parts of most rivers is under 3 feet of ice. Water temperatures range from about 32°F to 39°F. In southern states, winter water temperatures usually run in the 40°F range—upper 50°F range in Florida.

We define this period by what catfish do, which is basically the same no matter where they're located. In winter, catfish face a long period of temperatures much

## THE CATFISH CALENDAR

| Gregorian Calendar | Jan | Feb | Mar | Apr | May | June | July | Aug | Sept | Oct | Nov | Dec |
|---|---|---|---|---|---|---|---|---|---|---|---|---|
| **Northern Range** | | 10 | | 9 | 1 | | 2,3,4,5 | 6 | 7 | 9 | | 10 |
| **Mid Range** | 10 | 9 | | 1 | | 2,3,4,5 | | | 6 | 7 | 9 | 10 |
| **Southern Range** | 10 | 9 | | 1 | | 2,3,4,5 | | | | 6 | 7 | 9 | 10 |

1. Prespawn
2. Spawn
3. Postspawn
4. Presummer
5. Summer Peak
6. Summer
7. Postsummer
8. Fall Turnover
9. Cold Water
10. Winter*

1,2,3,4,5,6
potential extensive
overlap of periods.

*Coldest water of the year.

*The 10 Calendar Periods of fish response can vary in length as much as 4 weeks from one year to the next. The periods aren't based on the Gregorian calendar, so they do not occur on specific dates each year. Instead, the Calendar Periods are based on nature's clock.*

*In addition, the Calendar Periods vary by regions of the country. Being in a warm climate, the rivers of the South have an extended Summer Period and a brief Winter Period. In contrast, the rivers along the US-Canadian border have extended Cold Water and Winter Periods. Channel cats in Florida or Texas could be in the Spawning Period while those in northern Minnesota are still in the Winter Period.*

*The unusual thing about the channel catfish calendar is the long period during which individual cats may be in one of 6 different periods at the same time. In most situations, this doesn't affect fish location and fishing patterns much.*

# CALENDAR PERIOD REGIONAL TIMETABLE

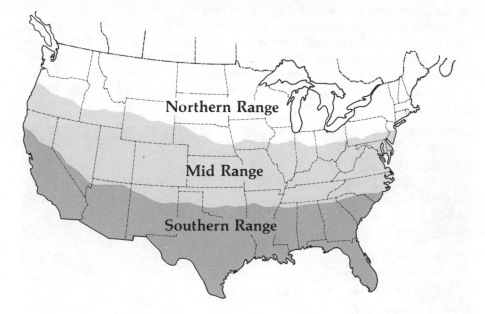

Northern Range

Mid Range

Southern Range

The timing of the channel catfish Spawn Period illustrates the region-by-region progression of Calendar Periods. Region (latitude), water temperature, weather trends, length of daylight, inter- and intraspecies competition for habitat and an internal clock are some of the factors influencing the exact timing of the spawn. Not all channel cats spawn at the same time even in the same body of water. While the bulk of the adult fish in a given river may spawn during a few days of ideal conditions, there will still be some early- and some late-spawning fish.

Regionally, the onset of channel catfish spawning may begin in early May in the South or as late as August in southern Canada. The following chart lists typical spawning months for channel catfish in representative areas:

## TYPICAL SPAWNING MONTHS

| AREA | MONTHS |
|------|--------|
| Florida | April - early June |
| Alabama/Georgia | May - June |
| Texas/Oklahoma | May - June |
| Kentucky/Tennessee | June - July |
| Missouri/Illinois/Iowa | June - July |
| Ohio | June - early August |
| Minnesota/Wisconsin | June - early August |
| Manitoba | July - August |

colder than they encounter the rest of the year. They go into a winter lethargy, a sort of suspended animation, as they lie in the deepest holes or deepest pockets off the main current flow, areas with slow-flowing water.

Scuba divers report seeing catfish behind boulders that break current. If there aren't enough boulders, catfish appear to snug behind whatever they find to reduce current. Then other catfish line up behind the first one, nose to tail in a chainlike formation, to reduce water resistance.

In smaller rivers, a holding hole might be 6 feet deep or less. In bigger rivers, holes may be 20 to 40 feet deep.

*A congregation of flatheads in a slack-water hole on the Mississippi River during winter. Big channel cats were mixed among flatheads. The fish were in a state of stupor; silt covered their bodies.*

In the middle and southern regions of the country, catfish don't completely stop moving and feeding during winter. A radio tagging study on the Missouri River showed catfish almost completely dormant during a bitterly cold winter. But during a mild winter they moved short distances. An extended period of warm weather in January or February can stimulate catfish activity near deeper river holes. The holes are easy to locate because the water's usually low. Since fish are highly concentrated in predictable locations, anglers can make tremendous catches.

During midwinter when cats are inactive and packed in river holes, it's often possible to snag them. This is illegal in most areas.

# SPRING SEASON
*Water Temperature: Rising*
*General Fish Mood: Neutral to Positive*

When ice leaves or early spring weather arrives, walleyes, pike, and sauger move quickly through the Prespawn Period into the Spawn Period. It's a time of rapid transition. Not so with channel catfish, which probably won't spawn for months. Even in far northern waters, where the Prespawn-Spawn transition is compressed, these periods may span months.

In rivers, early spring usually means continued cold and turbid water. Northern areas experience snow melt and cold spring rains. Southern areas get cold spring rains. The water begins to warm gradually, and catfish activity increases.

In early spring, catfish might still spend most of their time in deep holes. Eventually, rising water temperature stimulates catfish metabolism. No distinct temperature marks this point. In southern regions where water temperatures have been in the 50s, catfish might start feeding when the water reaches the low 60°F range. In northern regions, 45°F usually means cats will prowl, but temperatures in the upper 50°F range are better.

Mostly, we sense when the first good run of cats will be aggressively feeding. Spring weather will have whipsawed from nasty to nice, but suddenly it's nice for days in a row. You smell a spring thundershower in the air and stand on your lawn, bounce a little, and feel a give in the soil. The lawn is about to come alive at night with the first strong showing of nightcrawlers. Trees are budding, frogs begin their evening chorus, and ducks, geese, grouse, and most of the rest of the animal world is suddenly alive with activity.

Catfish are moving, but still avoiding direct current. And there's usually more current now than any other time of year. Current concentrates fish in areas where they find relief from it. The fish may be in the core of a hole, the deepest spot, but more likely they move toward shoreline holding areas.

This is the season for live baits or sour baits. Cats find plenty of fish that have died over winter and are beginning to decompose as water temperatures rise.

# PRESPAWN PERIOD
*Water Conditions: Rising Temperatures*
*and Stabilizing River Flows*
*General Fish Mood: Positive*

What river walleyes do in fall, channel catfish do in spring: move, usually upstream, sometimes into smaller feeder rivers, searching first for food and secondly for spawning habitat.

No sharp demarcation exists between the preceding period and this one. The periods blend naturally as water temperature continues to increase into the 60°F range and river flows stabilize. The main difference is catfish behavior. Their metabolic rate is much higher, so they need more food and are also better able to search for it. Higher water also lets fish move to a variety of areas.

The earliest upriver movements are motivated more by the need to feed than by a spawning urge. Because cats can move to more areas than they could earlier in the year, they don't need to accept the limited forage in holes where they spent winter.

Barriers such as big dams and low-head dams temporarily stop movement

# CHANNEL CAT GROWTH RATE

| Location | Average Length at Age (inches) | | | | | | | | |
|---|---|---|---|---|---|---|---|---|---|
| | 1 | 3 | 5 | 7 | 9 | 11 | 13 | 15 | 17 |
| Red R., Manitoba | 10 | 11 | 15 | 20 | 20 | 27 | 27 | 33 | 34 |
| Several Kansas Lakes | 3 | 10 | 13 | 17 | 19 | | | | |
| Salt. R., MO | 3 | 8 | 12 | 16 | | | | | |
| Oklahoma Average | 4 | 12 | 16 | 20 | 24 | 25 | 26 | | |
| Des Moines R., IA | 2 | 8 | 12 | 17 | 21 | 25 | 27 | | |
| Lk. Moultrie, SC | 3 | 11 | 17 | 24 | 29 | 32 | 36 | | |
| Kentucky Lk., TN | 4 | 9 | 12 | 17 | 22 | | | | |
| Lk. Havasu, CA | 3 | 7 | 9 | 14 | 18 | 19 | 23 | | |
| Lk. Erie | 3 | 9 | 12 | 14 | | | | | |
| Potomac R., MD | 8 | 13 | 18 | | | | | | |
| Wisconsin R., WI | 5 | 9 | 12 | 16 | 19 | 22 | 24 | 27 | |
| Missouri R., NE | 2 | 9 | 13 | 17 | 16 | | | | |
| Lk. Oahe, SD | 1 | 8 | 13 | 17 | 20 | 22 | 24 | 24 | 25 |
| Pony Express Lk., MO | 4 | 13 | 18 | 22 | 24 | 26 | 25 | | |
| Mississippi R., IA | 5 | 12 | 16 | 20 | 23 | | | | |
| St. Lawrence R., Quebec | 4 | 8 | 10 | 12 | 13 | 14 | 16 | 17 | |

*Channel catfish growth rate has been studied throughout their range. Cats lack scales, the most commonly used aging structure for other fish, but pectoral and dorsal spines and vertebrae can be sectioned and examined microscopically. Year marks (annuli) can be counted and measured to determine age and growth. This table describes average growth rates for various populations. Note the high growth variability and the many years required for a cat to reach trophy size. Cats, like many fish, probably make most of their yearly growth gains during the period from late spring through midsummer. Population growth rates are determined by abundance and type of forage, quality of habitat (including water), length of growing season, and intraspecific competition. The oldest channel cat on record was a specimen about 40 years old from the St. Lawrence River. The oldest fish grow very little and age determination isn't precise.*

and concentrate cats. This period compares somewhat to the prespawn movement of steelhead in rivers, with fish constantly moving, stopping to hold in spots offering food and protection from current, then they moving again as feeding opportunities diminish.

Catch a fish or two from a small spot and come back in a day or two and catch three more. The spot has been restocked by the restless movement of the fish.

In high water without impassable barriers, catfish may move 75 miles or more—channel cats have moved as far as 111 miles in 36 days. When water is high and fish are finding food, they keep moving. At times, however, they move only a few miles.

Where catfish spawn is determined by where they are when spawning time nears. Cats don't always return to locations where they spawned before. They often return to general areas, however. Many catfish in the lower portion of the Red River in Manitoba, for example, return to the same slough off the main river each year, despite varying river levels. Catfish move upstream, looking for food and future spawning sites.

Prespawn movement often continues until cats reach an impassable barrier like a dam. They'll search the area for possible spawning locations like holes in riprap or rocky outcroppings near the dam. If the area below the dam is too silty, catfish drift downstream to look for spawning sites. Spawners may spread over a long stretch of river.

The Prespawn Period offers the potential for the year's best fishing. The fish are moving—searching and actively feeding. Be there.

## SPAWN PERIOD

*Water Temperature: 75°F or Higher*
*General Fish Mood: Positive-Negative*

Catfish spawning may span a month or more, so the spawn doesn't have the negative impact on angling it would have if all cats spawned at the same time. Also, channel cats bite almost anything near a spawning hole, so find a spawning area and you may find good fishing.

*Prespawn migration usually continues until catfish reach a dam. Cats may use the tailwater area as a foraging area and may also spawn there. More likely, however, they eventually drift downstream to look for appropriate spawning sights as the time approaches.*

The spawn is triggered by the length of daylight (photoperiod). Day length is sensed in the brain, probably in the pineal gland. Linking spawning in part to day-length is one guarantee against having eggs hatch too early or late, which could happen if spawning time was based solely on water temperature. In addition, catfish have an internal biological clock that causes maturation of eggs even if external stimuli are absent.

Catfish are motivated to spawn by water temperatures of 75°F or above. According to some studies, temperatures approaching 80°F are ideal. Catfish kept in water too cool for spawning, spawn when water temperatures are quickly raised to 75°F, if the time of year is appropriate.

Spawning, then, is regulated by the interplay of an internal clock, the day-length and water temperature.

Spawning can take place as early as May in the South and August in the North. In Missouri, dates range from late May to early July. The most common spawning month across the channel cat's geographic range is June.

To begin the spawn, a male channel cat seeks a hole or pocket in a bank.

Catfish in ponds with no suitable places to form holes won't spawn, but if artificial spawning structures are introduced, they'll readily spawn.

The hole should be secure, preferably with only one entrance big enough to admit the male and female. A small entrance not much larger than a fish's body is ideal. Big fish spawn in big holes, small fish in small holes. If the hole's entrance isn't much bigger than the male, he'll lie with his head toward the entrance, nearly filling it, to effectively guard eggs and fry.

In smaller rivers, crevices near rocky riffles offer possible spots for spawning holes. Undercut banks, muskrat holes, and objects in the water—hollow logs, car bodies, tires, buckets—are all possible spawning sites.

First, the male sweeps the hole to clean and enlarge it. Eventually the male lures a female into the hole. The female ejects eggs in a sticky, cohesive clump and the male fertilizes them.

Females produce from 2,000 to over 70,000 eggs, depending on the size of the fish. Then the female leaves or is driven from the hole by the male. She produces one clutch of eggs a year. Males, however, may spawn more than once if the spawning season is extended. The supply of available males often exceeds the number of sexually mature females.

*Cutbanks and cover, a prime combination for prespawn and spawning channel catfish!*

The male is a good guardian. As mentioned, his massive head usually fills the entrance to the nest. He's aggressive in his defense of the eggs. Anything stuck near him will be hit or bit. Holes with two or more entrances probably suffer egg loss because the male can't guard them as well. He also aerates and keeps silt off the eggs by fanning them with his fins.

Little is known about what happens next in the wild, because observations are based on catfish in clear hatchery ponds where they may behave differently. But we do know that eggs hatch in about a week. Then fry spend about a week in the nest being protected by the male before they enter the river and begin life among predators.

Some observers say the young slip into the river and are immediately on their own. Others who observed cats in small ponds report that males protect young for several days after they leave the nest. Survival of the young is probably better in turbid water than in clear water, as reduced visibility in turbid water conceals the young from predators.

## SETTLING PERIOD
### (Encompasses Postspawn and Presummer Periods)
*Water Temperature: Upper 70s to Mid 80s*
*General Fish Mood: Neutral to Positive*

This period, important in fishing for some fish, isn't vital to catfishermen because the catfish spawning period is so spread out. Even in ponds where water temperatures and day-length are identical for all fish, not all catfish spawn at the same time.

Catfish probably go through a type of recuperative period after spawning, but to an angler, it doesn't matter if a few fish are recuperating, because at any given time, most of them aren't. Some fish are almost always feeding.

This period probably occurs in late June to July in much of the catfish range. Catfish are on the move again, often moving downstream from spawning sites, looking for deep, cover-laden holes that offer security and food. Downstream movement isn't automatic. If the spawning area offers good summer habitat, they may linger.

If water levels are high and rising, channel cats are as likely to move upstream as downstream during this settling period. More typically, though, water levels are dropping, so catfish move downstream, often leaving small tributaries to enter bigger rivers. These movements are more pronounced in small creeks than in big rivers.

## SUMMER
### (Encompasses Summer Peak, Summer and Postsummer Periods)
*Water Temperature: 80s or Above*
*General Fish Mood: Positive*

The Summer Period includes much of July, August, and September in most regions of the channel cat's range.

Summer means prime-time fishing. Fish are in predictable locations. They feed aggressively, although not all the time. They have plenty of food available, at least during the beginning of summer, so they put on much of the year's growth during this period that doesn't end until water begins to cool during fall.

Find the best holes with the biggest catfish and fish them with the right baits at the right time.

*Stable summer weather means consistent fishing as cats settle into predictable locations and feeding patterns.*

## COOLING PERIOD
*Water Temperature: Cooling from 80s*
*General Fish Mood: Positive to*
*Neutral to Negative*

As late summer becomes fall, longer, cooler nights and cool rains reduce river temperatures. In early fall, catfish location depends mostly on river level. During stable levels, catfish continue holding in holes where they spent the summer. Heavy rain during September or October may pull catfish upriver. Generally, though, especially when water temperatures begin to cool into the 60°F range, cats move downstream toward bigger, deeper water where they'll more likely find very deep wintering holes.

Eventually, the biggest, deepest holes gather large groups of catfish. As water temperatures continue to fall, catfish activity is confined to the immediate vicinity of this wintering hole.

Catfish in confined quarters can mean good fishing. Obviously though, it's important to fish the right holes.

## Chapter 6
# WHEN TO CATFISH
### Peak Periods For Fine Fishing

Some fishermen fish for catfish because they like being on a river. They're happy to watch the river slide by, and they don't worry about peak action periods. Fine. But catfish are like other fish. Certain times of the day and year they're more active and catchable. To catch the most and biggest catfish, concentrate on key times.

Peak times may not be the times you hear about. Somehow, the idea exists that catfishing is a nighttime affair. At times, though, fishing is best during mid-day. And even when night fishing's good, the action usually isn't consistent all night. Peaks and valleys in activity occur, and we want to tell you about those we've identified over many years in the rivers we've fished.

Catfishing is also supposed to be best during the hottest time of the year. Good, yes. Best? Sometimes. Too many anglers underestimate coolwater cat-fishing because the word is that cats are a warmwater fish. A survey of I.G.F.A. line-class catfish records (channel cats, blues, and flatheads combined) showed that hot summer months, when more anglers are fishing, produced only half as many catfish as cooler months. The prespawn bite is probably the best bite of the year. But cats congregate during late fall. Find them and fish during a warming trend, and you may have tremendous fishing.

Generally, too, catfish are supposed to bite best when water is rising. General-ly, yes. Absolutely? No. Absolutes rarely exist in catfishing.

So when are the best times to go catfishing?

## SPRING

Spring offers a period of weather transition. Streams warm and often become high and silty. This is a long and important period in the catfish angler's calen-dar, a period unique for challenges and opportunities.

One challenge is finding fish. Cats are on the move, generally heading upstream in search of food and a place to spawn. Where cats were yesterday isn't where they might be tomorrow.

On the other hand, catfish are almost desperate to feed after virtually hiber-nating during winter. Even in the south, activity and feeding are greatly reduced when water temperatures fall below 55°F. Warming water soars metabolic rates and the need to feed in order to grow. Females and males must be healthy to successfully spawn, and females need extra nutrition to complete egg maturation.

Fish are determined to feed, yet cold, high, silty water hinders them. Though channel cats adapt to these conditions, they don't thrive in them. High water does concentrate cats, though, along shoreline structural elements that break current. They may not bite aggressively, but you'll know where they are. Slow down and thoroughly fish fewer spots.

"Good" weather is stable weather. Stable weather and stable water conditions are keys for great spring catfishing. A period of little rainfall and warm days and nights reduces water flow, clears water, and increases water temperature, which stimulates cat activity. Rising water usually isn't a blessing in spring; stability is.

But spring is a time of unstable weather with frequent storms and cold fronts. Don't wait for a week of good weather before planning a catfish trip. Look for a stretch of 2 to 4 warm days.

Spring often produces wonderful catfishing. This is also one of the best times to fish the evening twilight period. The importance of vision in the catfish's feeding strategy is underrated. Although they use many other senses, they bite best when they can see well. So in spring, expect less action when water is silty, and particularly at night in dirty water. Take advantage of spring's all-day fishing because when conditions worsen, the evening bite disappears.

## The Morning Peak

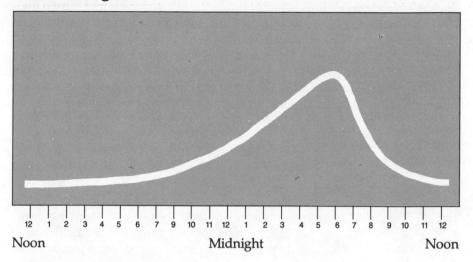

| | | | | | | | | | | | | | | | | | | | | | | |
|---|---|---|---|---|---|---|---|---|---|---|---|---|---|---|---|---|---|---|---|---|---|---|
| 12 | 1 | 2 | 3 | 4 | 5 | 6 | 7 | 9 | 10 | 11 | 12 | 1 | 2 | 3 | 4 | 5 | 6 | 7 | 8 | 9 | 10 | 11 | 12 |

Noon        Midnight        Noon

*No simple chart can accurately illustrate catfish activity for each catfish species in every type of water during each season. This chart, however, illustrates a general trend in catfish activity on many bodies of water after catfish have spawned and settled into a summer pattern.*

*Catfish may feed during the day or night, depending on the type of water, water conditions, and weather. Generally, however, bigger catfish become more active after dark during summer. Activity often peaks in an intense early morning feeding period too many fishermen miss.*

## SUMMER

As spring fades to summer, rivers become warmer, lower, clearer, and more stable. As we noted in the last chapter, good catfishing covers a broad range of calendar periods. From prespawn through the end of summer, the sport doesn't change much.

Cats hold in distinct holes. They've found the best river spots, and predictable feeding patterns develop. Cats quickly learn where food is and how to most efficiently forage.

Summer days stretch up to 16 hours. Fishing is better at dark or after dark, with a typical flurry of activity at sunset. The sunset period is overrated on most waters, though, because often only small cats become active. While fishing then is often better than during the day, it isn't the best time to fish. In many rivers, fishing picks up at sunset and builds steadily through the night, peaking at dawn.

During stable summer river conditions, the dawn peak is from about two hours before sunrise until several hours after. The length of the peak varies, but expect better action on the dark side of dawn. One variable may be the relative success cats have had feeding. If they fill their bellies early, the peak drops off sharply as the sun rises. If feeding conditions aren't quite so good, cats may still bite when office workers take their first coffee break. Cats feed actively because not finding prey may mean having to wait until evening to try again. This aggressive feeding almost always halts by mid-morning, although you can catch cats all day if you concentrate on fish in a neutral mood holding in snags or at the base of riffle areas.

Cats are like many other fish. Walleyes and chinook salmon feed at night, often with peaks around sunrise. It's as if the fish sense approaching daylight and feed frantically before it's too late. Or catfish may enjoy a brief sight advantage over prey as light changes at daybreak. We don't know why, but we do know the dawn period is a special time for cats to feed. This is the time to be on the river throughout the Summer Period.

Doug Stange discussing key fishing periods with old Zacker:

"You mean you didn't want someone to see you fishing, or fishing legally with a pole line?" I'd asked.

"No use ruinin' your reputation," he'd chuckled.

Mostly he was joking, though. Mostly he didn't want anyone seeing his spots. Mostly he fished at night to keep his secrets. The boys would set baits just after dark and pick them up just before daylight, for when big cats first get hooked they make a terrible noise before settling down and sulking on the bottom. Sure. Leave the lines in for 24 hours on smaller-fish water. But not on big-fish water.

And then he'd said something important, something that reinforced an important observation of my own.

"Too often big cats bite during the early daylight hours," he'd said. "You couldn't afford to leave a line in and make a commotion then. Other fishermen wouldn't turn you in, but they'd sure steal your lines and your fish.

"For my money," he'd continued, "the best time for big cats runs from 'bout 4 to 8 in the morning. Big cats feed at night, but they need to see, feel and smell things to be successful. They need light, but not too much light. That's one reason the full moon's so good. But most of the time, big cats that don't feed successfully at night get fed full quickly in early morning. That's the best bite. As morning progresses, the bite gets worse and worse as more and more cats feed themselves full."

## SPECIAL CONDITIONS

General rules work for many situations, but there usually are exceptions. During summer, for example, cats generally spend daylight hours in deeper water away from strong current. But a recent drought in North Dakota and western Minnesota affected the Red River, which flows north from the North Dakota-Minnesota border into Manitoba. Water levels dropped so low that cats searched for the most available current.

Three summer conditions generally affect catfish: cold fronts, rain, and changing dam flows.

Cold fronts produce poor fishing, especially for bass and walleyes. In a typical weather cycle, cold fronts occur every few days. Before a front passes, the weather usually turns humid and skies are hazy. The air feels muggy.

Then a band of cold weather moves through, possibly bringing a storm. After

*While stable summer weather keys predictable catfish activity, a gathering storm, a break in summer stability, often puts cats on the prowl—so much the better if the storm is accompanied by a rise in water level that moves bait around in the river.*

the front passes, the air becomes cooler and dryer. Skies display the deep blue of tourism photos. Clouds are high and wispy and the air is fresh.

No one knows exactly why cold fronts affect fish, although the change in sunlight penetration is suspected. Barometric pressure increases markedly, but few anglers or biologists even speculate how this might affect fish behavior. Do summer cold fronts hurt catfishing? Yes, but not disastrously. In general, fish in moving water systems seem less affected by fronts than fish in still water. Stable weather, however, keys better fishing than periods of frequent fronts, so the longer the interval between fronts, the better the fishing.

Fronts, however, often produce rainstorms, which may improve catfishing for a time. This is especially true during August dog days when fishing is good, but a little stale. Then a thunderstorm brings cloud cover that often improves daytime fishing.

Heavy rain raises water levels; current picks up, and food washes into the river and drifts downstream into catfish holes. Most importantly, we believe, baitfish

*Stable summer dam flows mean predictable catfish activity. Sudden increase in flow, however, often keys sudden feeding forays by increasing the quantity of food available to catfish.*

living in small pools or on flats isolated from big cats by stretches of shallow water move downstream into holes, and cats respond to this infusion of new food. Rising water also gives catfish access to areas that had been too shallow.

Similarly, summer tailwater fishing often turns on and off as dam gates open or close. Thus, your calendar of best times to go fishing is often dictated by the power-generation schedule.

Most dams are built to control water levels and generate electricity. Many dams have gates that are adjusted to let water through or over the dam to bypass power-generating turbines. As gates are closed, little water flows except through the turbines; as gates are opened, water rushes through.

Flood-control dams usually regulate flows consistently unless floods occur. Tailwaters are stable and predictable, so catfishing follows the typical summer pattern, progressing to a peak at sunrise.

Dams built primarily to generate electricity release water irregularly. Electrical demand rises and falls sharply. Major differences occur between weekend flows when power needs are less and weekday flows when businesses demand electricity. Electrical demand is also lower at night.

Increasing flow usually improves tailwater catfishing. Minnows and other small fish, sucked through turbines during generation, emerge as cut-bait catfish delicacies. Increased current also changes the world below the dam. Crayfish are dislodged from their bottom hides and smaller fish relocate. Catfish feed more efficiently as prey is moved and pinned by current into predictable places.

Catfish respond to increased flow below dams by feeding more actively, just as they do to rising water in rivers.

Lunar influences on catfishing? We've talked to cat anglers who swear the best angling occurs around the full moon, and we've talked to good cat anglers who fish the dark of the moon. Without analyzing statistical catch data, lunar influence remains open to conjecture. We'd suggest, though, that several days before and after the full and new moon probably spur better fishing.

Lunar influences, however, probably are secondary to factors like water clarity, water temperature, current flow, time of night, and other factors we've discussed.

Doug Stange discussing with Zacker the effect of the moon on catfish:

And I'd asked him about the moon—"Do you fish by it?"—and I knew I'd struck upon an important topic by the pause he took before answering.

"The moon, the full moon," he said, "works powerful on big cats. The best days are those before the full moon, maybe starting five days before.

"You know, folks think all a catfish can do is smell and taste things. But they see darn good, and they like to feed at night in light. But there's somethin' about the full moon that makes them active, too.

"Never cared much for the dark moon, 'cause I think the fish might bite best during the day then; but then I never fished much then because it was too easy to be seen."

## FALL

Fall can mean wonderful fishing, and it's typically a time when fewer anglers fish. In northwest Iowa, for example, the trend usually went something like this:

Fishing during at least the first three weeks of September was an extension of summer fishing. By early October, however, cats usually were moving, spurred by cooling water to search for the deepest of deep holes in long stretches of river. The key was knowing large stretches of river well enough to have pinpointed the biggest and deepest holes. As fall progressed, those holes gathered more and more cats as they moved to appropriate wintering areas.

Certainly by the third week of October, fishing was wonderful in these areas if stable warm weather and stable river levels prevailed. Three of four days of cold fall rain brought cold, dirty water and increased current, which usually halted fishing.

If the river was clear and low in November, catfish would still bite during the day under mild stable conditions. Most of the holes that held cats during summer were devoid of cats then, however. Few cats were active even on good days, but the concentration of fish made up for the lack of aggressively feeding fish. Fall was also prime time to catch a few walleyes and pike.

Almost no one fishes cats in fall. In farmland areas, set out at dawn with a

# Important Periods During The Lunar Month

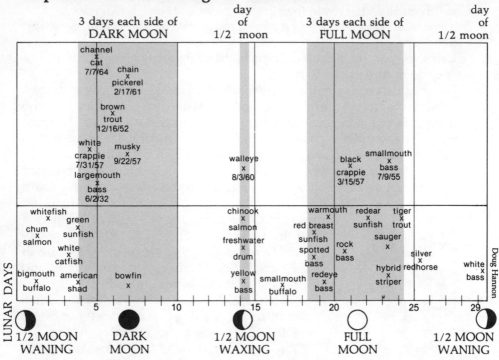

*Selected world-record gamefish catches.*

canoe, a shotgun, and a fishing rod. As you float downstream you can jump-shoot wood ducks, and you're sure to crack a few squirrels. Beach the canoe at a deep catfish hole and drop a line for an hour or two. That's living!

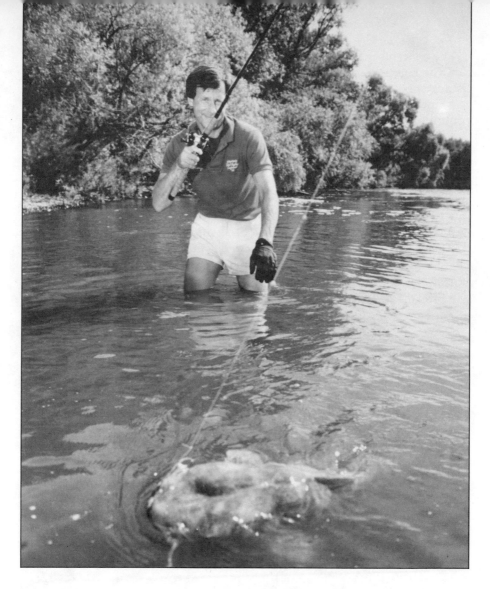

# Chapter 7
# LOCATING CATFISH
## How To Read Rivers

Locating catfish consistently depends on easy-to-employ strategies to identify the best portions of rivers and the best spots in those portions. No complex concepts here, just critically important ones. Apply them each time out and you'll dramatically improve your catch and your appreciation of the sport.

Key concepts include:

• The biggest mistake most catfishermen make is spending too much time fishing spots that don't hold many catfish.

• Finding channel cats in most rivers is easier once you learn to analyze the continuing river patterns of riffles, holes, and runs.

• During most yearly periods, the lives of catfish revolve around river holes and associated riffles and runs.

• Holes are not created equal. To analyze which holes have the most potential, learn how stream elements interact to fulfill catfish needs.

• The biggest, deepest, most cover-laden holes usually gather the most catfish.

• To find these holes, instead of fishing just one or two on each outing, walk or float farther and fish faster, looking for active catfish while you compare holes.

• Once you know where the best holes are, you can make the best judgement about when to fish them and how much time to spend there, relative to other holes.

• Streams and rivers share the same basic elements, but on a different scale.

## SMALL STREAM CATFISH LOCATION

The easiest way to understand catfish location in rivers is to look at small streams. Small streams are easier to get to know because the catfish world is compressed into a small area. In a large river, major holes may be half a mile apart. On a small stream, half a mile might contain 10 holes. You can move easily and see lots of water. More importantly, the continuing combination of riffles, holes and runs, and the cover elements that may exist in them are obvious. Small steams offer the easiest and quickest education in river make-up and how catfish react to it.

*Small rivers offer the easiest and quickest education in river make-up and how catfish react to it. The more you see and fish, the better you become at judging the water—true of rivers of all sizes.*

Catfishing on small streams translates directly to catfishing on larger rivers. Yet the anatomy of larger rivers is more subtle and confusing. If larger rivers are all that's readily available, you can learn to catch cats effectively, but it will take longer.

The typical small river is about 15 to 50 feet across. You can easily cast across it and move along the banks on foot, crossing without difficulty.

In Chapter 4 we mentioned the continuous riffle-hole-run series of river composition. Time now to discuss these in detail, for you'll need to judge the merits of each series of riffle-hole-run elements in deciding where to concentrate your fishing.

## RIFFLE-HOLE-RUN

As water meanders through a stream bed it flows over substrates of varying hardness. Riffles form over hard-bottomed areas and are shallower because current doesn't wash away hard bottom. Riffles form natural dams that obstruct moving water. A pool of water builds at the head of a riffle. Eventually water flows over the riffle, quickening over the constricted area like water forced through a hose nozzle.

*A hard-bottom riffle constricts water, making it flow forcefully downriver, cutting a hole where hard bottom meets softer bottom at the base of a riffle.*

Riffles in rocky trout streams may be over a quarter-mile long before rocky substrate meets softer substrate and the fast-flowing constricted water begins to scour a hole. Hard substrate isn't common in most areas where catfish rivers are located; so riffles usually are comparatively short, followed immediately by a hole. In most catfish streams in farm country, riffles rarely run for 30 yards—more likely 20 feet. Most dams are built on these natural dam areas because the river narrows there and firm bottom provides a solid base for a dam.

The turbulence of constricted water running over a rock-gravel riffle oxygenates water. Crevices in rock and gravel provide habitat for invertebrates like larval insects that serve as forage for fish.

The force of current flowing against the softer substrate at the end of a riffle scours a hole. So a riffle ends in a hole. A riffle's ruffled surface is obvious on most rivers. Look for fast, busy water—the riffle. A hole will be formed just below.

Holes, also called pools, are the home of catfish. They're wider and deeper sections of rivers. Depth varies according to local geology and current patterns, as well as the size of the river.

In a small stream, a typical hole during a stable summer period might be 30 feet long, 20 feet wide, and 4 feet deep. The biggest and deepest holes might be only twice those dimensions. Comparisons in size, depth, and available cover in holes are important, however, as we'll describe.

Holes gradually become shallower at their downstream end as suspended materials sink when water slows. The tail end of a hole becomes a run.

Runs are river flats—stretches with no significant depth changes. The bottom usually is sand and silt with occasional rocks and patches of gravel, plus debris—wood, tires, brush. In some regions, though, runs may be entirely composed of sand or rock. Catfish move through runs as they travel, but rarely hold for long unless abundant overhead cover offers protection for resting security. Flats are generally too shallow for cats to hold there unless cover is present.

Catfish make forays onto flats to feed, especially the deeper section of a flat

"Tell you somethin'," Zacker offered. "Don't mean squat where you set a baited line in a hole if fish aren't feeding when you set the bait. But you got to be patient and you got to have the right bait. A big cat knows what he wants to eat and he knows the hole he lives in like you know your kitchen.

"I've watched them big ones on a moonlit night in June when the water's clear. They lay up in the deepest part of the hole or maybe under a snag. You can fish 'em till hell freezes over and never even make 'em move—until they want to.

"When they start movin', they go 'round the hole a time or two, sort of to warm up before they ever eat somethin'. By that time the healthy fish, including smaller cats, have scattered and only the injured ones or the stupid ones are left. Big cats eat fish that need eatin'. But if there ain't no injured fish—like on a baited line—they set up in a proper place, and then everything's fair game."

"But what if you were specifically pole fishin'; you know, sportfishing?" Doug Stange asked. "Seems to me that the head end of a hole, where a shallow riffle or glide flows into the hole, is consistently the best possible spot."

"Sportfishing!" he snorted. "Times sure change. Now some folks say our fishing with lines wasn't right. Now you gotta race around in a fast boat and catch fish no bigger 'an we used for bait and win money. That's sport. That don't make sense. But that's fine. Seems to me that folks should just let other folks be, long as there's fish and game.

"As far as where you fish," he continued. "The place a big feedin' cat checks most often is the head of a hole. That's where they'll find a bait the quickest. Just remember that's where they set up when everything's fair game. Tell you what: I think those big cats can smell what's in the water 3 or 4 holes up from where they're at, and they been around long enough to know. Anything that enters the hole from the top side, they know it. And once they're set up, they rarely feed back."

"Back?" Doug asked.

"Yes, back," he said. "That's what I was tryin' to say. Once they're set up proper toward the front of a hole, they don't much bother with things—baits—anywhere else. Once they start feeding, the head of the hole—where the current comes from—is the key."

at the rear of a hole and the shallow portion of a flat immediately above a riffle. These shallow flats serve as nursery areas for fish fry and holding areas for minnows, chubs, suckers, and small catfish. Carp often feed on these flats and gar roam there, too. But adult catfish tend to prefer the more immediate confines of a hole area.

Like riffles, runs vary in length depending on bottom composition and river size. In our typical small river with a hole 4 feet deep and 20 feet long, the hole might be followed by a 30-yard run, before the river curves or runs over another area of hard bottom—a riffle—and the cycle repeats.

Holes, specific holes during summer and fall, are the center of the catfish world. Holes must be deep enough to provide security, and the surrounding area must offer food. The hole collects living and dead food, drifting or moving downriver.

Channel cats tend to move forward into current when they become active and feed. The upper end of a hole is a key feeding area. There cats find a definite edge, a dramatic change in current and depth. The tail end of a hole often tapers so gradually that it fades into the run. Rarely so the upper end of a hole where a riffle spills into the hole.

The scouring force of current at the upper end of holes often exposes rocks or boulders that break current and serve as catfish holding stations. Debris may also wash into this portion of the hole and divert current. Cats sometimes rest there when they're inactive, but more often they move deeper into the core of holes or into cover in holes. Active cats use slack water behind boulders or debris at the head of a hole as feeding and holding spots. Generally, the area from the bottom of the riffle to shortly downstream of the deepest part of the hole—the forward section of the hole—is the best feeding area.

The deepest part of the hole usually follows the tail (downstream end) of the riffle. Again, a hole's width and depth depend mainly on current and bottom. The core of the hole may also offer rocks or boulders for cats to hold near. Usually, though, current slows enough in the core of holes to let catfish lie anywhere.

Two critical elements of the catfish world, two major features of holes, determine how good a hole is. We've already mentioned cover objects that break current. Cover is always a potential attractor. But cover near distinct current has more potential than cover, say on a flat. Cover near the top of a hole where current has force is especially attractive. Channel cats use current as a conveyor belt to bring food to them. Yet they can't expend all their energy swimming against strong current. They use cover objects to break the force of current and funnel food into specific spots—percentage feeding areas for cats and percentage fishing areas for fishermen.

Cover may be a boulder. In the tail of the pool, boulders may be partially silted over, but near a riffle, current sweeps away debris and scours depressions in front and behind boulders. An old tire may be cover, or logs or tree roots. Even a sandbar is cover if it deflects current and creates an eddy or backwash area where current swirls in a circle or bends back upriver.

To catfish, cover serves as a feeding station or rest area, attractive in part because cover is different from the rest of the river. Mainly, though, cover helps gather food and lets catfish lie comfortably near current, the supplier of food.

## Snag Principles

Some river snags attract catfish; others don't. When evaluating a snag, ask these questions: Is it thick? Is it large? Is it associated with relatively deep water—a deeper hole? Is it associated with an expansive hole?

If the answers are yes, there are bound to be channel catfish relating to the snag, unless the area is fished down.

When river level is down, cats usually don't move long distances. Fishing pressure may remove many of the cats from a snag. It takes a big rise in water level to get cats moving. When that happens, a good snag will gather another group of cats.

## Active Cat Holding Areas in a Typical Hole

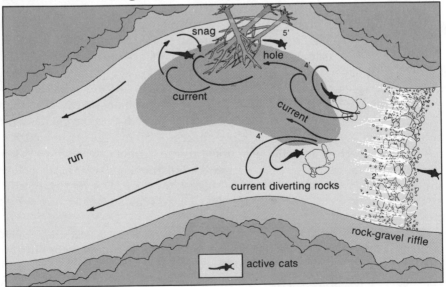

Inactive cats usually hold in the snag or in deeper water in a hole. Active cats feed near the snag, but are as likely to leave the snag and (1) move ahead of the riffle to feed in the fast, slick water, (2) find a spot to hold and wait for food below the riffle, or (3) roam the hole searching for food.

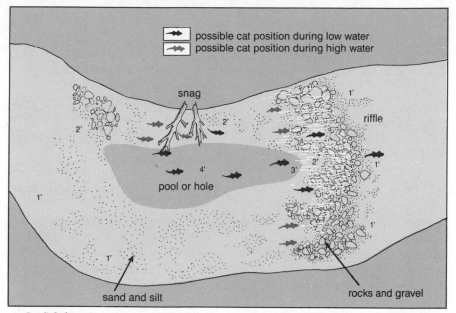

possible cat position during low water
possible cat position during high water

snag

riffle

2'

2'

1'

pool or hole

4'

3'

2'

1'

1'

1'

1'

1'

sand and silt

rocks and gravel

*Catfish location changes, depending on feeding mood and current. Active cats tend to stay at the head of the hole, although they'll also swim around the entire hole to check it out. Inactive or neutral fish hold in the core of the hole, or in or behind cover.*

*Heavy current forces catfish behind cover objects usually found along shore. Low flow draws cats to deeper water away from the bank.*

*Drift a bait through each possible spot. Usually patterns emerge quickly. If you catch cats at the head of one hole, they'll probably be at the head of the next hole, too.*

Cover objects aren't equally important. Catfish may occasionally use a large boulder near the end of a hole where current slackens, but not as often as a boulder toward the head of the hole. With increasing current, though, the rear boulder might be better. Then, too, if current flows heavily against one side of a hole, identical boulders on the opposite side receive different use by catfish. Unless current increases drastically, the boulder on the slack side won't attract cats as often as the boulder in faster water. Fish both boulders, however, and you'll be able to judge which areas are best, based on present current conditions.

Snags are the other important feature of a catfish hole. Snags may occur anywhere, but often result from current washing against a bank, exposing tree roots, causing the tree to topple and gather debris. This usually happens on a flat only during the spring flood stage. The best snags lie near or just downstream of the core of a hole, where current slows. Snags on flats may also attract catfish if the flat's deep enough. But cats on flats usually run small.

Snags and cover aren't as important for their physical characteristics as for their location in a hole. Location determines how catfish use them. Cover in fast current near the top of the hole is primarily feeding territory. A snag in quiet water at the lower half of a hole is primarily a holding or resting area. Snags near the core of a hole are resting and feeding areas. A snag in fast water right below a riffle would likely be important only as a feeding area.

This isn't to say cats won't rest in the core of a hole—they will when a snag isn't present. They also rest in reduced current behind cover objects. It's a matter of priorities. The biggest cats are likely to use the best feeding and resting areas. Snags in key areas key catfish location. We've never seen cats fighting for spots, but the presence of big fish in the best spots suggests that competition occurs.

Remember that some snags are better than others. A snag in deep water probably is better than a snag in a shallower part of a hole. Complex snags consisting of dozens of branches are better than more simple snags. A snag lying in current is better than a snag in slack water.

Catfish prefer snags offering depth and overhead protection, depth being the more important. Cats use simple snags in deep water more than complex snags in shallow water.

Streams, then, are composed of riffles, holes, and runs. Key elements of a hole are its depth and cover, perhaps a snag. The hole is the home of the catfish—a big one-room home. In that home, the snag or the core of the hole usually is the bedroom, the top of the hole the kitchen. Catfish usually rest around or under the snag or in the core of the hole, but may occasionally snack there, especially when it's near the kitchen. Active cats move around the hole, checking areas that gather food. Eventually, though, they move to the head of the hole, the kitchen, at least for a time.

## PRIME HOLES, PRIME STRETCHES

Where will you fish a small stream?

Many catfishermen fish the first convenient hole. Classically, that's a hole near a bridge. Or they might drive down a road that ends at the river and fish the first good-looking water nearby. Often they'll open a lawn chair and crack a cola. They'll probably prop their rod on a forked stick left behind by other anglers.

Something wrong?

You bet. First, they're fishing the same spot fished by most anglers. Holes get "fished down" or "burned out," even when catfish are caught and released, especially during times when catfish aren't moving much. Don't spend most of your time on the holes that have had most of the catfish removed or even caught and released. Cats are quick learners, remember.

The best fishing in a small river will be in prime holes in prime stretches. Remember, some holes and some stretches of river are much better than others. By sheer luck, a bridge hole might be a prime hole, but the odds are against it. Even then, it's going to get fished down.

What's a prime hole? We've been talking about elements or aspects of holes; now it's time to pull back for a broad view. Catfish move up or downriver, often traveling long distances. They survey many holes, judging their comparative worth as holding or feeding areas. Eventually the biggest and the most cats find the best holes.

Every hole in a river might hold a few cats, but better holes attract more cats. Those are the holes to concentrate your fishing on, but they're the holes most catfishermen don't find because they don't walk or float far enough to compare river stretches and holes.

How well does a particular hole meet *all* the needs of the catfish? A prime hole will be larger and deeper with long adjacent runs to produce lots of food, plus cover objects, especially near the top end, and perhaps a big snag in the core of the hole. Everything comes together in one spot to give catfish security, food, and a resting spot. When cats travel by, this hole holds them.

Find such a hole and you'll find catfish, especially if there aren't comparable holes nearby. With similar holes nearby, catfish may distribute evenly among them.

Usually, though, a river stretch with more good holes also attracts the most catfish.

Learn to recognize prime holes by experience—seeing and fishing them. That, again, is easiest done on a small river. But move. Look and compare. The more river you see, the better you can judge about where the fish will most likely be. It's work, but fun too, when you use a fishing rod for your research. Just be willing to move more and fish less when you first begin exploring.

Most rivers tend to have prime stretches with better habitat, thus better holes. In a 10-mile stretch of river, there might be a 2-mile prime stretch with more good holes holding more and bigger catfish than the other 8 miles. The other 8 miles might contain sandy runs, marginal holes and a good hole here and there. Find a good hole in the 8-mile stretch, and it might produce as well as some of the holes in the prime stretch. The prime stretch, though, will hold more cats.

*Obvious holes often get "fished down" during periods of stable water flow. Releasing big cats helps, but it takes high water to get cats moving throughout the river, to naturally restock holes. Move. Look for holes that haven't been fished much.*

Spend most of your time on prime holes in prime stretches, fishing other prime holes only occasionally.

*The best catfish in any stream inhabit prime lies in prime holes, usually in prime stretches of river.*

## SCOUTING HOLES

Rivers are dynamic—constantly changing. A portion of river might look the same from the highway, but just out of sight, a loop in the river might produce a deep hole and a timber snag. You must see what you'd otherwise miss.

By now you know that the only way to learn to evaluate holes is to fish lots of them. Move, but walk or float with a purpose. Compare, compare, compare. Analyze each hole. How big is it? Does it have good cover? A snag? Are there other good holes nearby? Are there tributaries to help restock this hole during changing water conditions?

Start with a map, a topographical map if possible. Look for stretches where the river meanders. Straight stretches won't contain as many riffles and holes as meandering stretches.

Walk or float a three-mile stretch, but don't spend too much time at any one hole. Look for deeper holes with more cover than other holes. Soon you'll know the best holes in that stretch. Then look at other stretches and compare, compare.

When you're fishing quickly—scouting—fish only for actively feeding cats. Drift a bait above the riffle, then through the riffle once or twice, then into the

*An obvious riffle, hole, and run.*

head of the hole around a cover object or two. If you catch a fish, you've learned a little about the quality of fish in the area. You'll also know that at least some cats are active because they're at the head of the hole.

No fish on those first drifts? Then move down a bit and drift a bait through the core of the hole. Then move to the snag, if there is one. Drift a bait along the front of the snag. Take a moment to soak a bait just above a snag. Move to the rear of the snag. Try a drift or two. Time to move, even if you're sure fish are present, but not active.

Off again, moving downstream. Check the next hole. There's always new and intriguing water around each bend.

Scouting works best when the water's low, particularly during prespawn and early fall when cats also are likely to be active. Low, clear water's an asset; high, dirty water obscures cover and snags.

Most catmen are amazed by how many more cats they catch when they fish quickly, moving, moving again, fishing only for active cats. It's one of the biggest steps you can make to better catfishing.

There are a few times, however, to sit and outwait catfish. That's only after you've seen lots of river and can judge where the best holes are. Only when you're absolutely sure, do you want to spend an entire morning or evening fishing one or two holes.

"About holes," Doug said as Zacker eased back on his bench.

"Holes! Holes is the home of those big evil-tempered cats!" he said as he raised himself on the bench again. "Mud cats live there and so do big forks. But those blues like to move more. You kin catch 'em in holes, but you can't always predict they're there."

"Prediction," I said, "that's another thing. Lots of catfishermen think old-timer big-cat guys had an aura about them: Like you had the ability to feel the presence of big cats like a well digger with a witching stick feels water?"

"Aw, crap! You just want to make me mad," he coughed and wheezed. He took a "proper" spit and proceeded.

"Any idiot can figure out where big cats are. They live in those holes. But not every hole: the biggest ones; the deepest ones; sometimes the ones with the most cover like fallen trees.

"Pole fishermen are so dang stupid—lazy! They walk or float a couple miles of river and then they set their butt down and rest. Resting's fine, but only when I know where a big cat is."

"What you're suggesting," I said, "is that a fisherman should take say a 10-mile section of river and walk it or drift it in a boat, looking and surveying the habitat. Instead of fishing each hole, just check it out. How big is it? How deep? How much cover is there? How many other holes are nearby? What are those other holes like? How do they compare with this one?

"Once a guy has an inventory of a pretty good-size section of river, he can make a prediction about where the biggest cats are. Once he draws a map, he can make some logical guesses. . ."

"No dang guessin' involved," he interrupted. "No danged guessin' 'tall. Ya darn right I had a map in my head. If I knew how every hole in a 10-mile section of river stacked up, I'd know exactly where the biggest cats were. Big cats are easier than little cats 'cause they're more predictable."

"So," I said, "a fisherman might want to pass by 15 consecutive good-looking holes to get to the one hole that's by far the biggest and deepest hole in say a 5-mile river section?"

"Danged right! Only some jackass city slicker thinks he's gonna catch a big cat without knowing his river. Course those guys think a big cat is 15 pounds. Humph!

"People who used to live on the river knew maybe 50 miles of it. I did. In those 50 miles they'd know there were really only 10 terrible (great) holes. That's where you fish. That's where you catch terrible fish. City slicker knows one mile of river and 4 holes and thinks he's what you writers call a 'river rat.' Caarap!

"And don't make no difference what size the river is, either. I'll tell you that. Only the biggest size of the catfish change. Show me a creek and the idea for finding the biggest cats is the same."

"But bigger rivers have bigger fish?" I asked.

"Course! Danged right! That's what I'm saying. More bigger fish in a hole, too. Bigger river like what the Missouri used to be before they crapped it up with dams, well, a good hole might have 15 big cats. You'd catch 5 or 8 of 'em and then fishin' would turn tough. You wait 'til the water came up again. Cats—but not always the biggest ones—move when the water comes up. Holes get restocked. When the water's down and the cats can't move, I can catch every fish in a hole. But I never did. We always left some. But catching a big cat is the simplest thing ever."

## LOCATING CATS IN MEDIUM-SIZE RIVERS

Master small rivers and it's easier to move to larger rivers, not a huge river, but one that makes most highway maps. Although you have to slow down a little and look more carefully, a bigger river is just a small stream on a larger scale. You probably can walk along these rivers and wade them easily when the water's low, but there may be spots where it's hard to fish both sides from one bank.

What do you see? Riffles, holes, and runs. What's in the holes? Cover and snags, though they may be harder to see in this bigger body of water. A riffle, instead of extending from shore to shore, might extend only halfway across. But it's still a riffle. It still sends quick, frisky water to scour a hole below. It'll be more difficult to see the size, shape, and depth of holes, but a few drifts with a bait will provide a feeling for the hole. Check a few backwash or eddy areas associated with the hole, too.

Scout. Move. Cover water. Use a boat perhaps. Don't concentrate on stale holes other people fish, especially when the best hole might be just out of sight around a bend.

Snags are less frequent in bigger rivers, because snags usually are shoreline extensions and there's more river per shoreline now. Again, look for the biggest, deepest holes with the best cover.

Larger rivers have more dead water than small streams. Learn to read current flow, looking for the "smaller river" within the larger river. Rivers naturally meander. Larger rivers today are tamed and tubed, but even when rivers run straight for miles, the small river within the larger river runs left, then right, cutting this way and that, finding hard bottom here and there, and creating riffles and pools. Look past the main body of slowly moving water to the lively little river you've learned to fish. Again, successful fishing depends on your ability to recognize the river areas cats ignore and those cats use.

Note tributary streams. Cats often move in and out of tributaries. A hole usually forms where the tributary meets the larger river, and this often is a productive hole. It may, however, be heavily fished.

Larger rivers may also have side channels. Think of them as small rivers attached to the bigger river. If they have current and holes, and cover and forage, they may be worth fishing. If they have only sluggish water, they won't be worth fishing except during prespawn when cats might run into them to escape heavy flow in the main river. Even then, though, there probably are better places to fish.

Bigger rivers often are dammed. Opportunity! Low dams, built to power mills, may still exist, but often are broken, creating large artificial riffles followed by holes. Such spots are catfish barriers and, as we've said, during certain periods gather catfish.

*Dams on small and medium rivers attract and concentrate catfish during late spring and early summer. By summer, water levels fall, and fishing pressure takes its toll on the fish available in the tailwater area. Unless the river rises and attracts cats upriver, you're best off searching elsewhere.*

Bigger dams are even more effective barriers. Deep water, current, and an abundance of food below many dams holds cats, especially in spring when they move upstream. Dams attract fishermen as much as they attract cats, though, so fishing pressure takes its toll, especially after cats spawn and settle for the summer. When cats are moving during spring and early summer, dams get fresh runs of cats. Not so during lower water in summer.

Use dams when they're producing, but don't go to the same place time after time. Catfishing doesn't have to be unproductive if you move. Learn where good stretches and the best holes are, just as you did on small streams.

If you move, effectively evaluate rivers, learn to read water, and concentrate on the most promising spots, you'll catch more and bigger cats in any-size river.

## LOCATING CATS ON LARGE RIVERS

Turn now to the largest rivers, for example the Ohio, Mississippi, and Missouri. Big rivers have a wealth of forage, and catfish are free to move to the best areas. Although locating good areas gets tougher, chances for bigger fish increase.

It's harder to know where to aim your effort. All that water! Overwhelming! And the skills learned on small streams are more difficult to apply.

Scouting a big river is done most effectively with a motor-powered boat. Drifting downstream is too slow. Most good spots are large, so you can drive and walk in to check them. From shore, check for depth and cover by casting a heavy sinker. In a boat, use a depthfinder. It's hard to see holes or even shallow spots under so much water. Sonar will tell you the shape of the bottom. A graph is fine, too, but rivers are full of carp, suckers, buffalo, drum, gar, and saugers. Don't expect a graph to selectively highlight catfish.

Fishing for cats on big rivers can produce a mixed bag. For a variety of species, including cats, try baits such as jigs tipped with minnows or crawlers, livebait rigs, or spinner rigs. Crankbaits are often more productive in a larger river, too, because cats are more aggressively competitive.

Big rivers seem so rich in fish that anglers often forget about fishing pressure. It takes a toll, especially near large cities, bridges, and boat landings. Traveling up or downriver from a major city can put you in a world of untouched catfish opportunity.

Riffle-hole-run structure exists in the upper reaches of big rivers, but in lower sections they disappear. Current breaks are more difficult to identify too, except for obvious huge breaks like wing dams.

The most productive spot on a large river is often a hole associated with a wing dam. Wing dams function like a riffle or rocky bar; they disrupt current, causing it to scour a hole.

Which wing dam? Look for wing dams where current digs the deepest, biggest holes.

Remember, too, that bigger rivers often contain a river within a river, an inner river meandering from bank to bank. The best wing dams often occur when the flow of heavier current in the main channel swings close to shore near a wing dam. River charts or channel buoys show where the channel cuts close to shore. Check with sonar, too. Careful! Wing dams are notorious for eating props and shattering lower units.

## DOWNSTREAM CAT LOCATION IN BIG RIVERS

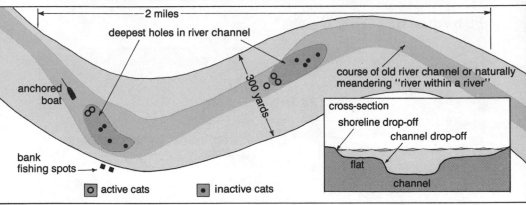

*Tailwater areas on big rivers often offer catfishing opportunity all year long. Downriver catfish holding areas usually are associated with holes in the old river channel or with holes behind wing dams.*

*A cross-section of a typical river shows a shoreline drop-off that becomes a shallow flat that drops off into the old river channel. Follow the river channel, however, and you'll find deeper holes in the channel. These holes, just like holes in smaller rivers, consist of a head, a core, and a tail end. Active cats usually move to the head of the hole. Inactive cats usually hold in the core or tail of the hole.*

*Portions of holes that swing close to shore can be fished from shore. The most effective approach, however, is to anchor a boat above the hole. Cast your bait downstream, let it settle, flip your Garcia 6500C into freespool, set the clicker mechanism, and wait.*

*During early morning and at night in summer, anchor at the head of the hole. If you catch several fish and fishing slows, move up or downriver to the head of a fresh hole.*

*During midday, fish the heads of holes first. Be prepared, however, to fish the core of the hole, waiting longer for action.*

Some wing dams stretch farther from shore. Buoys often mark the ends of wing dams, but use your eyes and sonar to judge the size of the wing dam and the shape and depth of the hole behind it. The best wing dams often are long enough so their tips extend into faster current. When wing dams occur in clusters, the first and last dam in a cluster often are the most productive.

Anchor a boat to fish wing dams, although you can sometimes fish portions of them from shore. Fish promising holes carefully. Say a hole's 100 feet long by 100 feet wide. Study the water for current breaks. Probe with a set rig or a bait beneath a float to determine what the water's doing.

Big-river holes take much longer to check. Instead of sampling 10 holes an hour as you could on a small river, carefully check one or two. Dissect the huge mass of water to determine how the parts relate.

Look for current edges. Wherever fast and slow water exist side-by-side, catfish are likely nearby. Backwash (eddy) areas are common on big rivers. You'll often find fish on the current edge where the eddying water slides upstream past the downstream flow. When an eddy moves along a bank, it creates two edges, one being the shoreline. Expect catfish on the deeper offshore edge of the eddy where it glides past the main-stream current flowing downstream. Check the shoreline edge, too.

## Fish-Attracting Wing Dams

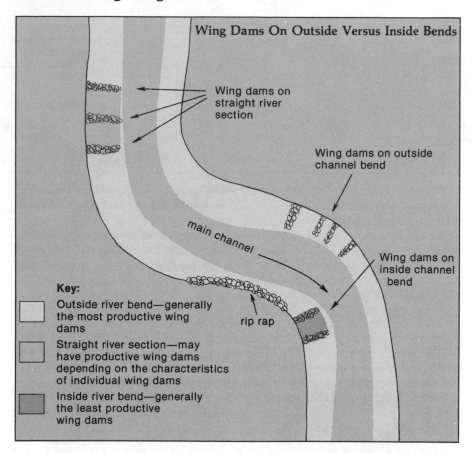

Wing Dams On Outside Versus Inside Bends

Wing dams on straight river section

Wing dams on outside channel bend

main channel

Wing dams on inside channel bend

rip rap

Key:
Outside river bend—generally the most productive wing dams

Straight river section—may have productive wing dams depending on the characteristics of individual wing dams

Inside river bend—generally the least productive wing dams

*A wing dam's characteristics determine if it will be used by fish. Generally, fish attraction to wing dams is based on the amount of current associated with the wing dams once the water level in a river pool stabilizes during summer. Wing dams on outside river bends receive more current than those on inside river bends. Wing dams on straight river sections may be as productive as those on outside river bends, again, depending on the current and the characteristics of the dam.*

Dams are more important on big rivers than on smaller streams, because dams on small rivers often get fished down quickly. A few cats are always present, but not enough for consistent fishing. Tailraces on big rivers offer more consistent flow and abundant food to attract cats all summer. If fishing pressure takes a few, more move in.

That doesn't mean dams are always the easiest or best place to fish a big river.

## A Good Wing Dam

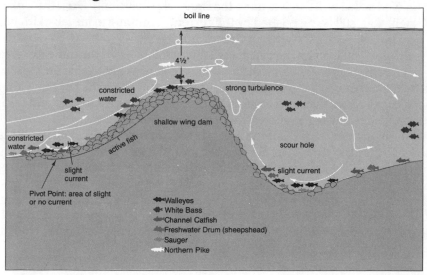

*Good wing dams offer a smorgasbord of fish activity during summer and fall. Those that attract fish receive plenty of current, but have shallow versus deep water over their tops.*

*Heavy spring current and shallow water over the top of the dam increases the scouring action behind the dam and results in a deep scour hole. Once the water level drops during summer, the combination of deep scour hole and moderate current attracts fish and offers them a place to loaf and feed.*

*Research by John Pitlo of the Iowa Department of Natural Resources indicates that dams with tops shallower than about 4½ feet during normal river pool tend to offer the most diverse habitat and attract the most fish. Good wing dams are where the action is during summer and fall.*

Tailraces offer huge water and confusing current. Cats concentrate in small spots that aren't easy for an untrained eye to spot. Often surface currents don't tell enough about what's happening below. Eddies are eddies, just as in a small river, but tailwater eddies may not provide an accurate picture of current conditions on the bottom, where catfish hold.

Since spotting good lies is hard, the emphasis switches to *feeling* your bait through spots that could hold cats. Probe with a bottom-bouncing bait rig. Fish through potential areas by feel and sight.

Say you're using a slip rig consisting of about a 2-ounce bell sinker slipped on your line through the swivel hole on top of the bell sinker. Your main line to the bait runs freely. The sinker is held in place with a swivel tied into your line 6 to 12 inches above the bait. As you'll learn in Chapter 10, leader length should be short (3 to 6 inches) in heavy current so your bait doesn't blow around and become snagged or be difficult for catfish to grab.

Say you've anchored near a likely break in current along shore or near or behind an obstruction in midcurrent. Say the water shifts direction here, or two major currents roll against each other creating a wall of water that obstructs both flows, thereby slightly halting the flow.

Cast your bait to the top of the current break and let it drop to the bottom. Tighten up and barely lift your sinker off the bottom. The pressure of the current on your sinker and line will move the sinker and bait along. Drop the sinker and it will skid, still being pushed by the current. Continue to lift-fall-skid, lift-fall-skid the bait along the edge of the current break.

Do this and you'll notice the bait doesn't always lift-fall-skid the same distance due to current differences along the bottom, differences not visible on the surface. With practice you'll to recognize—feel—slack spots along the bottom within general current areas that attract catfish. Catfish use these areas to hold and feed. Finding them is the key to successful fishing in tailwater areas.

Big rivers also offer side channels and oxbows that function like smaller rivers attached to the main river. They attract cats mainly during prespawn, particularly if they have significant current. If a flowing side channel runs against a causeway or barge mooring area, current may scour holes that hold cats. Current breaks—rocks and debris—also attract cats in side channels, as they do in smaller rivers.

The key on big rivers is finding one or two good spots and spending enough time on those spots to learn them intimately. Structural elements may change from year to year, but good areas usually remain good for many years.


## TRACKING CATS

The lack of attention paid to catfish by the outdoor press extends to fisheries management agencies. Little information on the ecology and basic biology of wild catfish is available, in contrast to the wealth of information on salmon, trout, and bass.

While catfish tagging projects have been conducted, questions remain about the movements of fish that aren't recaptured by anglers or biologists (the vast majority). Tag returns also don't reveal information about complex movements between tagging and recapture. A fish recaptured at its tagging location could be sedentary or could have just returned from a journey.

Radio and sonic tags have been widely applied to many species to more closely monitor movements. Recognition of catfish popularity with fishermen led to recent studies by the Missouri Department of Conservation and the Wisconsin Department of Natural Resources that provide insights into seasonal movements of channel cats in large rivers. Fish from the Missouri and lower Wisconsin rivers (just upstream of Pool 10 on the Mississippi) were tagged and checked for several years.

## Channel Catfish Wintering Locations

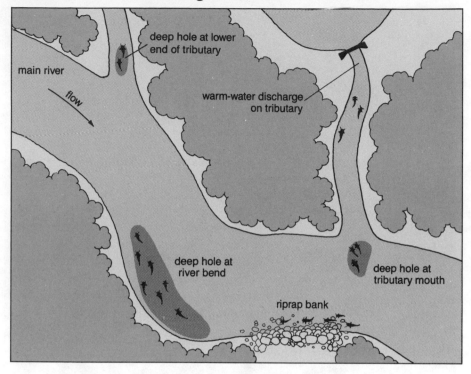

## WINTERING AREAS

Tim Grace (Missouri DOC) led a project that studied the winter habitat of channel and flathead catfish in the central Missouri stretch of the Missouri River. Tributaries in the study area included the Osage River and several smaller creeks. Ten channel cats were radio tagged during the fall of 1982 and followed into the next spring. In 1983, eight more were tagged.

The winter of 1982 was mild and cats moved mostly downstream. Some fish were sedentary while others moved up to 73 miles. Some short upstream movements were noted, including two cats that entered the Osage River. This shift was noteworthy because the Osage is warmed by reservoir releases upstream at Lake of the Ozarks. These cats apparently were attracted by the thermal effluent. Other cats abandoned the warmed Osage for the Missouri during the same period. Catfish residing in warmer water were more active.

Some cats shifted location during midwinter. Some fish moved short distances up tributaries and wintered in 10- to 20-foot-deep holes, while other cats chose deep wintering holes at the mouths of tributaries. Shifts couldn't be tied to environmental factors like temperature or river stage. Winter 1983-1984 was much colder and catfish moved less, following a downstream shift at the onset of winter.

Channel cats usually chose the deepest available holes, sometimes 25 to 30 feet deep. These holes offered relative environmental stability, including reduced current. Huge aggregations sometimes formed with several

## Channel Catfish Seasonal Movements

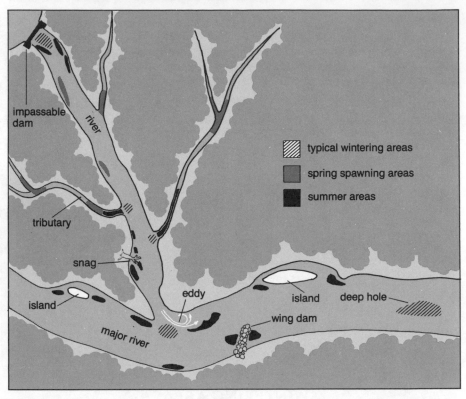

thousand cats crammed into a 5- or 10-acre area. Flathead catfish sometimes used the same wintering holes as channel cats, but generally favored deep holes behind dikes over holes at tributary mouths.

In late March or April, cats began moving upstream, often into tributaries with potential spawning areas. Upstream movements continued into June, when spawning typically began.

An even closer look at catfish wintering areas was possible when Minnesota and Wisconsin Department of Natural Resources fisheries personnel donned scuba gear during February 1979 for a look at Mississippi River aggregations in Pool 4. Divers reported scores of adult cats, primarily flatheads with channel cats mixed in. Cats huddled behind rocks, sticks, or other catfish, where current was minimal. The fish were flat on bottom, facing upstream in 16 to 25 feet of water.

Catfish appeared dormant with hardly any gill movement and could be handled with little response. Some were covered with a layer of silt, suggesting a long period of dormancy.

### SEASONAL SHIFTS

Don Fago of the Wisconsin Department of Natural Resources led a research group that followed 130 radio-tagged channel cats in the lower Wisconsin River from 1983 to 1986. The final report hasn't been published yet, but Don and his colleague, Gene Van Dyck IV, shared their preliminary observations.

Some cats remained in small home areas, while others made long excursions.

Such variability in movement has also been noted in tracking studies of other species.

Wintering areas were similar to those described for the Missouri and Mississippi rivers. Some cats shifted wintering areas in midwinter. The deep hole where the Wisconsin flows into the Mississippi was popular with this population.

In spring, fish that wintered in the Mississippi typically moved into the Wisconsin. High flows and increasing temperatures often coincided with this shift. Tributaries of the Wisconsin also attracted cats over the 92-mile study area.

*Once you forge catfishing skills on smaller waters, the step to big rivers is exciting. Conditions on big rivers are more stable. It takes time to learn a few spots on a big river, but once you do, they'll produce more consistently. Still, never hesitate to look at and evaluate new waters. The list of catfish rivers offers more than a lifetime of good catfishing.*

Cats that wintered just below the Prairie du Sac dam moved downstream, however.

Some cats returned to spawning areas they'd used the year before. Maximum life for radio tags was about a year, so individuals couldn't be tracked for extended periods. Since many cats were more than 10 years old, they had likely experienced many of the river's choice locations. Catfish movements from spot to spot were often direct, as though the cats knew where they were going.

During spawning season, cats often were in the smallest river stretches occupied during the year. These spots offered logs, rocks, undercut banks or other crevices for laying and protecting eggs. Summer locations often were nearby, usually downstream of spawning sites. Again, homing to previously occupied locations was noted.

Summer brought generally restricted movement. The catfish that moved from the Mississippi River at the mouth of the Wisconsin River to St. Louis in less than six weeks was an exception.

Fall signalled a major locational shift, almost the opposite of the spring upstream movement. Cats didn't make a mass migration, but gradually shifted toward wintering areas—deep sanctuaries from severe weather.

Preferred catfish habitat awaits computer analysis, but catfish used snags and holes on the Wisconsin. Cats also tended to move in groups, but weren't close-knit like schools of suckers. Wintering areas attracted large numbers of cats, but they apparently sought appropriate conditions, not company.

*A happy In-Fisherman magazine reader with a flathead from a winter aggregation.*

## Chapter 8

# CATFISH TACKLE

### Trends In Tackle For Today's Catfisherman

Traditionally, catfishermen have used whatever tackle was cheap and available. Because bass are popular in geographic regions with the most catfish, cat anglers usually have used tackle designed for bass fishing and often not the best of that.

It's time for that tradition to change. No need to buy a lot of expensive gear. But a modest investment in good tackle guarantees more fish and more fun.

In perspective, bass fishermen run boats costing up to $20,000, and may stock hundreds of lures that may cost $5 apiece. Catfishermen can own a superb rod and reel combo, plus hooks, floats, and other rigging devices for a little over $150. For two top-line outfits plus supplementary tackle, you'd be hard pressed to spend $500 on tackle that should last a lifetime.

Some of the tackle we recommend isn't presently carried in baitshops and large sporting goods stores. That will change. But when items aren't widely stocked, we mention where to get them, usually from mail-order catalogs.

We refer frequently to European bank-fishing techniques. European shore-fishing has a glorious history. In the British Isles and continental Europe, intense competition often exists for limited numbers of fish on limited numbers of waters. European bank anglers have developed sophisticated techniques for the pressured fishing they face.

In short, Europeans are years ahead of most American anglers in refining bank-fishing skills and equipment. Americans, on the other hand, are years ahead of Europe in boat-fishing skills. Depthfinders and trolling motors, for example, are almost unknown in Europe.

European bank-fishing skills should interest catfish fans since most catfishing is a bank-fishing affair. In the next decade, many advances in catfishing will result from creative adaptations of European tackle and tactics. We want to get the trend moving as soon as possible.

## BETTER CATFISH RODS

The problem with bass rods as cat rods is they're too darn short. Even 6½-foot crankbait rods, a fair compromise length, are too short. In most situations, longer is better in catfishing rods.

Why?

• You can cast farther with a longer rod, an advantage for a shore-bound angler, plus cast long distances without snapping bait off the hook. Long rods let you gently boost a bait to speed with a fluid sweep of the rod, rather than having to make a whip-crack cast with a short rod.

• Long rods are better for keeping line tight during the fight. Pick up slack, remove line stretch quickly and make a good hookset with a long rod, too.

• You can fish around obstructions better. A long rod allows more effective drifts to a variety of snag areas. Long rods offer more reach and control.

• Most importantly, long rods let you accurately drift baits. Keep more line off the water. Move your rod tip and mend line to keep bait drifting exactly where you want it.

About accurate drifts. Throw a stick into a river and it floats downstream naturally, responding to current. Tie a string to the stick and throw it in, however, and current catches the string and pulls the stick unnaturally. Likewise, a float and bait drift unnaturally when current works on fishing line. Current pulls the bait toward you, out of position, ruining part of a drift. The more line in the water the bigger the problem. Long rods let you keep more line out of the water.

Lessen current drag by using a long rod to hold line above the surface. Correct drifts by "mending" line as fly fishermen do, by throwing a loop of line back upstream to keep a float and bait drifting true when current pulls a downstream bow in your line and threatens to pull the bait or float and bait out of position. With a long rod, your bait drifts more naturally, where you want it. It stays in the fish zone longer, increasing the chance to trigger cats.

With a 6-foot rod, plus your extended arm, you can reach about 8 feet out or up. A 12-foot rod provides almost twice the reach and control. Reach around obstructions to fish the far side of snags or cover breaks. Hold the rod tip high to make accurate drifts. Cast 100 yards. Drift a float 50 yards—100 yards. Set the hook effectively at that distance. Light, strong, sensitive, carbon (graphite) 11- or 12-foot-long rods are pleasant to fish with all day. Prices are right, too, considering you get 3 times more graphite than in the typical bass pole.

We've fished with long Euro-style rods for almost a decade. We would never

# LONGER RODS

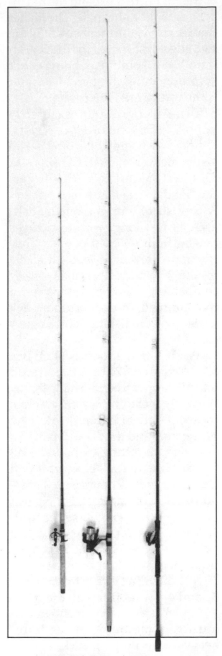

### Traditional Casting Tackle

*Any 7½- or 8-foot flippin' stick, Garcia 6500C reel, 17-pound test Berkley Trimax or XT, DuPont Stren or DuPont Prime, or 20-pound Bagley Silver Thread, or 27-pound Gudebrod or Cortland dacron.*

*Comment: Most-available all-round combo for most fishermen.*

### Euro-Style Spinning Tackle

*Cabela's or Wazp Brand 11-foot, 1¾-, 2¼-, or 3-pound test-curve rod, Daiwa 2600 Long Cast reel, 12- or 14-pound test Berkley XL or DuPont Stren, or 15-pound Bagley Silver Thread.*

*Comments: For long distance work— stealth—especially from shore, or in any situation that calls for holding a rod tip high or around cover. 2¼-pound test curve most versatile rod.*

### Euro-Style Casting Tackle

*Cabela's or Wazp Brand 11-foot, 1¾- to 2¼-pound-test-curve casting rod, Garcia 6500C reel, 17-pound Berkley Trimax or Berkley XT or DuPont Prime or DuPont Stren, or 20-pound Bagley Silver Thread.*

*Comments: For long distance work— stealth—especially from shore or in any situation that calls for holding a rod tip high or around cover. Euro-casting tackle is more powerful than Euro-spinning tackle.*

again fish without them.

For many catfish anglers, a 7½-foot flipping stick designed for bass is the easiest step to a longer rod. It's the shortest basic rod we recommend for catfishing. A flipping stick offers a fair measure of reach, control, and power; and they're readily available and competitively priced.

The next step, one most of you will make, the sooner the better, is to a Euro-style bank rod, the ultimate catfishing rod. And it won't cost any more than a flipping stick.

American rods are power rated by the lure weight the rod can handle. Euro rods are power rated by the "straight" weight the rod can handle. Euro rods are

## STURDY GRAPHITE MUSKIE ROD FOR HEAVY-DUTY CATFISHING

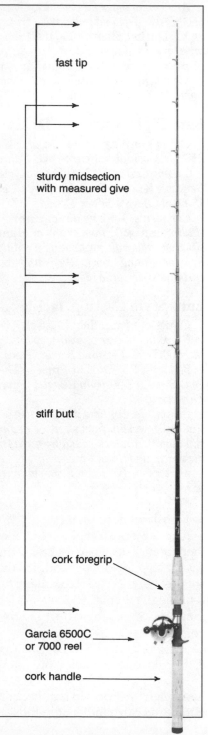

fast tip

sturdy midsection with measured give

stiff butt

cork foregrip

Garcia 6500C or 7000 reel

cork handle

graded in "test curves," the amount of weight needed to bend the rod into a parabolic right angle. The higher the test curve, the more powerful the rod. Ideal test curves for catfish run from 1¾ to 3 pounds. Choose either spinning or casting models, and some rods work either way.

Two American sources currently supply European-style rods, although we presume others will soon enter the market. Cabela's (812 13th Ave., Sidney, NE 69160) offers the "Predator" series, which presently consists of four graphite models, each 11 feet long, with test curves ranging from 1¾ to 2¼ pounds. They may have a few models still available testing 3 pounds. Eventually many companies will offer this powerful rod. Granted, though, it's too heavy for 90% of the fishing most anglers face.

Wazp Brand Products (P.O. Box 837, Minden, LA 71058) offers a broad line of European bank-fishing tackle, presently including several graphite rods appropriate for catfish. Most are 12 feet long and test about 2 pounds.

Long rods testing 1¾ pounds will handle big fish. We've whipped channel cats to 29 pounds on them—no sweat in open water. For big fish in heavy cover, of course, go with shorter, heavier, more powerful tackle. We've pulled cats to 20 pounds from snags with 2-pound-test-curve rods, though. Yet it's fun to handle 2-, 3-, and 4-pound fish with them.

So far, we've recommended two outfits, a medium- or medium-heavy-action flipping stick, and an all-purpose Euro-style long rod testing 1¾ to 2¼ pounds.

The traditional choice for huge cats in cover or heavy current has been a heavy saltwater rod with a heavy fiberglass blank coupled with a saltwater reel such as the Penn 309. A better alternative for most situations is a sturdy muskie rod that handles lures ranging from about 1 to 4 ounces. It should be at least 6 feet long, better 6½ or 7, to facilitate casts.

## REELS AND LINE

Many reels work well for catfishing but baitcasting reels probably are the best choice. Look for rugged construction, reliability, castability, a free-spool button, plus plenty of line capacity and a "clicker" mechanism. Most bass reels that hold plenty of 15- to 30-pound-test line will work, but most don't offer clickers. The free-spool feature in conjunction with a set clicker mechanism works well for setline fishing or still fishing. Hit the freespool button and engage the clicker. The clicker indicates when line is being taken, while it keeps slight, steady tension on line. Steady line tension is desirable on two counts: (1) To keep a bottom-fished bait in place, yet offer the opportunity to let a cat take a bait; and (2) to keep slight, steady tension on the cat once it takes the bait.

Doug Stange discussing free-line drag resistance and line test with Zacker:

"Doesn't the drag resistance bother?" I asked.

"Small cat talk," he answered. "Big cats don't care 'bout no pressure as long as it's constant."

"Do we wait to set?" I asked.

"Never!" he shot back. "Big cats crush and kill and swallow. When he moves, he's got the bait 9 times out of 10. When you get to the rod, engage it, set and hold on. Once I set, I never gave an inch; never let the cat run. Hold him. Turn him over. Make him roll and thrash 20 feet away from you, but never give him his head. You win or lose. And if you start losing you use heavier line. Cats don't care about whether the line is 70 or 80 pounds. Maybe in a reservoir or big river these days you can let a fish go a bit. But we never had such good drags, and my method works. Danged right!"

One casting reel currently offers everything a catfisherman needs. The Abu-Garcia Ambassadeur 6500C is the standard against which other reels must be measured. The 6500C is a fine size for all-around angling, easily handling lines to 40-pound test. If you'll be tug-o-warring with monster cats near snags, the slightly larger 7000C handles line stout enough to pull stumps.

What's wrong with inexpensive star-drag trolling reels, the traditional choice of many bank cat anglers who cast only a few times a day? Boat anglers use them, too, and they work reasonably well from a boat, though the 6500C is less bulky and we believe better built. There's no comparison in the ability to make smooth casts. To improve catfishing catches, most fishermen need to fish more—move around and do more casting. The 6500C far surpasses traditional saltwater or trolling reels for casting.

Spinning reels work too, although they don't offer the power or line-pick-up speed of a baitcaster. Reels with a freespooling feature like Shimano's Baitrunner are useful for set lining. We also use Daiwa's "Long Cast" SS2600 and TG12600H reels. The extra-wide spool facilitates long casts and can hold plenty of 17- or 20-pound-test monofilament.

About line. Cats usually aren't line-shy, so lines from 12- to 20-pound test serve a wide variety of situations. Fish 12- to 15-pound-test line on smaller rivers and 15- to 20-pound-test line on big rivers. We usually use 14-, 15-, or 17-pound test.

High-strength, small-diameter monofilament line like Berkley's Trilene XL, Dupont Stren, and Bagley's Silver Thread are good for most fishing. For heavy-duty work in cover, try Trilene XT or dacron line from Gudebrod or Cortland.

About dacron. In most situations in rivers, don't worry about cats seeing line. They're probably more line-shy by feel. Stiff, wiry monofilament is more likely to turn a catfish off than soft dacron. Sounds strange, but at times we spool reels with mono line and use a dacron leader or snell. Most folks would do just the opposite.

*The Garcia 6500C and 7000 presently are the standards by which baitcasting reels for catfish are measured.*

## TERMINAL GEAR

Terminal tackle for catfishing is as straight forward as a line-drive base hit. A simple, strong, sharp hook works. The Eagle Claw 84 or the Mustad 92671 are the hooks we use most of the time. Many of you will want to experiment with "turn-style" hooks, too, however. You may conclude they increase hooking percentage. We rarely use hooks with baithold barbs because the baits we use rarely require them. The extra barbs also tend to gather debris. Buy hooks in lots of 100 to save money. You lose lots of hooks.

Hook size depends on bait type and size and the size fish you're after. We stock sizes from #4s for small baits in small rivers for smaller cats, to 1/0 to 5/0 for most general catfishing, to 6/0 to 9/0 for record-class fish using huge baits.

We stock #6 or #4 trebles, too. The Eagle Claw 374 and the Mustad 3551 are good choices.

Try the "Quick Strike" or "Vic Bellars" (VB) hook by Partridge for bottom fishing in cover-free water. This hook has a small single hook soldered piggyback

# Favored Hook Styles

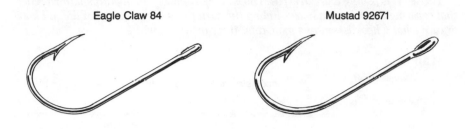

Eagle Claw 84

Mustad 92671

*The Eagle Claw 84 and the Mustad 92671: Good basic hook-style choices for most cat-fishing situations.*

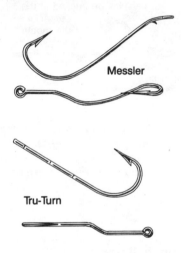

Messler

Tru-Turn

*Many fishermen believe ''turn-style'' hooks increase hooking percentage.*

*The VB hook from Partridge.*

to the shank of a bigger single hook. Impale bait such as cut or whole dead fish on the little hook, leaving the big hook exposed on the outside of the bait. When a cat takes the bait, set immediately and you'll consistently hook fish. A number of tackle stores carry these hooks, or order them from Cabela's (812 13th Ave., Sidney, NE 69160) or Bait Rigs Inc. (Box 4153, Madison, WI 53711).

Leave the hook point exposed whenever possible. Don't hide the hook point in a bait unless it's very soft bait such as paste. Let the hook stick out of firmer baits. In woody snags, you might want the hook covered, but fish it exposed everywhere else. Catfish that haven't been caught before aren't bothered by hooks. With a buried hook point, often you don't get the hook past the barb on the set, or the hook sets into the bait, not the fish. An exposed hook hooks the catfish.

Carry and use a hook file. Catfish aren't hard to hook, but sharp hooks

# Exposed Hooks

*If you're missing many cats on the hook set, you're doing something wrong. You should catch almost every decent cat that hits. Most good catmen do.*

*The secret is fishing with an exposed hook. Unfortunately, many catfishermen believe that covering the point of a hook—hiding the darn thing from a fish that doesn't know or care what a hook is—means more cats. It means the opposite.*

## Hair Rig

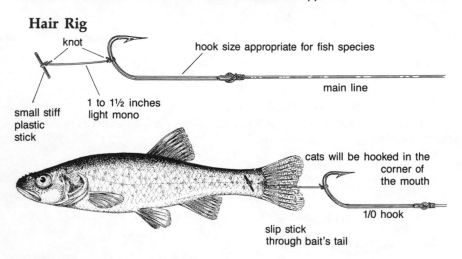

## knot
## hook size appropriate for fish species
## main line
## small stiff plastic stick
## 1 to 1½ inches light mono
## cats will be hooked in the corner of the mouth
## 1/0 hook
## slip stick through bait's tail

*Consider the hair rig, a popular English bait-rigging method that places an exposed hook near, but separated from a bait attached by an inch-long portion of light monofilament. Not only is a bait easier for wary fish (they have a lot of those in heavily fished English waters) to pick up, but the exposed hook means instant hook penetration on a set.*

## Fishing Blood

## Dough Baits

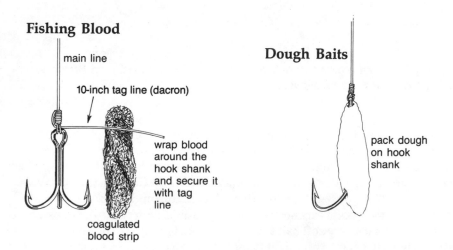

main line

10-inch tag line (dacron)

wrap blood around the hook shank and secure it with tag line

coagulated blood strip

pack dough on hook shank

*Dough baits? Pack them on the hook shank. Chicken livers or blood? Leave five inches of extra line dangling beyond the knot on your hook. Use it to wrap the blood or liver on the hook shank. If you use mesh to hold liver, barely slide the hook through the mesh, leaving the point and barb exposed.*

**Whole Fish**

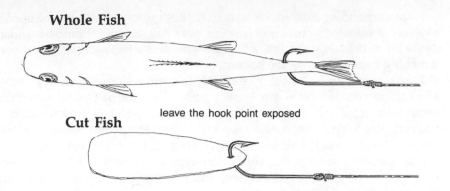

leave the hook point exposed

**Cut Fish**

*If you use a whole minnow or chub, don't push the hook point back into the fish. Slip it once through the head or tail and leave the point exposed. If you fish a strip of sucker meat or a frog, crayfish, or waterdog, slip the hook through only once. Leave the sharp point exposed and glistening in the sun.*

*You will lose more baits to snags. But hooks and baits are cheap compared to time. How much is frustration a pound? You never want to miss one of those fat ol' barrel-bellied cats, be they blues, flatheads, or channels. You don't have to. That's the* point.

penetrate easily to improve hooking percentage.

Slip sinkers: The traditional choice is the egg sinker, but since it tends to roll on the bottom in current, it's not the best choice. A bell sinker works better, and bank or pyramid sinkers work well in heavy current. If you can't find bell sinkers, walking sinkers used by walleye anglers are superior to egg sinkers.

Lead shot: Look for two qualities in at least some of your shot: softness and round shape (no "ears"). Soft shot can be pinched on by finger pressure without pliers or teeth. Eared shot are handy, but may drift oddly in current and snag more easily. BB and 3/0 shot from Water Gremlin are the most useful sizes. Good soft, round European shot is imported by Wazp Brand Tackle and can be ordered from them or from Cabela's.

## SET WEIGHTS

Lindy-Little Joe
Walking "Slip Sinker"

3/8 to 2 ounces
bell sinker

Get a box of #10 or #8 swivels. Straight swivels are adequate for most situations, although many rigs also require three-way swivels.

## FLOATS

We've fished cats from Massachusetts to Arizona, from Manitoba to Georgia. We've seldom seen catfishermen using floats (bobbers). *Using floats correctly is one of the simplest, but most potent ways* to catch more and better cats with less trouble.

Why don't catfishermen use floats? Two mistaken ideas. First, many people think catfish feed on bottom all the time. Second, people think floats are good only for suspending baits above the bottom. Both wrong! Floats can be used in a variety of ways to improve presentation, get a bait where it should be, and indicate bites. Primarily, though, a float lets you drift a bait accurately and keep it moving smoothly along the bottom.

Floats keep your bait moving efficiently into areas cats inhabit. They move a bait along a distinct path—you know exactly where the bait is and something about what it's doing. A float combined with a long rod allows true drifts. If you're fishing 6 feet down, the only line in the water is the 6 feet below your float; most of the rest is in the air where it isn't affecting the drift. Learn, too, about current patterns, water depth, and bottom type by the way your float behaves. Plus, you won't get snagged as often, and when you do, it's easy to use the buoyancy and bulk of the float to get free.

*Floats keep bait dancing along the bottom, moved accurately and naturally by current into areas where catfish hold to feed. ''Stemmed'' floats are easier to see at a distance. ''Slip floats'' let you make efficient casts and quick depth modifications.*

Contrast the float system to the usual bank-fishing drift set-up, a bait drifted with shot anchoring it. An angler fishing in 6 feet of water, 10 feet from the bank has a lot of line in the water being dragged by current. That means inaccurate drifts, snags, and difficulty detecting bites.

Or contrast that to an angler using a set rig. A set rig, as you might guess, is a rig anchored in place in a catfish hole. It "sets" there. No drifting goes with the presentation. Because the bait is sitting on bottom in one spot, it may not be seen by many cats, if any. Maybe the bait washes into a crevice where a big cat can't get it, even if he wants it. Then, when a cat takes line, if the "set" is in current, the pressure of current on line creates slack. The more slack, the less the angler knows about what's going on, and the loose line is likely to snag bottom and make the cat spit the bait. Then too, often the cat spits the bait and the drifting line bumping in current and on the bottom feels more like a catfish than a catfish.

Slip floats eliminate many of these problems. Walleye anglers use slip floats because they can reel the float to the rod tip and cast without having the float in the way. For catfishermen, a slip float's major advantage is ease of changing bait depth. If you drift a bait through a riffle and it drags bottom, swing it in, slide the float stop down, and have the bait tipping along the bottom in seconds.

Again, some of the better slip floats and stops are European designs. Wazp Brand Products imports neoprene float stops. Northland Tackle (3209 Mill St. NE, Bemidji, MN 56601) and Cabela's carry them, too.

Wazp's 3½-inch Cigar float with a highly visible fluorescent top is our mainstay. It casts well and holds up a good-size bait. This float works well in slow to medium current with most baits.

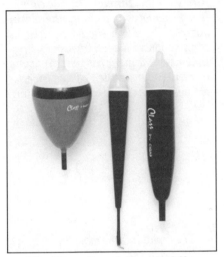

*The Wazp Brand Gazzet, Minnow Slider, and Cigar.*

When we fish heavier current or heavier baits in heavier current, we use Wazp's Gazzett slip float in the 2- or 2¾-inch size. The inverted pear shape holds up a bigger bait and rides heavy current more smoothly than slender floats.

Other bobbers work, too. Goldeneye Products (Box 35267, Minneapolis, MN 55435) makes a pyramid-shape slip float. Freshwater Tackle (13435 Jay St. NW, Anoka, MN 55304) makes a slip-on-off slip float. Walleye-style slip floats are fine, too, but usually aren't offered in the size needed for fishing catfish-size baits in current.

Don't worry about cats feeling a bit of resistance from the float. You *want* slight resistance for a steady connection to the fish. It's sudden tension followed by slack or vice versa that spooks fish.

## STRIKE INDICATORS

A float serves as a bite indicator. You need alternative indicators for setlining. A bell clamped to the rod tip to make noise when a cat jerks the line is a traditional, sometimes effective, but comparatively crude choice.

When cats take a bait you often want them to be able to at least begin to run with the bait; not far, but they shouldn't have to pull against solid weight. Neither do they need perfectly slack line. Steady resistance is the key. The challenge is to make a set sensitive enough to indicate a bite, but not so sensitive to be easily activated by wind. A reel clicker is a good bite indicator. Spinning reels with a free-spool feature can be used for setlining by clamping a bit of foil to the line to indicate when a fish is moving line.

Commercial indicators that work well are battery powered devices that attach to the rod. Some adjust for sensitivity and produce both sound and a light signal. One such indicator is the DS fish alarm sold by Bass Pro Shops (1935 S. Campbell, Springfield, MO 65807). More sophisticated electronic indicators are used in Europe, but aren't marketed yet in the U.S.

Make an excellent strike indicator by cutting a 6-inch X 1½-inch rectangle from a plastic bleach or detergent bottle. Coil the strip, loop a rubber band onto it to hold it coiled, drop it in boiling water for 20 seconds, then dip it in cool water. The plastic holds its coil shape after the rubber band is removed.

Cast your bait and set the rod in holders. Then pull extra line from your reel to create a V between the reel and the first guide. Slip the plastic loop on your

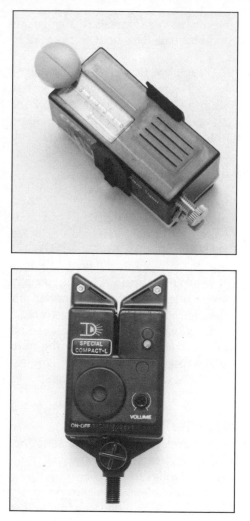

*The DS fish alarm fixes to your rod. Run your line through the line clamp. If a fish moves your bait, the alarm buzzes. The alarm should be used in conjunction with a reel freespool setting that gives line to the fish when it wants to run. We prefer the ''clicker'' mechanisms on the Garcia 6500C baitcasting reel.*

*The Optonic is the most popular and most advanced electronic alarm in Europe. The indicator attaches to the top of the front bank stick. Lay your rod in the rest with the line running through the indicator. A photoelectronic cell indicates the slightest line movement. The Optonic offers multiple sound settings so you can tell which indicator beeps.*

line to hold it in a V position. Add extra plastic loops over each other to hold the V position in wind. When a cat takes line, the indicator pulls up toward the rod. Strike immediately if you're using quick-strike rigging. If you're not, let the cat run momentarily against the free-spool mechanism. Set with the indicator on your line and remove the plastic loop as you fight the fish. In high wind add a "monkey climber" wire (sturdy wire about 14 inches long) to hold the bite indicators steady until a cat moves the line.

In addition to the strike indicator, in current or wind you may need a line snubber to keep your line from moving freely from the reel. Here again, the baitcasting reel with a clicker shines—no need for a line clip. If you use a reel with

## Plastic Indicators

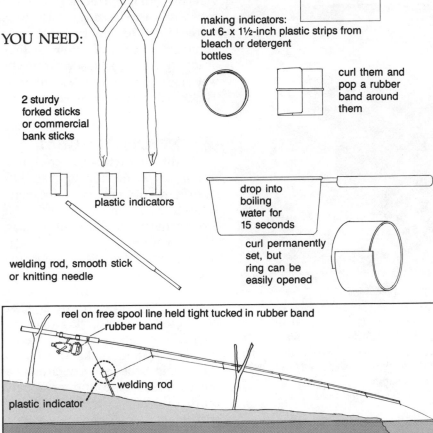

YOU NEED:

2 sturdy
forked sticks
or commercial
bank sticks

making indicators:
cut 6- x 1½-inch plastic strips from
bleach or detergent
bottles

curl them and
pop a rubber
band around
them

plastic indicators

welding rod, smooth stick
or knitting needle

drop into
boiling
water for
15 seconds

curl permanently
set, but
ring can be
easily opened

reel on free spool line held tight tucked in rubber band
rubber band

welding rod

plastic indicator

1. *Tighten line, engage reel and lay in forked sticks.*
2. *Add one indicator to line between reel and first rod guide—pull indicator almost to ground.*
3. *Indicator rises to indicate strike.*
4. *In wind—wrap several plastic indicators over each other to add weight;—position rod tip below water so line isn't blown;—insert welding rod into ground and slide indicator on rod to keep indicator from blowing around.*
5. *After a strike, remove indicator with a flip of your fingers.*

a free-spool feature, wrap a rubber band high on your rod grip. Pinch a loop of line under the rubber band to keep line from spilling freely off the spool.

## ROD HOLDERS

The tradition is forked sticks. The Europeans are again a step ahead, however. Wazp Brand Products offers classic European rod holders mounted on aluminum bank sticks paired with extendable rod rests. With this rig you can position your rod at various angles.

Set the rod according to wind and current conditions. The object is to keep the rod handy for setting the hook while minimizing the effects of current or wind on your line. The most common set is with the rod resting parallel to the water. Set the rod tip higher to minimize the effect of current on line, or low (touching or just beneath the water) to minimize wind interference. The adjustable rest makes it easy.

*A "proper" European bank set: Fore and aft adjustable double bank sticks, with an Optonic (electric strike indicator) screwed to one front stick. Note the plastic indicator hanging on the line between the reel and the first rod guide.*

## INCIDENTAL GEAR

Tradition dictates a cooler of refreshments and a lawn chair. Obviously, that ties you to a few locations. While there are times to park on a hole to tempt the big cat you're sure is there, those times are rare. The skillful catfisherman usually relies on mobility.

Choose whatever wading gear you like. River temperatures are often pleasantly cool in warm weather, so wading wet is common. To avoid mud, leeches, and cuts, wear jeans (tied at the ankles) and socks and tennis shoes. Hip boots or waders may be more comfortable and provide a modicum of protection against snakebite.

Boat choice is determined by where you fish. For small and medium rivers, jon boats are the time-proven favorite because they're stable and draw little water. With a 14-foot jon boat and small outboard, you can move wherever you want to go. Small semi-V aluminum boats work much the same way. Toad Smith and Doug Stange often fish cats from the small aluminum semi-Vs they use for duck hunting.

On big rivers use almost any boat equipped with sonar to locate wing dams, deep holes, ledges, and other river structure.

The mobile angler on foot needs a way to carry gear, like the multipocketed vest trout and steelhead anglers use. Doug Stange uses an ancient shoulder bag with a huge pouch and several pockets. A backpack works well, too, or a book bag. Keep your hands free for tasks like climbing banks or balancing atop algae-covered boulders.

What goes in the bag? The gear we've mentioned, plus a fillet knife, flashlight, bug repellent, sun screen, a towel or two, cotton gloves, a hookout tool (Baker Manufacturing Company, P.O. Box 28, Columbia, PA 17512) or long-nosed pliers. Flex Lights (the little lights used by trout anglers at night) are handy when

# Carrying Gear

Doug Stange's shoulder bag—easy to carry and stocked with everything he needs for a cat session. Doug also often uses a backpack for his cameras and a seven-course lunch.

Toad Smith rivets 5-gallon buckets together—handy to carry gear and sit on. Toad's small small-stream cats are in the fish basket.

How big is it? We'll find out with a weigh sack. Non-abrasive material keeps the cat wet and holds him firmly and safely while you weigh him. Weigh sacks: Coming soon to North America. Try Wazp Brand Products, Minden, Louisiana. (It's a 24-pounder!)

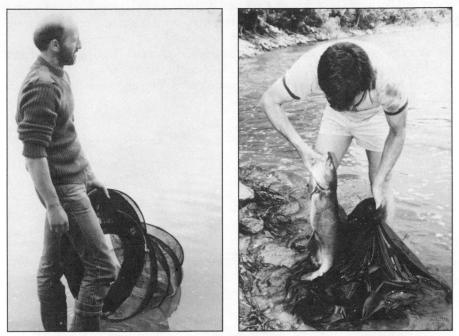

*Euro-style keep sacks: On the left, the Wazp Brand Products "Keep Net." Plastic rungs give the net shape yet allow it to be packed flat. The other sack is a square bag made from porous nylon. Both sacs are easy on cat skin.*

*Quick, easy and successful release straight from the bag.*

you need light and both hands are busy. Include a biodegradable soap. Carry cut bait in Ziploc bags. If you plan to keep fish, bring a stringer or a European-style keep sack for cats you might release later.

After that, you're on your own. A sandwich? A soda? A handful of jigs? Keep it light. The beauty of a catfish bag is that—except for cut bait—you can keep the gear together. When you go fishing, grab a rod or two and your bag. Add bait and you're ready to wade!

Stop that, junior! If you keep popping your eyes out like that. Someday they might just stay popped out. You want to go through life looking like a Walleye?

## Chapter 9

# CATFISH BAITS

### Myth, Mystery, And Truth About Best Baits

No area of catfishing offers more mystique than the topic of catfish bait. That makes this an unusually important chapter. Many catfishermen can take a tremendous jump in fishing effectiveness by switching to more effective baits. Some of those baits already exist. Other baits will result from present European technology or American technology yet to come.

Our earlier comments on catfish anatomy and eating habits provide a background for choosing baits. You know this about catfish and catfish feeding:

• Catfish are omnivorous, eating almost any living or dead food they find in their environment.

• While catfish will eat almost anything, they get used to feeding on what's available. Large cats in particular get used to feeding on fish more consistently than any other food.

• Catfish have an extremely sensitive sense of taste and memory of items they've eaten before.

• A catfish's sense of taste and your sense of smell have little in common.

How do those points relate to your choice of bait? The main points, which we'll develop include:

■ The least effective baits for big cats often are artificial pastes. Some are better than others; pastes with a more natural chemical make-up outperform exotic concoctions catfish haven't experienced.

■ Natural baits are usually best, although other concoctions have the potential to produce if they adequately represent natural baits.

■ "Grocery store" baits like shrimp or liver are more natural than many commercial stink baits, but still exotic because they don't occur naturally in the catfish world.

■ Offer channel cats food they recognize. The basic strategy is to fish with baits that are plentiful in their environment.

■ Cut bait—parts of suckers, minnows, or other fish are the most easily used and universally effective natural bait.

Give cats respect! They have an extraordinary tasting mechanism and a powerful memory. They eat almost anything with gusto if it's something they recognize from past experience.

What do too many people use to catch discriminating cats? Commercial stink baits are concocted from chemical compounds such as anise, animal parts, cheese, flour, gelatins, various preservatives and binders. Here you have a fish with one of the world's most highly developed palates, and you want to fool him with some weird-tasting chemical salad?

It isn't that catfish won't eat exotic compounds. But big cats, the guys with experience, tend not to take them readily or aggressively until they're used to doing so. If you fish with artificial concoctions, you're apt to get only bumps and nudges from cats. You'll decide they aren't biting, but actually they're playing with this strange new thing that has entered their world. They're curious and wonder if it's food, so they whap it and ding around with it. Eventually they *may* eat it.

Catch catfish with most exotic pastes, and you can bet your favorite rod you probably haven't caught the biggest cat in that hole. Today's paste baits tend to be small-fish baits. A trophy channel cat has been around. He has a superb memory bank of things he's eaten, and he has the natural caution of any large, old animal. He'll keep his distance from the strange-smelling concoctions that might take small, super-competitive fish. To catch a trophy cat, feed him something he knows.

Fish with cut bait or some other natural bait, and cats usually move confidently to the bait and take it. That's particularly important when you drift a bait in a riffle where a cat doesn't have long to decide to bite.

Remember, cats are highly intelligent, extremely aware of their environment and equipped with world-class tasting organs. The idea that cats can be caught on anything that smells bad enough just isn't so.

All artificial baits aren't bad and some day they will be better. Scientific studies of taste and smell are now being carried on in Europe and North America, attempting to identify key chemicals in natural baits that appeal to catfish. Once identified, we'll be able to fashion an artificial bait with those chemicals. It's hard to believe an imitation will beat the real thing, but we expect compounds to appear that are more convenient and still have the appeal of natural baits.

Of course, chicken liver, shrimp, or other atypical baits catch catfish. Heck, cats eat almost anything and the chemical make-up of those baits is enough like the chemical make-up of their accustomed forage to make them worth using at times. But cats tend to be suspicious of anything they aren't familiar with, and these baits are different enough to make fish tentative until they get used to their presence and taste. If liver or shrimp are fished in a hole often, cats get used to them, feed on them, and anglers decide they're great baits. In commercial pay ponds, artificial pastes are a popular bait choice. They work because cats are in a competitive situation and eventually become familiar with pastes.

Zacker discussing baits:
"Tell you somethin' about baits," he said. "Little cats eat anything, anything 'tall. Big cats is danged selective. For my money, the bigger the cat, the more he likes fresh bait. I ain't sayin' smelly baits ain't good and they won't take 'em; I'm sayin' that they just flat like fresh stuff better.

"Take a big mud cat. He's a mean sucker, the meanest fish swimmin' for my money. Danged right! He's the toughest, orneriest, meanest customer that swims in any natural (fresh) water. He won't ever pick up a dead bait, much less a ball of stinky crap. He wants somethin' live and big, like a big sucker or, better yet, one-, two-, or three-pound carp. Mud cats eat carp like peanuts: crack, and a head shake and then he's (the carp is) gone. Only time a big mud cat takes dead bait is spring. They take cut (filleted slabs) carp or sucker then.

"Big forks is kinda the same; I mean they ain't gonna go out of their way to take smelly baits when they're used to havin' the rule of their roost and eatin' live stuff or stuff that ain't been dead long. One-pound suckers or creek chubs—live ones—are good. Or big chunks of fresh-cut sucker or chub. Just cut the side (fillet) off a big sucker and hook it through once with a 5/0 hook. Don't ball the dang thin' up or you can't get hooks."

We mentioned this "conditioning" phenomenon before. In the Cincinnati area, folks riding Ohio River tour boats throw French fries overboard. You'll catch catfish on French fries in those waters. Does that mean French fries are a great bait for catfish? No. It means cats readily take food they know.

Another example. Grasshoppers can be good catfish bait, but they aren't nearly as effective in May when grasshoppers aren't as common as in August, when large grasshoppers often end up in rivers...and in channel cat bellies.

Much of the mystique of "secret" or super-potent catfish baits relates to the

Jan Eggers

*World record 75.74-pound carp caught by Leo van der Gugsen in Lac St. Cassien, France, May 1987.*

In European countries, carp are esteemed by anglers who may spend days at a time pursuing huge fish made wary by years of fishing pressure. Carp grow more cautious following catch and release, the usual disposition of these prized fish.

Success demands delicate presentations and exquisite baits. Expert English carp angler Kevin Maddocks has tested reactions of carp in tanks to amino acids, to improve his catch with scented paste baits. Amino acids are molecules that serve as building blocks for peptides and proteins and are contained in all foods fish eat.

Maddocks noted high sensitivity to amino acids and various reactions by carp. While not as wary as carp, channel catfish and bullheads sense more dilute concentrations of such substances than carp can. Development of future artificial baits for cats will likely mean incorporating chemicals that occur in natural foods into pliable formulations.

Keys for successful paste baits include long shelf life, ease of application onto hooks and remaining on the hook while wafting the concoction into the water. But ability to make cats bite is the final criterion. Natural substances seem most promising.

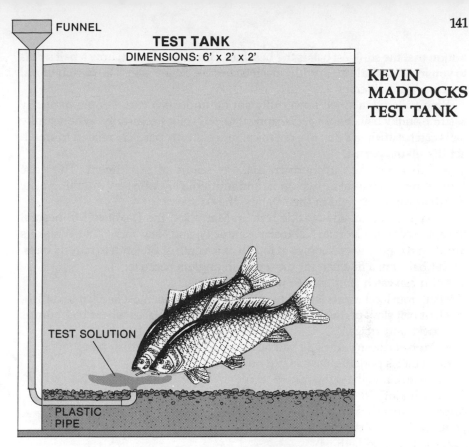

FUNNEL

## TEST TANK
### DIMENSIONS: 6' x 2' x 2'

**KEVIN
MADDOCKS
TEST TANK**

TEST SOLUTION

PLASTIC
PIPE

| TEST TANK RESULTS FOR CARP | | | |
|---|---|---|---|
| **Good Reaction** | **Fair Reaction** | **Poor Reaction** | **No Reaction** |
| Immediate response by fish on introduction of acid solution, fish rolling on gravel and against side of tank. Fish also mouthing gravel and digging into area of outlet. Continuing high activity, even clearing gravel around pipe outlet. Fish attempting to eat everything in tank and around them. | Fish responding to acid solution several minutes after introduction. General increased activity around outlet area, occasional rolling and turning over gravel, definite feeding reaction. | Fish seemed stimulated in some way and reacted slowly after acid solution had been introduced. Occasionally mouthing gravel but no turning or rolling and no homing into outlet area. | No apparent response to any solutions introduced. |
| | | Alanine<br>Proline<br>Cystine<br><br>Combination No. 31:<br>Asparagine/<br>Isoleucine<br>Glycine/Histidine/<br>Phenylalanine<br>Combination No. 37:<br>Tyrosine/Lysine/Phenylalanine | Methionine:<br>DL<br>Argenine<br>Glutamine<br>Threonine<br>Leucine<br>Serine*<br>Phenylalanine:<br>DL<br>Tyrosine<br>Aspartic Acid<br>Glutamic Acid<br>Methionine |
| Valine<br>Lysine<br>Combination No. 35:Phenylalanine-/Lysine/Cystine | Phenylalanine<br>Histidine<br>Glycine<br>Isoleucine<br>Asparagine | | |

*This acid had an adverse effect on the carp which showed signs of respiratory difficulties, eyes rolling, and obvious distress. Its use is therefore not advised.

N.B. All acids tested were 'L' versions unless indicated otherwise.

From: *Carp Fever*, Kevin Maddocks, Beekay Publishers, Withy Pool, Bedford Rd., Henlow Rd. Beds., England SG1 6AE.

notion that the stinkiest bait is the best bait. But as we've said, how a bait *smells* to you in air has little to do with how it tastes to a cat in water. The two chemical processes are different.

Ripe baits often smell powerfully strong and catch cats. People naturally assume stinky baits have special appeal to cats. Not necessarily. When stinky baits catch catfish, it's due to a chemical process only partially related to smell. Yet the myths persist.

Another mistake catfishermen make is failure to experiment. They use something, catch a cat or two on it, and immediately won't try anything else. If catfish were that rigid in their habits, they'd starve.

We've conducted side-by-side tests in Manitoba, the Dakotas, Minnesota, Iowa, Wisconsin, Georgia, Nebraska, Kentucky, and New York. "Old Whiskers Brew" and others always comes in fourth or seventh or fifteenth to natural baits.

Cut baits are a fine bait for most catfish anglers because:

- You can catch your own to reduce bait costs.
- Bait from local waters is readily available and the bait most familiar to catfish.
- Cut bait stays on the hook better in current and places where bait bumps rocks and snags.
- Cut bait doesn't smell as bad as many commercial catfish baits.
- Cut bait is portable, easy to put on a hook and easy to cut to the right size.

We fish a lot of baits, but we're convinced that cut bait is superior bait. If you don't have a reason to fish something else, try cut bait. Other baits may be better at times, though! Read on.

Hold it! Billy... this isn't our catfish bait - these are those little meatballs mom made for her bridge club... huh ho...

## NATURAL BAITS

*Cut Bait:* By cut bait, we mean portions of larger baitfish, or whole or nearly whole smaller fish. You don't have to use fish that come from the river you're fishing; catfish aren't that selective. Many fish work well, especially oily fish like shad or suckers. Try suckers (often available at bait stores), mooneyes, carp, chubs, shiners, or almost any minnow.

Some catfish anglers step on the head of a fish they use for bait. Cut bait should leak natural juices into the river. Whether you cut your fish or step on them, you'll notice a decline in productivity when you've fished the same bait

*Toad slicing suckers by flashlight. You may want to wash your hands before handling the end of the flashlight that goes in your mouth. Toad doesn't bother and, as far as we can tell, doesn't mind.*

*Cut bait! In this case the side (fillet) removed from a baitfish (sucker).*

long enough.

In rivers where you don't expect cats over about 6 pounds, stick to smaller cut bait. Pieces 1 inch wide x 3 inches long by 1/2 inch thick are about right. In bigger rivers with bigger cats, cut bigger baits. Where 20-pound channel cats are common, our baits are 1 x 5 x 1/2 to 1 inch.

No special rules exist for cutting bait. With a sucker about 4 or 5 inches long, you might cut off the head and tail. With a big sucker, fillet the sides and slice them into appropriate-size pieces. Baits with coarse scales, like sheepshead or carp, should be scaled before being cut. Cut so you leave a firm piece that holds a hook well. Run the hook through the corner of the bait, leaving the hook point exposed.

Match the size of cut bait to water temperature. In cold water, use smaller baits than in warm water. A 2-inch piece of bait that would be a tidbit during summer might be just right in spring and fall. If you don't have a large fish to cut, try impaling 4 to 6 minnows on a hook. Often they work almost as well as cut bait.

Freshly killed cut bait usually works best. As soon as you kill and cut it, put your bait on ice. Keep it cool until you use it. Sometimes you'll catch more fish on bait that's "soured" by leaving it in the sun for awhile. But soured bait often is more difficult to fish because it tends to get soft.

*Live minnows:* Early or late in the year, live minnows or chubs are often the best bait. Keeping them alive may be a problem, especially if you're moving along a stream. A frozen "blue ice" packet dropped in a minnow bucket will extend

Zacker talking bait rigging with Doug Stange:
"Where you hooking your livebaits?" I asked.

"Never hook one near the head even when your bait's settin' in current," he replied. "Big cat'll crush that bait and swallow it before you know it; and chances are 50-50 when you set the hook or he swims away from your set line that the hook'll dig back into the bait. I seen it a hundred times before I figured it out.

"You gotta hook a bait in his thinnest part and that's the part farthest away from their head: right in the danged tail."

"Top side or bottom side," I asked.

"No difference, but I always hooked mine in the top. And remember," he said, "keep the barb of your hook exposed, 'specially with a big slab of cut bait."

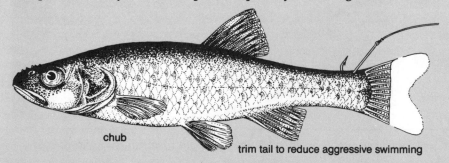

chub

trim tail to reduce aggressive swimming

the life of your minnows by keeping the water cool.

Try live minnows during the Prespawn Period until temperatures reach about 65°F and then again in fall after the leaves begin to fall. A live minnow on a slip rig works in most situations.

Since live minnows are most productive when temperatures are cool, use minnows 3 to 5 inches long. Switch to a larger bait when you think you know where a huge catfish is holed up and he won't bite on other baits. It'll be tough for him to ignore a distressed chub for long. Fishing live minnows in a deep hole in fall can produce spectacular results.

Hook minnows through the back near the dorsal fin, not through the lips. In heavy current, hook them close to the tail. In quiet water, hook them close to the dorsal fin to give them freedom to swim in an arc.

*Crayfish:* Crayfish are common in most rivers and prominent in the channel cat's diet. We've had our best fishing with crayfish in late spring when they breed and late summer when they molt. Crayfish make a fine bait for trotline sets, too but be ready to switch if cats aren't interested.

*Crayfish: Dynamite at times!*

The most common way to hook crayfish is up through the tail. Remove the pinchers to keep crayfish from grabbing the bottom. Fish them just off bottom with a float so they can't crawl under rocks. Many anglers squash the head or thorax to spread the scent. Use whole crayfish for larger fish or crayfish tails for smaller cats.

*Frogs:* Many catfishermen think frogs are magic. The problem is that too many catfishermen fish only with frogs. In many seasons of fishing frogs versus other baits, we have yet to see frog catches overwhelm catches on other baits. Thus, our opinion stands that they're a good, but somewhat overrated bait. Frogs can be terrific during the last portion of summer when they are particularly abundant. But even then, fresh cut bait or freshly killed baitfish often work as well or better, and may be easier to get.

The most common type of bait frog is the widely available leopard frog, the same critter you probably dissected in high school biology. Other common frogs may be available where you live.

Frogs can be used dead or alive, but a freshly killed and partially squashed frog probably is most popular. You'll probably also find that large frogs that are dead for long and stiffen up tend not to produce so well. Obviously, frog size should match the size of the cats sought. We snip off the lower legs of dead frogs and slip the hook through the lips or leg.

Tadpoles, by the way, catch cats, but tend to fall apart once they die, which is quickly. They look like succulent morsels that no catfish could resist, but they haven't been a good bait for us.

*Waterdogs (salamanders):* Waterdogs are the larval form of the tiger salamander.

*The leopard frog is a popular late-summer bait. The authors haven't found them to outperform fresh cut bait, but you may find otherwise.*

This is another bait that seems to vary in productivity.

In tests we ran one year, waterdogs from 4 to 6 inches worked better than any bait in farm ponds. But waterdogs have been a dud for us in rivers. Catfish in our tanks seem eager to kill waterdogs, then not eat them.

Waterdogs must be alive or freshly killed to be productive. Hook them through the mouth. This bait falls in a category that catches cats, but is more trouble and less productive than cut bait.

*Grasshoppers:* Though they are small, grasshoppers can be a wonderful catfish bait in late summer when they're abundant. In late summer grasshoppers may be the main part of a cat's diet. We usually hook them through the thorax on a light hook, or place several 'hoppers on a hook.

Grasshoppers are often seen in streams in August, especially on windy days. They're caught in current and carried to pools by riffles. Fish 'hoppers on a drift through fast-running shallow riffles. Floating grasshoppers often settle in slack water areas, then sink to the bottom, so fish your 'hoppers in those areas too.

*Nightcrawlers:* Catfish rarely encounter nightcrawlers in rivers, but they're an attractive bait nevertheless. Crawlers, however, are appealing to smaller fish, so your bait gets pecked to death and you catch a mixed bag of small fish too. Carry crawlers to catch suckers and other fish you'll cut up for bait.

Gob several fat crawlers on a hook. Nightcrawlers, like most baits, lose their juicy flavor after about 15 minutes in the water, so rebait frequently. As always, leave the hook point exposed.

Crawlers are most effective in spring and early summer in small rivers, ponds, and reservoirs, the time of year when it's easy to pick a pail of crawlers off your lawn at night.

*Leeches:* Catfish also hit this popular walleye bait in late spring and early summer. Leeches are a clean bait that's easy to handle. Like crawlers, they attract small fish. Though leeches work, they're rarely the best bait.

*Clams:* The same is true of clams. Cats that live around clams and mussels eat dead ones, so clams aren't a novelty bait. Clam meat is tough enough to hold on a hook when you bounce it down a riffle or around a snag. But clams don't catch cats as well as cut bait, and they're harder to collect. When clams get a little ripe, they get soft. Most of the time, why bother.

## SOUR BAITS

Many natural baits can be used as "sour baits," though cut fish are the easiest sour bait to use this way. Sour baits are natural baits that are dead...real, real dead. Baits become sour baits when they ripen. Sour baits smell awful, though that isn't why they work. A ripe piece of meat varies chemically from a fresh bait and probably has a more intense flavor than fresh cut bait.

There's a reason and a time to use sour baits. Fish and other animals that die in winter don't entirely decompose because the water is so cold. In spring, many of these dead animals become "floaters." Decay increases as the water warms. Meanwhile, rising water catches these ripe morsels and moves them. Many end up in eddies. In a reservoir, floating shad are driven this way and that by changing winds. In time, floaters become sinkers.

Zacker: "There's one time big forks like smelly baits, though. In spring you get those ripe carp— the floaters—that died in winter. There's no smell so bad. Cut the side off those fish and you got a good bait for forks of all sizes."

From the channel cat's point of view, a new source of food has suddenly become super-abundant. It might bother the squeamish, but cats dine heavily on the rotting food. During this time of year, ripe baits often outfish fresh cut bait.

Sour baits work when water temperatures range from about 50° F to 65° F— about the time nightcrawlers come out, your lawn blooms, and the first spring thunderstorms move through.

To make sour bait, cut boned fish into 1-inch x 3-inch x 1/2-inch sections, place them in a jar with a tight-sealing lid, and ripen them in the sun for several days. The best fish to use is an old carp, and sheepshead is almost as good. Any dead fish will do, but carp flesh is tough so it's easier to fish with. No matter how much plastic you wrap the baits in, they're going to be smelly. Wear rubber gloves to handle the baits if you plan to be around people for the next several days.

When waters warm to normal late-spring and summer temperatures, winter-kill isn't available, so the effectiveness of sours drops. Time to switch baits.

## SUCCULENT SOUR CARP
Ingredients:

A 1- to 6-pound carp; substitute sucker, mooneye, or any fish with tough skin.

A quart jar or two (with lids).

A cup of water.

**Step 1:** Fillet the carp, leaving the skin on. Scaling is a good idea, but isn't absolutely necessary.

**Step 2:** Cut the fillets into sections approximately 1 inch wide, 1 inch thick and 2 to 3 inches long. If the carp's a large fellow and the fillets are too thick, trim off meat until the chunks are about 1 inch thick.

**Step 3:** Pack the strips loosely into a quart jar and add a cup of water. Screw the lid on loosely and let the jar sit in the sun for several hours. Dig a hole about one foot deep in a spot that the sun hits for most of the day. Bury the jar. Allow the contents to fester inside the jar for several days if the weather's warm, or for several weeks if the weather's cool.

**Result:** Sweet, succulent, sour carp.

## BLOOD

Blood, like sour baits, is a special bait, a natural bait, not a novelty bait like most pastes. Chicken blood is blood, about the same stuff cats know from wounded minnows, a concentrated substance cats like.

Fish blood any time of year, but it's particularly effective in late summer, which isn't the easiest time to catch catfish, partly because of fishing pressure, which often peaks then. Use blood and you often have an edge on the competition.

Get blood from a chicken "processing" plant by talking politely to the foreman. Scoop the congulated stuff into a bucket. When you get home, pour it on a screen so the runny stuff slides through. You'll end up with caked blood.

Snip the cake into sections about 3/4 inch wide and 8 to 12 inches long. Strip the blood chunks into 1/4-inch sections by lifting and peeling strips off the chunk. Put them in a coffee can and keep cold. Preserve blood by freezing it, a process that toughens blood and makes it easier to keep on a hook. Freezing and refreezing, though, tends to make blood flakey and more difficult to use.

You can also buy blood. One source is Bob's Bait, Star Rt. 2, Box 14, Nixon, Texas 78140. Bob will ship it to you in plastic vats. Although fresh blood is probably better, Bob's blood often works fine.

Blood is not the same as paste bait with blood in it. Paste is paste; blood is blood. Try the real thing. Blood is channel cat bait. Flatheads usually want something alive. We haven't had much experience with blood and blues.

Toad Smith's method of keeping blood on a hook is probably best. Tie a plain #4 or #6 treble hook to your line, but leave a 10-inch tag end past the knot. Wrap a piece of blood around your hook, then spiral the tag line around the blood to hold it in place. Tie it to the main line with a half hitch or two.

Or use dacron to tie on blood. Tie on your hook. Then tie a 10-inch piece of 10- or 12-pound dacron to the hook eye. Spiral it around the blood and tie it to your line.

Finally, you can use steelhead rigs designed for spawn bags. These devices hold loose bait in a pouch of nylon mesh. Seal the top of the bag with a few knots of tough thread. One of the niftiest devices for doing this is made

Let the blood drain on a screen. Cut it in 1/4-inch thick by 1-inch wide by 8- to 12-inch long strips.

Keep the blood in a coffee can on ice. Wrap a strip around a #6 treble hook.

Leave a tag line of about 10 inches dangling from the end of the knot attaching the main line to the treble. A 10-inch tag line of dacron works well.

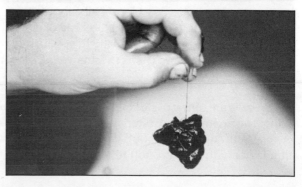

Wrap the blood with the tag line and tie it off with a half hitch or tuck the line between the blood and hook.

by Baitmaker, Melnak Tackle, 6 Van Allen Rd., Scarborough, Ontario M1G 1C2. The sacks also are handy for fishing clams or liver.

Like other baits—in fact, more than other baits—blood doesn't fish for long. A blood bait rarely lasts 15 minutes.

One of the best uses of blood is for chum. Freshwater anglers don't understand chum the way saltwater anglers do, and American anglers don't use it as advantageously as Europeans. Throw food into an area to draw fish and put them in an active feeding mode on the bait you're fishing. Don't worry that you'll "fill up" the cats if you chum because cats are inclined to pig out when they're in a feeding mood. Blood in particular sets catfish feeding, especially in late summer.

*The Baitbagger and bagged bait.*

How to chum? Let's say you've identified a good drift in a promising catfish hole. You run a good bait, probably a cut bait, through the area a few times and don't get a bite. Early in summer that means there are few catfish around or they're in a negative feeding mood. But this is late summer, when cats are often less aggressive. Lob a few blood baits about 10 feet above the snags or eddies you think hold cats. Now, drift a blood bait or cut bait. If you have chum sweetening the area and turning on the catfish, you'll often catch fish with any good bait.

Blood isn't magic and it isn't the answer all season, but it is effective at times.

## DIP BAITS

Dip baits are runny paste baits—paste without binders. Dip a sponge or plastic "ring" worm in the goo, often mixtures of things like animal brains, limburger cheese, and sour cream. Foul! Work the sponge through the runny dip bait until it loads with the goo. You're ready to fish.

*Dip worms or dip sponges are used to hold dip baits. Use a stick to push the bait into the goo. It's seldom necessary to let a cat run far with a dip bait. Hold your rod and set as soon as the cat moves with the bait. Dips wash away quickly in current. Keep dipping!*

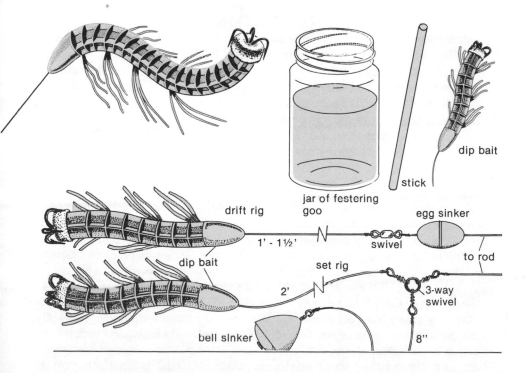

jar of festering goo

stick

dip bait

drift rig

1' - 1½'

swivel

egg sinker

to rod

dip bait

set rig

2'

3-way swivel

bell sinker

8"

*Dip baits and pastes by the dozen. The North American bait manufacturer's most consistently productive way to trigger catfishermen.*

Dip baits work, but rarely take big cats. They work best in late summer, but we'd usually rather fish blood then.

## PASTE BAITS

Most paste baits are combinations anglers think catfish like. But catfish usually don't immediately recognize them as food. Many commercial pastes are marketed as containing a secret ingredient. But cats respond to what they know, not to exotic secret substances they haven't encountered. At best, paste baits try to duplicate the appeal of natural baits.

Expect future improvement in paste baits when it's possible to isolate the most potent chemicals in natural baits and make them available in paste. Presently, we consider pastes baits for small to average-size cats.

## STRATEGIES

Fish paste baits or dip baits and you're probably fishing bait catfish don't readily recognize as food. But they'll explore almost any intriguing object that enters their pool. Fish novelty baits differently than natural baits, though.

With natural baits, you won't usually spook cats. A cat will pull a bait down and drown a float without minding it a bit. A cat will grab a bait with a big hook sticking out of it. If the bait is natural, a cat will run against your reel clicker or other tension. Catfish hang onto real food in a big way when they're hungry.

But they rarely hang onto novelty baits. We call pastes or dip baits "contact" baits because you must be prepared to set the hook right now! Cats pick these baits up, mouth them momentarily and then spit them. Stay in contact with your bait and set quickly to consistently catch catfish. Even then you'll

*Premier English bait manufacturer Duncan A. Kay mixing a batch of his paste for American catfish. Doug Stange verifies that the stuff is amazing in it's constitution and ability to stay on the hook. Duncan's baits should be available in North America soon.*

miss lots of cats because so many small ones mess with pastes and dips.

We've mentioned chumming in connection with blood baits. Chumming is an excellent, seldom-used strategy. No point in chumming when you're moving along a stream, skipping from spot to spot. But when you identify a good spot and set up to fish it awhile, chumming can turn the odds in your favor.

## ARTIFICIALS

Leadhead jigs aren't really artificials, though many anglers think of them that way. A leadhead jig is no different than a baited hook with a sinker ahead of it, except leadhead jigs place the bait and weight together. Fished like other live or dead bait, catfish bite the bait, not the jig. The jig is just an efficient way to present a bait. Because the weight and bait are in the same spot, you can fish a jig-rigged bait with precision.

Jigs are versatile. Drift a bait down a riffle. Cast a baited jig into a hole or eddy and work it around. While there's no reason to let a cat run with a jig before you set the hook, cats aren't bothered by the lead of a jighead. No need to set as quickly as with paste.

Channel cats also hit crankbaits and jigging spoons, but these are special application lures and not common ways of taking catfish. Jigging spoons for example, work well in certain reservoir locations where catfish feed on injured shad. Crankbaits that duplicate shad are effective for reservoir catfish feeding competitively on shad.

# BAIT COMBOS BY SEASON

*Bait choice is a matter of personal preference and usually develops from experience with what works in a particular water or region. Many productive possibilities occur during different seasons; however, the following combinations represent one approach for spring through fall. Keep at least one natural and perhaps one attractor (stink or blood) bait with you (at least while you fish).*

| SEASON | NATURAL BAIT | | ATTRACTOR BAIT | |
|---|---|---|---|---|
| | **1st choice** | **2nd choice** | **1st choice** | **2nd choice** |
| **Spring** | live or freshly killed baitfish | none | sour fish | none |
| **Early Summer** | live or freshly killed baitfish | crayfish | chicken blood | prepared dip or paste baits |
| **Summer** | live or freshly killed baitfish | frogs, crayfish, or grasshoppers | chicken blood | prepared dip or paste baits |
| **Fall** | live or freshly killed baitfish | frogs | chicken blood | prepared dip or paste baits |

The catfish bait was out all night, Dad, and the raccoons didn't go near it... I guess it's ready.

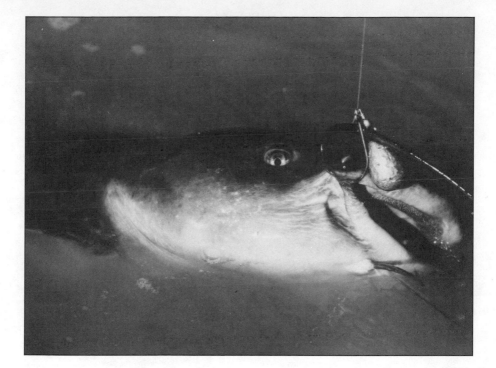

Chapter 10

# CATFISH RIGS

Old Rigs And New For Controlled And Consistent Fishing

While catfish may be very discriminating about scents and tastes that make up baits, they usually aren't picky about the rigs fishermen use to present baits. Catfish rigging, therefore, remains a simple affair—too simple in too many instances. A few basic rig modifications—nothing complicated mind you—can improve your fishing success by fishing efficiently in each situation. We'd like to introduce you to the basic rigs we rely on as well as a few rig options from Europe that may apply in special situations.

## DRIFT RIGS

Drift rigs present bait drifting naturally with current as it carries bait along a path where it will be seen by catfish. Obviously, you want to drift baits as naturally and efficiently as possible, so the bait looks like a "real find" when it reaches the catfish.

*Shot Rig*—The most basic and widely used drift rig. Consists of a hook and shot on the line above the hook to carry the bait along the bottom. Shot shouldn't be so heavy to interfere with the drift; therein the problem, for changing current conditions in most drifts mean the rig will move too fast at one point and

# Drift Rigs

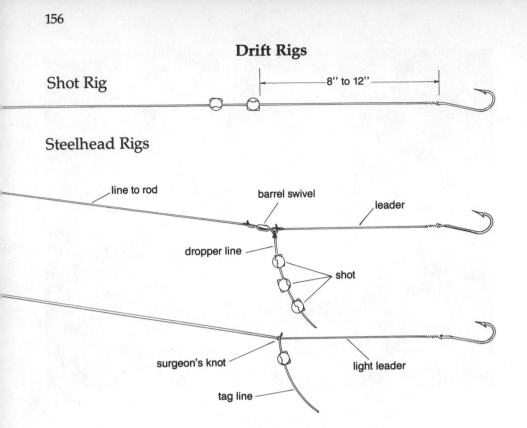

Shot Rig

8" to 12"

Steelhead Rigs

line to rod

barrel swivel

leader

dropper line

shot

surgeon's knot

light leader

tag line

too slow at another. Because of the effect of current on the long length of line usually in the water, the rig also tends not to drift naturally in current. Still, we often use this rig in small streams to drift a bait through a riffle and into the small hole below the riffle where we let the bait settle. In most cases, however, other rigs fish more efficiently.

*Steelhead Rig*—A modification of the basic shot rig. Consists of a swivel tied to the end of your main line, with a short section of lighter (than the main line) leader tied to the end of the swivel. Tie another short section (say 6 inches) of line to another portion of the swivel and attach shot to the tag end. Often the shot will snag instead of the bait, and you can save the bait portion of the rig by stripping the snagged shot from the tag line. Attach more shot and you're back in action.

The rig was made for efficiently bouncing a bait along bottom in steady, strong current for fish that react quickly to passing baits. Catfish, however, don't react as quickly to passing baits as steelhead and trout. In most catfishing situations, the problems with the basic shot rig also apply to the steelhead rig. Still, it's a pleasant rig to fish, especially during spring in small streams with steady current flow.

We usually eliminate the swivel by using a surgeon's knot to tie a section of lighter leader onto the main line. Leave a 4- to 6-inch tag end on the knot connection and pinch the shot onto the tag line.

*Slip-Float Rig*—A superior option for efficient drifts in most situations where water doesn't run too fast or too deep (beyond about 10 feet). Consists of a stop knot or neoprene float stop on your main line above the float (bobber) to set

## Slip-Float Rigs

### Tying Your Own Stop Knot

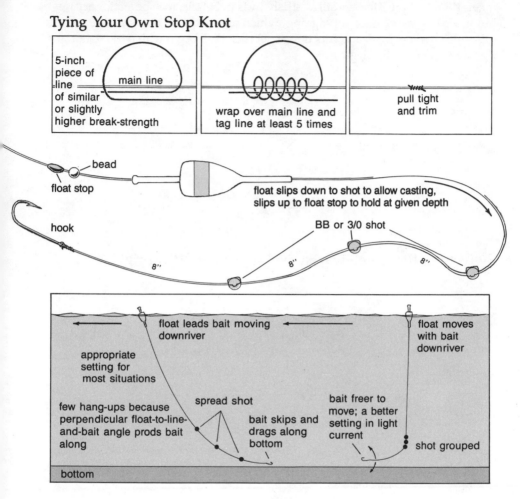

| 5-inch piece of line of similar or slightly higher break-strength — main line | wrap over main line and tag line at least 5 times | pull tight and trim |

bead

float stop

float slips down to shot to allow casting, slips up to float stop to hold at given depth

hook

BB or 3/0 shot

8"   8"   8"

float leads bait moving downriver

float moves with bait downriver

appropriate setting for most situations

few hang-ups because perpendicular float-to-line-and-bait angle prods bait along

spread shot

bait skips and drags along bottom

bait freer to move; a better setting in light current

shot grouped

bottom

depth. Often a bead on the line prevents the stop from sliding through the top of the float, which slides on the line below the float stop. Add a hook and shot to anchor the rig. To facilitate casting, the float stop reels through your rod guides onto your reel as the float slides to the end of your rod. The rig slides to the predetermined depth when it hits the water.

Keep your shot pattern below the float simple. Group enough shot to get your bait near bottom quickly and keep it there; and at the same time set your float so it's visible, yet offers minimum resistance to fish. Clump shot, then, from 6 to about 18 inches above the bait, depending on how much movement you want from the bait. In heavier current, clump shot closer to the bait. In slow current, move shot away from the bait. Twelve inches is a standard set.

As covered in Chapter 8, floats must be the right design and size to handle current conditions and bait size. It bears repeating that one of the most important steps most catfishermen can make to catch more fish is to replace traditional drift rigs with a slip-float rig.

## SET RIGS

Set rigging means casting a bait into a set position (sometimes it drifts before it gets there) where it stays until a catfish finds it. Set rigs may be stationary rigs, but more likely consist of slip rigging, which allows cats to move with the bait. Obviously, drift rigs can also function as set rigs. We'll begin with basic stationary rigs and move to slip rigging.

### Basic Set Rig

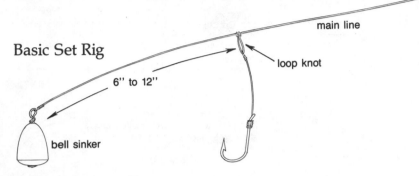

### Swivel-Set Rig (three-way-swivel rig or Wolf River rig)

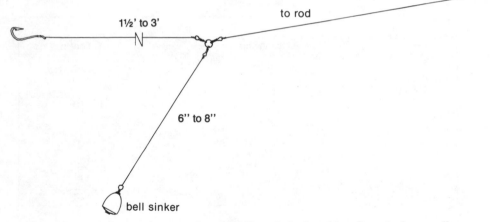

*Basic Set Rig*—Most often used as a bullhead rig, but it's a fine rig for smaller cats. Consists of a bell sinker tied to the end of your main line with a loop knot sporting a snelled hook, usually 6 inches to a foot up your line. Tie in as many loop knots and snelled hooks as is legal.

*Swivel-Set Rig*—Commonly called the three-way-swivel rig or Wolf River rig and often used as a trolling rig or a drift rig in big rivers. Typically consists of a three-way swivel tied to your main line, plus a 6-inch to 2-foot section of slightly lighter (than the main line) leader tied to a free rung. Add a lighter drop line, 6 inches to 1 foot long, to the other free rung. Place a bell sinker on the drop line and your hook rigging goes on the end of the leader.

The advantage to this rig is that it can pivot in place. Picture a 6-inch drop line as a leg standing perpendicular to the bottom. The rig can swing in a half-circle 6 inches forward or back. The rig, therefore, although stationary, can move enough to allow a cat to turn so you can make an efficient set into the corner of his mouth. Lengthening the drop line allows more give.

# SLIPPING SET RIGS

*Basic Slip Rig*—The most common catfishing rig in North America. Consists of an egg sinker sliding on the main line, held in place, usually 6 inches to a foot above the bait, by shot pinched on the line. The drawback is the egg sinker that easily rolls and drags in current. Roll anything along a typical catfish river bottom for long and you're snagged. Add a bell sinker or walking slip sinker such as the Lindy-Little Joe Lindy Rig sinker to your line to improve the efficiency of this basic rig. Snell length becomes instantly adjustable with the addition of a neoprene float stop instead of shot to stop the sinker.

## Basic Slip Rig

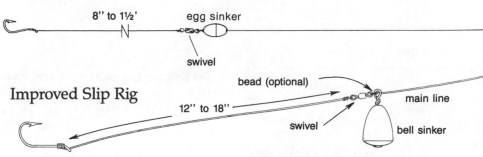

## Improved Slip Rig

*Swivel-Set Slip Rig*—Our favorite slip rig, but because it takes awhile to set up, we usually opt for the more easily tied basic rig when fishing snag-infested water. Consists of a bell sinker on one end of a 6-inch piece of mono with a swivel tied to the other end. Slip your main line through the end of the swivel and tie on a hook. About a foot up your main line, add a shot, anchor swivel, or neoprene stop knot to hold the swivel in place.

*Double Swivel-Set Slip Rig*—A modification of the basic swivel-set slip rig. Add a second terminal hook line to the free-running swivel. Fish two baits at once, the same bait or different baits.

## Swivel-Set Slip Rig

## Double Swivel-Set Slip Rig

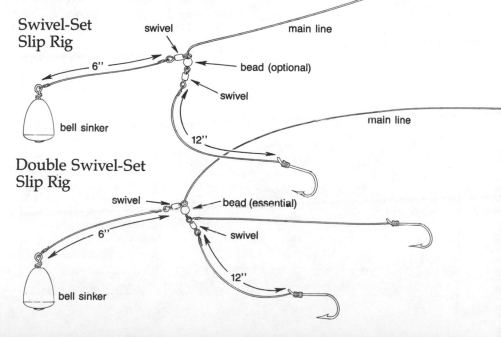

# SHOT PLACEMENT DETERMINES BAIT ACTION

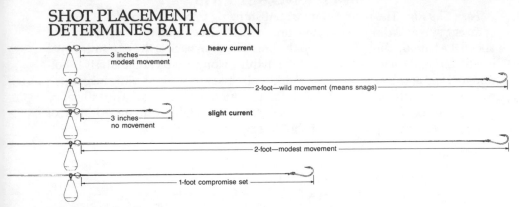

## Buoyant Ledger

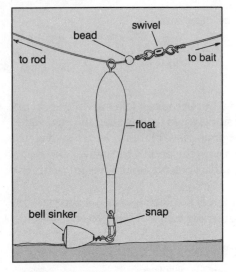

*The Buoyant Ledger is a simple improvement of basic bottom rigs. It keeps line off the bottom and away from debris.*

*The Collin Dyson Sunken Float Rig suspends live or dead bait. A suspended bait draws more takers than one lying on the bottom. The Buoyant Ledger and Dyson Sunken Float Rig are available from Angling Designs.*

## Collin Dyson Rig

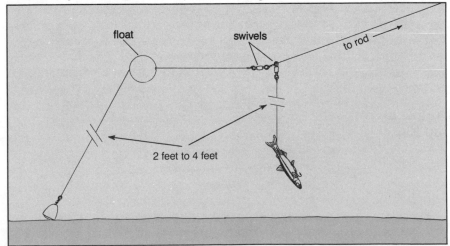

# EURO RIGS

*Buoyant Ledger*—The simplest rig consists of a hook or floating jighead like the Phelp's Floater (Northland Tackle, 3209 Mill St. NE, Bemidji, MN 56601), 18- to 24-inch leader, swivel, and bell sinker that attaches to the "buoyant ledger," a float designed to keep line off the bottom. Your main line goes through the swivel on top of the ledger to allow the bait to slip when a fish takes the bait. Buoyant ledgers are available from Angling Designs, P.O. Box 75085, Milwaukee, WI 53215-7585, and Wazp Brand Products, P.O. Box 837, Minden, LA 71058.

*Collin Dyson Sunken Float Rig*—Allows more adjustment for suspending baits off bottom. This rig is also available from Angling Designs. Check the diagram for rigging.

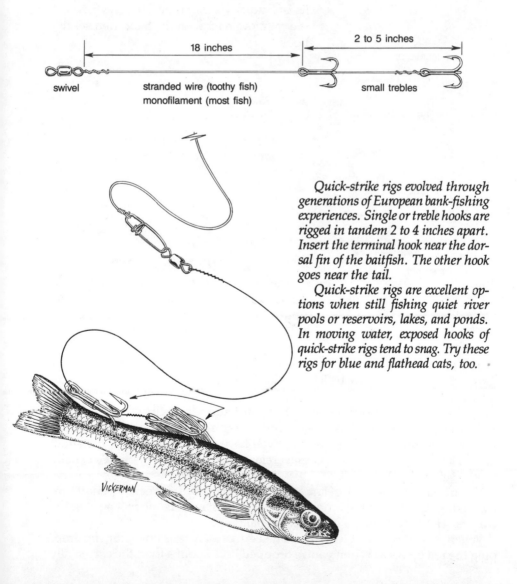

18 inches          2 to 5 inches

swivel     stranded wire (toothy fish)     small trebles
           monofilament (most fish)

Quick-strike rigs evolved through generations of European bank-fishing experiences. Single or treble hooks are rigged in tandem 2 to 4 inches apart. Insert the terminal hook near the dorsal fin of the baitfish. The other hook goes near the tail.

Quick-strike rigs are excellent options when still fishing quiet river pools or reservoirs, lakes, and ponds. In moving water, exposed hooks of quick-strike rigs tend to snag. Try these rigs for blue and flathead cats, too.

VICKERMAN

# JIG RIGS

It's not double talk to say rigs aren't jigs, but jigs are rigs. We've mentioned that rigs with the weight close to the hook fish more precisely, especially in current. Live- or deadbait rigged on a leadhead jig is the most precise way to present those baits. Think of the leadhead jig, not as a lure, but as a method of bait presentation.

## Leadheads For Cats

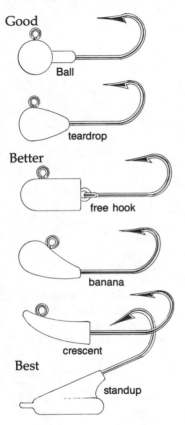

Good

Ball

teardrop

Better

free hook

banana

crescent

Best

standup

Jigs with standup heads weighing 1/4 to 1/2 ounce and sporting a 1/0 or 2/0 hook work best. Put bait on the hook and fish it like a set rig. Stay in contact with the bait; don't set your rod down; hold it, constantly monitoring the bait. When a cat grabs hold, the weight doesn't seem to bother him; the head of the jig isn't much heavier than a big crayfish. Let the cat move a bit with the bait; then set the hook.

*Leadhead jigs with worms or fish, fished on the bottom, are great for bullheads and cats.*

## SET-RIG HOOK SETS

The hook set. The moment of truth. A cat grabs your bait and moves away. Your heart pounds and your palms sweat. Most of the time, you'll catch the cats that take your set bait. The key is to eliminate rigging problems.

The problem with an egg-sinker slip rig is that you must let your line go as the cat moves away, or else he'll feel "odd" tension. If you don't let your line go, the cat has to move the sinker in order to move. If the sinker momentarily hangs up, the hook point may prick the cat and he'll drop the bait.

Sustained, moderate tension rarely bothers catfish; intermittent tension-slack tension-slack does. With a slip-set rig, you have at least one foot of sustained give to let a cat move before you must release line or set the hook. It's usually best to set the hook.

Picture the 6-inch section of line anchored with the bell sinker as a pendulum. By pulling your rod tip toward you, you can move the bait one foot against the current. Hold there until a cat takes the bait.

When the cat moves off with the bait, keep constant tension on him by dropping the rod tip back. When you've dropped back about a foot, the cat usually

## Set-Rig Hook Sets

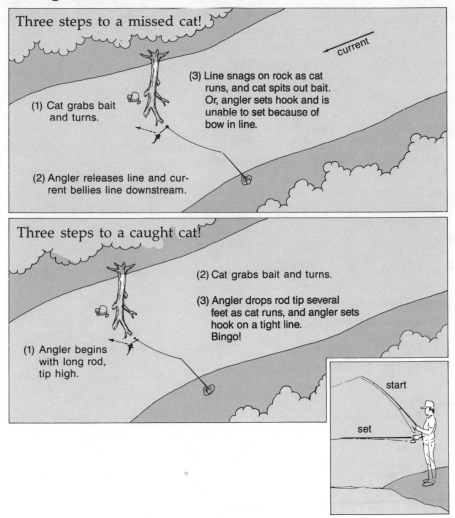

Three steps to a missed cat!

current

(3) Line snags on rock as cat runs, and cat spits out bait. Or, angler sets hook and is unable to set because of bow in line.

(1) Cat grabs bait and turns.

(2) Angler releases line and current bellies line downstream.

Three steps to a caught cat!

(2) Cat grabs bait and turns.

(3) Angler drops rod tip several feet as cat runs, and angler sets hook on a tight line. Bingo!

(1) Angler begins with long rod, tip high.

start

set

has turned. Set the hook. If you've matched your bait and hook size to the size of the catfish in the river or stream, the cat will have the bait in his mouth and you'll catch him, usually in the corner of the mouth.

Letting a cat run causes problems. Often, when a cat starts to run, the fisherman releases line. The fisherman thinks the cat's still running, but usually it's current dragging the line downriver. By the time he tries to set the hook, there's a huge bow in the line. He'll be lucky to hook the fish.

Another problem. The line may snag on something and make the cat drop the bait. Or the cat may retreat into the snag with the bait, making it impossible to haul him out.

When a cat grabs a set rig in current, give a little, then take a lot—make a good hook set. You'll miss a few, usually smaller cats, but your hooking percentage will increase.

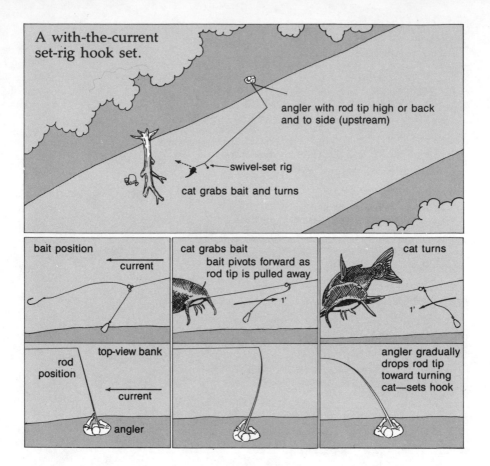

A with-the-current set-rig hook set.

angler with rod tip high or back and to side (upstream)

swivel-set rig

cat grabs bait and turns

bait position

current

cat grabs bait
bait pivots forward as rod tip is pulled away

cat turns

rod position

top-view bank

current

angler

angler gradually drops rod tip toward turning cat—sets hook

## SLIP-FLOAT RIGS

Slip-float rigs are the most overlooked option for effectively fishing snags. A properly rigged slip float keeps a bait poking along the bottom, with current pushing it into pockets and corners where cats lie.

Can you accomplish the same thing with a bait and several shot? Yes, but it's a matter of efficiency. When you cast a shot rig into current, the current works on your line, as well as on your bait. Once the bait and shot are on the bottom, current bows your line and drags the bait toward you, as well as downriver with the current. That means snags. And rarely do you know exactly where your bait is.

Watch the float and you'll learn about current conditions around a snag, too. There's only so much you can tell by looking at the surface. The movement of a bait and float will help you pinpoint current breaks, deeper holes and other good spots.

A slip float slides up your line until it reaches the float stop. Fish it any depth you choose. When you cast, it slides down your line and stays out of the way.

The proper-size slip float depends on the total weight of your terminal rig. Say you've filleted the side off a one-pound sucker and have cut one fillet into three chunks. That portion of fillet will weigh about an ounce out of water and

## Slippin' the Float

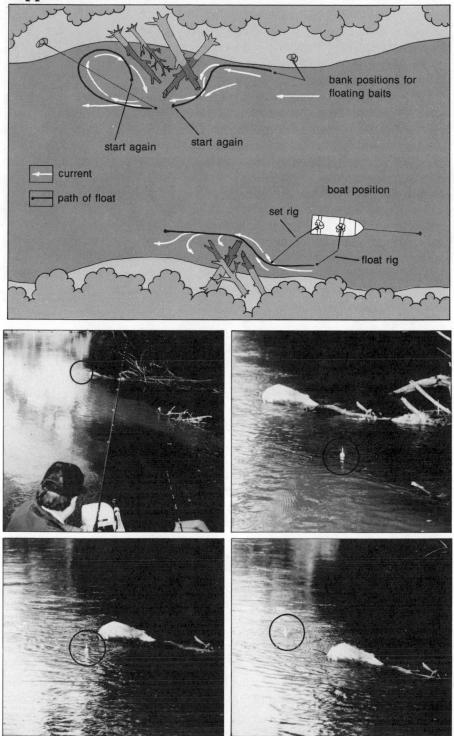

bank positions for
floating baits

start again   start again

→ current

path of float

boat position

set rig

float rig

*Drifting and wading a river on a lazy summer day.*

less in water. You'll need two or three 3/0 shot to get the bait near bottom. The combination of shot and bait requires a larger float.

You want the bait weighted so it skips along the bottom, with your float preceding your bait as they move downriver. Place your shot about eight inches apart, starting about eight inches above your bait. A float that sails downriver and doesn't jiggle means the bait isn't bumping bottom. Move the float stop farther up the line until you get a jerky, hesitating motion from the float.

With a long rod you can direct a float where you want it to drift. Say you want to fish a snag 30 feet away on the other side of the river. Cast the float rig across the river 20 feet above the snag. Don't engage your reel, but do hold the line with your index finger. Hold your rod tip high. At first the current will carry your float and line straight downriver at the same speed. But as the bait occasionally hangs on the bottom, as it should, your line will begin to bow in the current and pull the float toward you and away from its intended course. To correct this, first let out a bit more line. Second, mend your line by lifting your rod tip to lift slack line off the water, and flip it back upstream.

On the first drift past a snag, keep your float and bait moving at least a foot or two outside the snag. Active cats will charge out to get the bait.

If that doesn't work, let the float and bait drift up against the snag. Then immediately pull them back a bit and nudge them downriver so they tumble along the snag. To keep them moving, give line. When the bait reaches the end of the snag, it will twirl for a moment in the backwash below the snag and then be pulled downriver with the current. You've worked past prime catfish-holding areas.

When a cat grabs a bait, the float will stop, be pulled under slightly and begin to move. Your reaction depends on where the float moves.

If the fish moves into the snag, apply constant, but not super-heavy tension as you drop your rod tip a foot or two toward the fish. Then set the hook. If you let the cat enter the snag, you aren't likely to drag him out.

It's our experience that cats that head back into the snag usually are solitary cats. You may catch only a fish or two from such snags.

If a cat runs toward you or upstream, wait until you have an angle on the cat before you set the hook. Having the cat turned away from you increases the chance that you'll set the hook into the side of his mouth, the ideal spot to hook and hold. The upper jaw of a channel cat is tough and much harder to penetrate.

By the way, always be sure to leave your hook point exposed. Channel cats don't know what a hook point is and they're used to crunching down on hard stuff like fish heads or crawfish bodies. If you hide the hook point in a piece of cut fish, too often the point doesn't leave the cut fish to enter a cat's jaw.

*Steve Quinn with a channel cat that took a portion of cut sucker drifted below a Wazp brand ''Gazzet'' float.*

Zacker discussing his favorite rig for big cats:
"You gotta weight the bait so it struggles. It don't have to struggle all the time, but when a big cat gets close, it does. I usually used a big cork and a slip sinker set-up.

"Say it's about 4 feet deep in an eddy area near the head of a hole. 'Bout 2 feet up your line (from your hook) you put a big swivel. Tie good knots. Then add a big egg sinker, like a 2-ouncer if you're using a 1-pound bait. If the live bait's too lively, you can trim his tail (cut off a portion of the tail fin).

"Then another 4 feet up your line, add a big cork. This cork ain't to keep your bait off bottom. The cork gets blown around in the current and keeps prodding your bait; makes it move and struggle. A big cat'll crunch your bait just for the sport of it."

"And when a big cat takes?" Doug Stange asked.

"You'll know; you'll danged well know," he said as he scratched the stubble on his chin. He nodded, and a smile crept across his face. "You'll danged well know!"

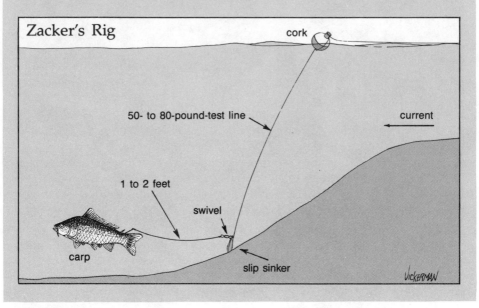

Zacker's Rig

cork

50- to 80-pound-test line

current

1 to 2 feet

swivel

carp

slip sinker

## Chapter 11

# STRATEGIES IN ACTION

### An Outing With The Authors

Time for Toad Smith and Doug Stange to take charge. Many of the fishing tactics in this book are the result of their time together fishing and refining strategies that work on rivers anywhere in North America. After 10 chapters you have the basic tools with which to forge your catfishing skills. Before you set out, however, watch how they use some of those tools on an outing that occurred just as this book was published.

You may be tempted to believe the strategies in this book are only applicable to rivers the authors actually have fished. Again, the point is that they've successfully fished dozens of rivers in many parts of North America, using these strategies. To prove the point, this outing was on a section of river the two had never seen before.

Of course, they were willing to fish this section of river because they had heard other fishermen were catching channel cats and flatheads there. By Toad and Doug's standards, that meant the probability of plenty of untouched cats, assuming that most catfishermen in the area fished as inefficiently as catfishermen in most parts of the country. If their assumption was right, their strategy of moving, moving, moving, fishing quickly for aggressive cats and using their knowledge of how cats relate to the riffle-hole-run make-up of rivers would mean lots of fish overlooked by other fishermen. They'd see lots of river, catch lots of cats, and after a day or so would also be able to judge where particularly large cats were holding.

In a phone conversation, they decided that Toad would bring fresh chicken blood and green sunfish and Doug would bring live suckers, the bigger the better. Doug would also carry some dip and paste baits in his large shoulder bag. Since the cats were prespawn, however, the two didn't expect to have to use more than cut suckers for channel cats and live suckers or green sunfish for flatheads. The chicken blood would serve as a standby bait if fishing for channel cats got tough.

A call to a baitshop in a town along the river suggested the river was just high

*That's the thing about baits for catfish. You can use crawlers to catch cats or to catch suckers to use to catch cats. And once you've caught suckers, they can be chunked for bait or used alive for big cats.*

enough so they could use Toad's 14-foot aluminum V-hull, powered with a 15-horse motor to move up and downriver. Great. They'd have to get out and pull the boat over some riffle areas, but most of the time the motor set at shallow drive would keep them moving. They'd be able to cover even more river.

D-day. The two meet at the baitshop on the river. Faded photos showed many fishermen holding small strings of channels that seemed to top out at 10 pounds, a bit small for a "large" small river such as this one. The flatheads were impressive, though—many 10s to 18s, some 20s, and a few 30s. Big fish for a small river. Perhaps there are more flatheads in this section than people think, they wonder. Perhaps competition with flatheads tends to keep the channel cats from getting larger. Still, apparently there are plenty of 4- to 8-pound channel cats.

"Where are local guys fishing? What are they fishing with? Ever hear of cat-fishermen making big catches—20, 30, 40 fish?" they ask.

"Twenty fish a day?" The baitshop owner frowns. "Fishin' ain't that good. Harry Cramer, the best catman in the area fishes every day all season and even he's never caught more 'n 10 in a crack. And that was at night."

"So where do folks fish, and what are they fishin' with?" Toad asks again.

"The hole below the dam's popular; so's Timmin's hole, Carter's hole, and the piece of river on Sam Johnson's land—he'll let you fish," the shop owner said as he pointed to spots on the map. "Don Lacey, 'bout 5 miles south's got a big cutbank hole on his land, too—drive right down to it. Rest of the river's kind of hard to get at. Put the boat in from the sand bar at Lacey's place, I s'pose.

*"Folks 'round here use just about anything, guess you could say."*

"But you'll have yourself a time with the water so low," he said as he eyed Toad's 250-pound carcass and pondered the boat carrying them and their gear through inches of water.

"Folks 'round here use just about anything, guess you could say," he continued. "Chicken liver's popular; so's shrimp. Some folks use crawlers; chubs is popular, too—live ones 'specially for flatheads."

"And those?" Doug asked, referring to his stock of pastes behind the counter.

"Sure sell," he said. "'Specially this blood flavor, ever since that fancy-pants magazine—*In-Fisherman*—ran that article 'bout chicken blood two years ago. Folks must be catchin' fish. Even get people come in and ask for these little gumball baits called Fiddler Candy," he shook his head.

Toad and Doug studied the map of the river.

"The river below Lacey's place?" Toad asked. "What's it like?"

"Well, can't say as I've ever been through there," he answered. "I've fished darn near everything below the Riverview Bridge, five miles south o' Lacey's, where the road runs 'longside the river, plus the other spots I mentioned. No need to fish below Lacey's, or even above Lacey's 'cause there's plenty of easier spots to get at. Plenty of cats. Just yesterday I got 3 myself, no problem."

"So you never fished this big bend area on Lacey's?" Doug asked, noting that the river ran straight for almost 10 miles south from the town dam and then suddenly made a quarter-mile veer and then another and another.

"Just told you," the shop owner said, beginning to get irritated. "Plenty folks fish Lacey's high bank hole, right there (he pointed at the spot) smack in the middle of that big bend area as you call it. But it's a mile walk into those other spots, and I s'pose a mile run in a boat above Lacey's or a mile float below Lacey's to get to those other spots. No need goin' to so much trouble."

"Betcha a dozen chubs Lacey's high-bank hole's where the biggest flatheads and channel cats come from every year, not counting the tailwaters below the town dam," Doug said. "Bet most of the fish get caught in May and June, and then fishing turns tough." Ten miles of straight river, then lots of curves—first break in continuous river, Doug was thinking. So much straight river, then suddenly a curvy section—a section that apparently no one bothered to fish except for one hole. Had to be plenty of other holes there, probably some of the biggest holes in that section of river. Had to be a ton of timber piled in the holes in the bends, too. Catfish! Both channel cats and flatheads!

"Well yes, come to think of it, that's just about where a lot of big fish come from every year. Course some folks won't say 'xactly where they're gettin' 'em. And yes, 'bout July the fishin' turns tough. Now how'd you know that?"

To Lacey's they would go. Permission granted, they drove to the sandbar and dropped Toad's boat in the water. Most of the suckers, the blood, a few sodas and sandwiches were on ice in a cooler. The rest of the livebait was in a keep sack in the river in case they decided to fish for flatheads at night. Each fisherman took two rods, one a flippin' stick rigged with a Garcia 6500C casting reel, the other an 11- or 12-foot Euro-style casting or spinning rod rigged with a Garcia 6500C (casting) or a Daiwa Long Cast 2600 (spinning). Even though they'd be fishing during the day, hardly prime time for big flatheads, the possibility of one biting called for 20-pound-test line on each combo.

Upriver or down? No difference except . . . neither fisherman had fished for catfish in several weeks. Fishing downriver would mean fishing as they went: Drift a bait through a good-looking riffle; fish cover near the head of the hole; fish the core of the hole, especially cover in the core of the hole; maybe fish the rear of the hole and move to the next riffle-hole area; and on and on. That meant

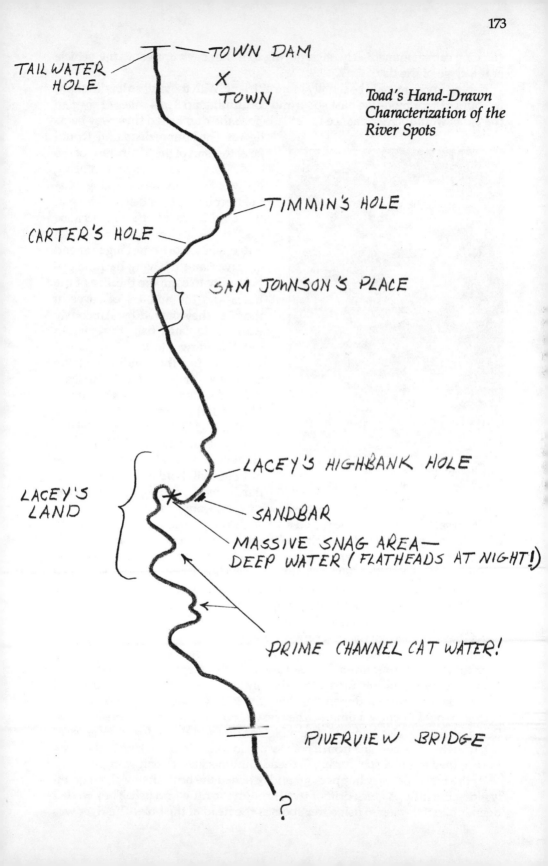

Toad's Hand-Drawn
Characterization of the
River Spots

catching catfish immediately, then having to motor back upriver to the vehicle at the close of the day.

Fishing upriver would be slightly more efficient. With the river so low, though, it would call for motoring past spots and continuing up 3 or 4 miles of river so the spots would have a chance to settle before the duo fished their way back down. The hour of dead time would be at the start of the trip instead of the end. The advantage in motoring upriver, however, was in seeing what the river had to offer before fishing it. It would be more efficient because they'd be better able to make judgements about how long to spend on given areas, having had the opportunity to compare the size of the holes and the amount of cover in them as they passed by. Anxiously wanting to catch fish, they would head downriver today.

*Cut bait and the inevitable flies.*

Evaluating the condition of the river—low and filled with snags— Toad decided not to use a float. "Fished the same situation two weeks ago," Toad told Doug. "Fish'll mostly be round snags. Riffles are too shallow. The head of holes and core of holes will hold a fish or two, but hardly worth fishing. Unless a hole has a good snag in it, chances are we won't even want to stop and fish it."

"We'll see," Doug said as he rigged a 3½-inch Wazp Cigar slip float on the line of his Euro-style rod. He'd go with a 3/0 hook and weight the rig with three 3/0 Water Gremlin shot or 4 Wazp SSG shot. His flipping stick would be rigged same as Toad's two rigs, with a 3/0 hook and one 3/0 shot. Fishing downriver, there would be no need for slip-set rigging with the water so low. Most of the time, they'd be anchoring above holes or snags and laying the lightly weighted bait on the bottom close to cover or in the core of a hole.

As they approached the first riffle-hole area, Doug had already filleted one side from a 12-inch sucker and cut it into three sections. Then, leaving the backbone intact, he removed the head and tail, discarded them, and cut the remaining bony chunk into three more sections. Six- to eight-inch suckers would be chunked or filleted, depending how thick they were. Only two or three suckers would be cut at a time, so the rest would remain firm and fresh on ice. Remember, they also had two dozen big suckers and three dozen green sunfish (caught hook-and-line from a borrow pit) in a keep sack soaking in the river, in case they found a spot for big flatheads and decided to fish at night.

At the first riffle, they hopped out and beached the boat, then walked quietly along the riffle. A quick drift or two through the riffle—no fish. They waded deeper into the water to fish cover spots at the head of the hole. The river was too low. The cover at the head of the hole was only a foot deep, deep enough for an early morning or evening bite perhaps, but too shallow for midday. Being Doug was fishing a float, he continued drifting his bait through the hole as Toad retrieved the boat.

As Toad returned, Doug was battling a catfish. "Cracked me right in the core of the hole," he said. "Bait didn't even get near the snag at the end of the hole.

"Let me make another drift before we get in the boat and anchor above the snag," he said as he released the 3-pound channel cat. The float drifted through the core of the hole— nothing—then approached the snag. Just as the float was about to disappear below the snag, it snapped down. "Fish!"

"Better set," Toad said, but Doug already had.

"Good one; darn good fish," Doug offered, arms straining to hold the cat out of the snag. The cat sliced across the hole, then back toward the snag, then toward the head of the hole. "Two more pumps. There." The cat wallowed on the surface, dove slicing left again, and finally rolled back to the surface and to the waiting fishermen.

"Maybe 6," Toad guessed as Doug slid the cat into the water. "Get in."

As they drifted toward the snag, Doug slid the anchor down and let the current tighten the rope to hold the boat about 30 feet above the snag.

*Toad posing for a quick photo with Doug's rig and the channel cat from the hole below the first riffle they fished.*

"Quiet," Toad said instinctively as he cast his bait within a foot of the face of the snag. "That'll bring 'em out . . . 'specially if there's a bunch in there and they're competing for food and space."

Before Doug's float could get near the snag, Toad, holding his rod tip at a 45° angle above the water watching his line for a pickup, had dropped his rod tip toward a fish. . ."Just let him turn a bit," he mumbled. "There! You bet! Knew it was a good one. . .it was just thump, he's got it, and then he moved off . . . no peck pecking like some little cat."

"'Bout 6," Doug said. "Lemme get a shot or two". . . click, click, click splash. The fish was back, and Toad had already replanted a fresh bait in front of the snag. Doug's float followed the current neatly around the outside of the snag as Toad continued to hold his bait in front of the snag. As Doug reeled the float back to the front of the snag, Toad was setting into another fish. "They're in there, but your float's moving the bait too quickly," Toad offered as he boated the fish. "Fish aren't crackin' that good right now. Gotta call 'em out and give it to 'em

*Anchored just above a snag. Fish on!*          *'Bout six!*

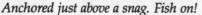

where they can find it when they get there."

Indeed. After fishing several series of riffle-hole-runs, the pattern for the afternoon was obvious: A few good cats (3 to 8 pounds) were holding in the core of holes, but mostly they were stacked in snags associated with the cores of holes. What about good-looking snags on flatter river areas?

"Peck, peck, pecker city," Toad would say as he swung another 1-pound cat into the boat. "Nibble, nibble and finally you get one of these. That's so typical of snags on river flats. Big cats'll hold with the little guys during spring when the fish are moving. But I've never seen little cats hold with big cats once a small river's down and fish have a chance to settle into a pecking order. These bigger cats are right where they should be, in cover in deeper water. Little cats are pushed into marginal spots. Start catching little cats and you know something's wrong. That's where most folks go wrong; they continue fishing every snag they see, instead of recognizing the real pattern and fishing selectively."

The boys could take a decent cat or two from snags on river runs (flats), but why bother when they could pull up to every snag near the core of a hole, anchor and use simple set rigs at the head of a snag and often take a half dozen good cats before moving on. No use wasting time in small-cat spots. No use covering water with the float when the cats where in precise spots. Soon the guys were running more, fishing less, but catching more.

After seeing more river, they made an observation. "I know where the big flatheads are," Doug told Toad as they motored back to the sand bar at Lacey's about 6 o'clock that evening.

"I know, too," Toad grinned. "You wanna?"

"You bet!"

*Fifty channel cats and an unexpected flathead cat later. . .*

The "you wanna—you bet" meant that even after catching and releasing 50 or 60 channel cats in 6 hours of fishing, the guys would take time to fry up a couple small cats for supper, then get rigged for flatheads after dark. They'd need flashlights, bug spray, a cushion or two, and coffee. Flatheads would also demand heavier tackle and livebait.

"Let's see if we agree on which hole," Doug said.

"Easy choice," Toad said. "There's 10 pretty straight miles of river before Lacey's place, then a curvy section for a mile or two. It's the first hole in the first bend below us, not more than half a mile away."

"Right," Doug smiled. "Half the timber blown in from the 10-mile section above us must be lodged in that hole in that bend—perfect cover for big flatheads—deep, too. It's the biggest and baddest hole I've seen in the 5 miles we covered today."

"You got it!"

As the guys headed downriver, they checked their gear. "Think 36-pound dacron and 30-pound mono will do it?" Toad wondered aloud. Both Toad and Doug were using muskie rods with Garcia 6500C and 7000 reels.

"It'll handle any channel cat in the river," Doug responded. "But can't be sure

## Simple Set Rig

bell sinker

shot

5/0 hook

2 inches

hook placement in sunfish, sucker, or chub

*Lively, wild bait. One key to flatheads.*

about flatheads. Twenties won't be a problem. Can't say about 30s; they're tough suckers. Just gonna have to put the muscle to 'em, keep 'em out of snags and hold on."

Since current was minimal, both men chose simple set rigs—a 1-ounce slip sinker set just a couple inches above a 5/0 hook with a shot. They'd keep snell length short near snags, so the baitfish couldn't swim into cover. Nighttime snags with 36-pound dacron can be a real nuisance. And they didn't want the baits to hide in tree branches.

"Once you know where to fish, rigging's easy, and lively bait's the key to flatheads," Doug said. "It's the reason these green sunfish are such a fine bait. Chubs are ten times better than pond-raised suckers, but wild suckers are as good as chubs. Bullheads or madtoms are tough to beat, too. Just hook 'em through the back, an inch or two in front of the tail.

"Before you decide where to cast the bait, make several casts with just a sinker," Doug added. "Reel in the sinker slowly so it bumps bottom. It's like a long-range sonar unit. You'll learn where not to cast (snags) and where to cast (clean spots near snags)."

They cast their baits out and set the rods in holders. Their reels were on freespool with the clickers on. Tension from the clicker was enough to hold struggling bait in place. When a cat took a bait, they'd know. As the sun set, they settled

*Trap set!*

alongside a small driftwood fire. A little light wouldn't spook the cats in this murky water. No bright lanterns, though. Keep it quiet and keep it dark. Big flatheads have been around awhile—'bout as wary as they come.

Zzzzzzt. Zzzzzzt. . . . . zzzzzt, zzzzzzt!

"Small channel cat or a mighty wary flathead," Doug said as he approached his rod. He left the rod in the rod holder as he watched the line with his flashlight. Suddenly . . . zzzzzzzzz, zzzzzzzzzz, zzzzzzz, zzzzzzzzzzzzzzzzzzzz . . . the cat moved off steadily. "Flathead," Toad mumbled excitedly as Doug gingerly picked the rod from the rod holder. "Don't let him run to a snag," Toad reminded.

The fish still moving, Doug set. "Flathead! You bet. Big one!" Doug's arched rod tip whomped-whomped-whomped up and down, signaling the powerful side-to-side head rips of a big flathead. Channel cats shake and power run. Flatheads power as they make those distinctive head rips. In shallow water they may also roll.

Finally, Doug led the fish onto a shallow flat, and Toad waded in to guide it toward shore. Get them swimming the right direction and they'll beach themselves.

"Twenty-five, maybe 27," Toad offered as Doug momentarily held the fish in Toad's flashlight beam. "Thirty-six, maybe 37 or 38 inches long. A good fish, but a bit skinny. The size of the fish in this small river surprises me. Must be a real fertile system."

By the time the sun rose, the two had caught 13 flatheads, the biggest, Doug's 27, along with half a dozen channel cats to 10 pounds. "First time anyone's touched that hole at night in 50 years," Toad said. "Think the fish in that hole are moving around, moving up and downriver to surrounding holes?"

"Naw," Doug answered. "When the water's low, those cats are stuck; they won't move until the water comes way up. Two hundred pounds of catfish from one small area might make you think there's an unlimited number of cats in the river, but that's not so. Most of the good fish from a long section of river are in that hole. If we'd kept everything we caught tonight, we would have put the hurt on the fish in that hole. They're real vulnerable in a situation like that.

"Mighty fine channel cats we caught today, too," he continued. "The reason we caught so many fish is because we're fishing fish no one else ever takes a crack at. But if everyone fished this way, especially if they were meat fishing, we wouldn't be able to catch so many fish, even using our system, because most of the fish would be gone.

"Think there's a 30 in that hole, Toad?" Doug asked.

"Aw yeah, gotta be; probably a 35. Like Zacker always says, once you get it figured out, big cats are easy, simplest thing in the world. Gonna take another night of fishing, though, and right now I'm ready for breakfast and a snooze. Bring Tabasco for the scrambled eggs?"

*A good day done!*

Chapter 12

# CARING FOR, CLEANING, AND COOKBOOKING THE CATCH

## Nutritious, Delicious, Renewable Catfish

Catfish are nutritious and delicious, and catfish populations are renewable if harvested wisely. To most fishermen, conservation implies protecting habitat and releasing fish. Agreed, those topics are important; we address them in Chapter 13. But wise use of fish that are kept, so they aren't wasted is also a conservation measure.

A delicious meal is the perfect end to most catfishing trips. Catfish are wonderful baked, broiled, steamed, poached, casseroled, stewed, or fried. How good they taste, however, is dependent on how well you care for catfish from the time you catch them until the time you eat them.

Fish flesh is fragile. It begins to deteriorate before the fish dies if fish are

## Nutrient Value

| Fish | Calories | Percent Protein | Percent Fat | Sodium (mg) |
|---|---|---|---|---|
| Burbot (eelpout, lawyer) | 80 | 17 | 0.9 | — |
| Carp | 125 | 17 | 5.9 | 44 |
| Catfish | 119 | 18 | 5.2 | 60 |
| Clams | 63 | 11 | 1.7 | 190 |
| Cod | 74 | 17 | 0.5 | 67 |
| Flounder | 88 | 18 | 1.4 | 54 |
| Freshwater Drum (Sheepshead) | — | 17 | 5.5 | — |
| Haddock | 77 | 18 | 0.5 | 98 |
| Halibut (Pacific) | 119 | 19 | 4.3 | 71 |
| Herring (Lake) | — | 19 | 3.3 | — |
| Lake Trout | 169 | 17 | 11.1 | 43 |
| Northern Pike | — | 19 | 1.2 | 52 |
| Oysters (Eastern) | 68 | 8 | 1.8 | 160 |
| Perch (Yellow) | 85 | 19 | 1.1 | 63 |
| Rainbow Trout | 154 | 21 | 6.8 | 43 |
| Salmon (Chinook) | 182 | 18 | 11.6 | 42 |
| Salmon (Coho) | 148 | 21 | 6.6 | — |
| Shrimp | 86 | 20 | 0.4 | 155 |
| Smelt | 86 | 17 | 3.9 | 80 |
| Suckers | — | 21 | 1.8 | 53 |
| Tuna | 122 | 24 | 2.2 | 76 |
| Walleye | 89 | 19 | 1.5 | — |
| Whitefish | 121 | 19 | 5.2 | 52 |
| **Other Common Foods** | | | | |
| Beef Steak | 266 | 17 | 26 | 61 |
| Beef Liver | 141 | 22 | 5 | 33 |
| Pork | 298 | 17 | 24.7 | 60 |
| Chicken | 127 | 23 | 7.0 | — |
| Lamb | 186 | 15 | 13.5 | 52 |
| Cheddar Cheese (1 oz.) | 113 | 7.1 | 9.1 | 198 |
| Egg (1) | 80 | 6 | 6 | 70 |
| Whole Milk (1 cup) | 159 | 8 | 8.5 | 122 |

*Fish are nutritious—high in vitamins, minerals and protein, and low in calories and fats. Research shows that increasing amounts of fish in the diet reduces cholesterol levels and the risk of heart attack.*

*These calculations for 3½-ounce food portions were made by Jeff Gunderson of the Minnesota Sea Grant Institute.*

—Information not available
Source: Adapted from information supplied by the National Marine Fisheries Service, and "Nutritive Value of American Foods in Common Units," U.S. Department of Agriculture. Agriculture Handbook No. 456, 1975, by Jeff Gunderson for *Fixin' Fish*, the University of Minnesota Press.

roughly handled and stressed until they die. Catfish seem hearty fish because they live so long on a stringer or in a livewell. But catfish are easily bruised, and bruised flesh doesn't taste good. Catfish should be labeled, "Fragile! Handle with care!"

Keeping fish healthy as long as possible before cleaning them is one step to better-tasting catfish. Fish flesh deteriorates even more quickly after a fish dies, especially if it's not handled correctly after it dies.

Bacterial growth is a principal enemy of fresh fish. After fish are killed, ensure fine table quality by retarding bacterial growth. Once fish die, gut them, making sure not to get sour bacteria-filled stomach and intestinal juices on the flesh. Gutting fish also bleeds them. Blood left in flesh speeds deterioration. Wash fish in cold water to remove bacteria. Then place them on ice to retard bacterial growth.

## ICING FISH

Crushed ice is best for chilling fish. It packs closer and cools quicker than large blocks of ice or frozen bottles of water. After gutting catfish, rinse them in cold water and then surround them with crushed ice. Don't let a fish soak in water, even cold water. Crushed ice keeps fish for up to three days, although table quality of the flesh deteriorates each day.

If you have to keep fish on ice longer, use super-chilling.

## SUPER-CHILLING FISH

Super-chilled fish can be kept on ice for up to five and perhaps seven days:

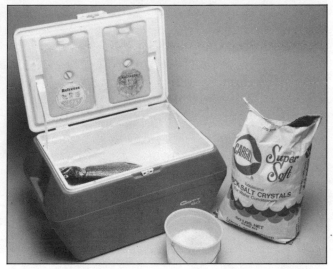

1. Line the bottom of an insulated cooler with several inches of crushed ice, leaving the drain open.
2. In another container, mix coarse ice cream salt and crushed ice, ratio of 1:20. For average-size coolers, that's a pound of salt to 20 pounds of ice. Wrap fillets or pan-dressed fish in plastic wrap. Layer the fish in the ice chest, making sure there's plenty of salted ice around each fish.

Super-chilling lowers the temperature to about 30ºF. Replenish salted ice as it melts.

## AT THE CLEANING TABLE

At the cleaning table, or wherever you clean your catch, sanitation is critical. Also be sure to have ice available to keep fish that have already been chilled and to cool fish that are still alive when they reach the cleaning table. Say you'll be filleting your catch. At the cleaning table you should have:

1. Cleaning utensils, including fillet knives and sharpening tools.
2. A bowl of cold water (add ice cubes) to soak fillets in for a short time to remove blood and bacteria.
3. Clean paper towels for wiping slime from fish and keeping the fillet board clean. Pat fillets dry after they've soaked, if you plan to keep them, not freeze them. (A solution of one teaspoon vinegar to three quarts water helps cut fish slime.)
4. Packaging material for freezing or refrigerating fish.

Proceed:

1. If fish are alive, dispatch them with a sharp blow to the head. Bleed them.
2. Remove the fillets, being careful not to rupture the digestive tract with your knife.
3. Place fillets in cold water to help remove blood and bacteria. With lean fish such as catfish, add ½-teaspoon salt to help neutralize acids and draw out blood.

## At The Cleaning Table

## Contaminant Concentration

You influence the table quality of your catch by choosing where to fish. For example, algae blooms may affect some lakes and ponds during summer. Some algae species give off chemical compounds that make fish taste "muddy." Use an appropriate recipe to cover this flavor or fish somewhere else.

Many waters harbor contaminants that are transferred to fish. Some bodies of waters are monitored and health advisories are posted. But many waters aren't monitored. Use cleaning procedures that reduce the contaminant levels in fish. These procedures help fish keep longer and taste better.

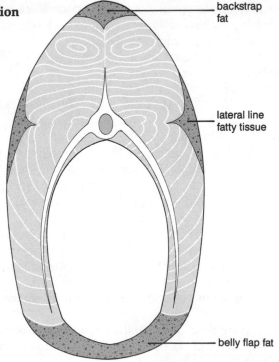

backstrap fat

lateral line fatty tissue

belly flap fat

Many contaminants are bound into the fatty belly flaps, backstrap and lateral line tissues. These areas taste strong and tend to turn rancid faster than leaner surrounding tissue. Remove these areas.

4. Discard the carcass, wipe the board and your knife clean, and start on another fish. Replace the water in the bowl when it begins to thicken with fish juices.

## CLEANING CATFISH—PAN DRESSING

1. On each side of the catfish, cut through the skin, beginning just behind the head and moving down toward the belly just behind the gill cover. About halfway down the side of the fish (just below the lower tip of the rib cage), begin a 45° cut just below the rib cage to the anus. On large catfish, also cut straight back along the center of the back, moving along the left side of the dorsal fin and then the right. The cut should extend at least an inch beyond the dorsal fin toward the tail. On very large catfish, it should extend even farther.
2. With a fish skinner, grip the cut skin just behind the head and remove the skin by pulling toward the tail.
3. Grip the dorsal fin at the base of the fin, beginning at the rear of the fin. Lift toward the head of the fish. Small fish require one lift to remove the dorsal fin and spines projecting into the flesh. Larger fish require two lifts. Very large fish may require an incision with your knife into the flesh along each side of the dorsal fin.
4. Separate the head from the "pan" portion of the fish by breaking the neck. Lift up with the head while pushing down on the pan portion of the carcass at the neck.

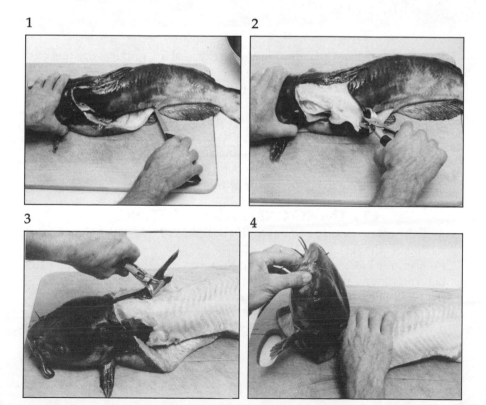

1  2

3  4

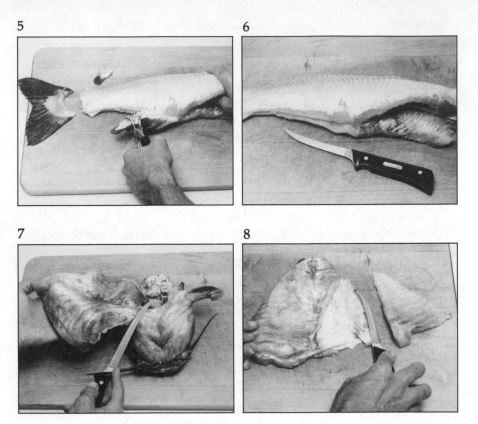

5. Remove the tail and anal fin. To remove the anal fin, grip it at the rear and lift toward the head of the fish.
6. This portion of carcass can be fried (small fish) or baked (large fish). Deep frying is the classic preparation for small fish—a la catfish and hushpuppies.
7. The carcass can be finished by removing the belly flesh.
8. Remove a triangular fillet from each side of the belly. Fishermen should be warned that belly flesh is fattier than most other portions of the carcass. Fattier flesh gathers higher levels of contaminants. Fatty fish portions also deteriorate quickly in a refrigerator or freezer.

## CLEANING CATFISH—FILLETING

1. Roll the cat on its side and cut to the backbone. Make an angle cut from just below the rib cage to the anus.
2. Reinsert the knife into the initial incision, turn the blade toward the fish's tail, and remove the fillet by cutting to the fish's tail as close as possible to the backbone. Cut through the rib cage as you proceed.
3. Cut through the flesh portion of the fillet down to the skin but not through it. Turn the knife toward the head of the fillet and remove flesh from skin by cutting progressively forward.
4. Remove the rib cage and the set of epipleural bones set at a right angle to the rib cage.
5. Remove belly meat if you wish.

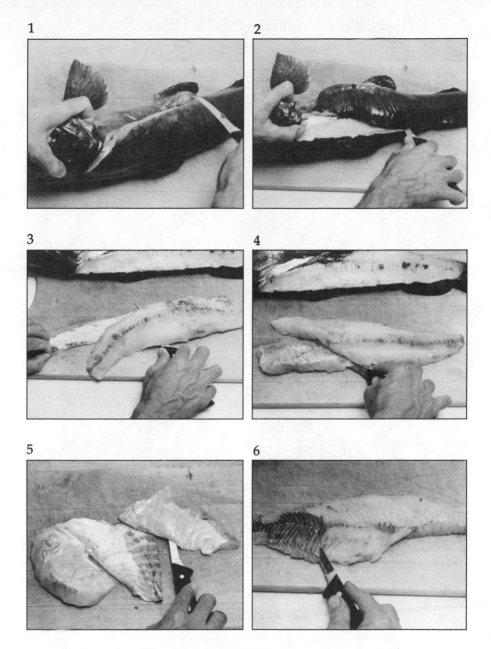

**1**

**2**

**3**

**4**

**5**

**6**

6. Remove any red lateral-line tissue (especially prevalent on flathead catfish).
7. Fillets can be fried, broiled, poached, baked, steamed, or used in casseroles, stews, or soups. Fillets cook faster and more thoroughly than pan cuts. The result is tastier flesh, in most expert's opinion.

# CLEANING CATFISH—OTHER METHODS

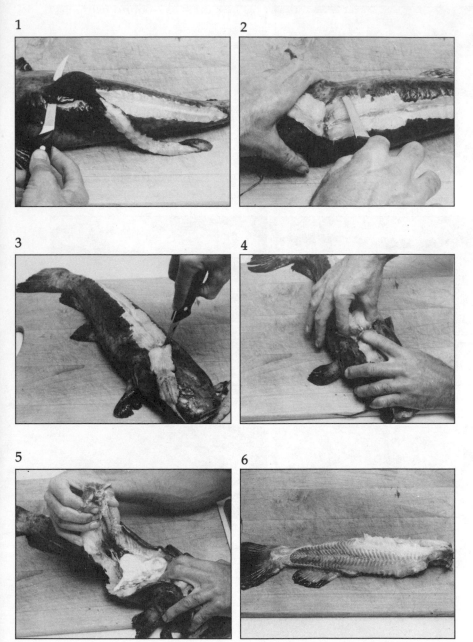

1. Beginning just behind the adipose fin, cut forward just below the skin, leaving a track about a half-inch wide. Cut below the dorsal fin to just behind the head where the back meets the head.
2. Make a slight incision on each side of the fish (about 1/2-inch deep and 1/2-inch long) between the skin and the flesh, just back of the end point of the first cut.

3. Cut through the backbone of the fish, which becomes progressively more difficult on larger fish. This method works best on 1- to 2-pound fish.
4. Slide your thumb and index finger of one hand into the incision per Step 2.
5. Grip the head with the other hand. Pull up and back with the "pan" portion of the carcass, removing it from the skin and the belly meat.
6. The finished product can be fried or baked. This is but one of many "other" methods of dressing catfish.

## PACKAGING FOR THE REFRIGERATOR

The best way to keep catfish in a refrigerator is on crushed ice. Fill a bowl with crushed ice and surround the fish with ice. Cover the bowl with cling wrap (Saran-type wrap). Drain the water occasionally so the fish doesn't sit in water. Keep your catfish *very cold* and *nearly dry*.

Most refrigerators are kept near 40°F. If you keep your fish on ice in a refrigerator, you can hold the flesh at about 34°F, allowing several additional days of storage—depending how fresh the fish were when refrigerated.

Another method works when you don't have ice, although not as well as the crushed-ice method. Pat clean fillets dry with paper towels. Moisten a clean dish towel. Line the bottom of a bowl with the towel and spread the fillets on top. Cover the bowl with cling wrap. This keeps the fillets cold and moist, not sloppy wet.

Do not keep fish in a plastic bag, especially soaking in water containing juices from the fish.

## FREEZING CATFISH

Properly frozen catfish keeps well and holds its flavor for months, although fish inevitably deteriorate the longer they're frozen. Too many fishermen use the wrong type of packaging, keep fish in the freezer too long, and store them at the wrong temperature.

Fish loses table quality in the freezer through *dehydration* and *oxidation*. "Freezer burn" (whitish, leather-tough flesh) represents an advanced stage of dehydration. Freezer burn is caused by using the wrong wrap or wrapping improperly. If your wrap doesn't keep moisture effectively sealed in, fish loses moisture and turns tough.

Oxidation is also caused by poor packaging. If you don't use the right wrap, or if you fail to remove air from the package before freezing, oxygen combines with polyunsaturated fats and oils in the flesh. These fats eventually turn rancid when combined with oxygen.

## PACKAGING MATERIALS

Seal your fish so moisture is held in, oxygen is held out, and no unnecessary air is left around the flesh. Some popular materials don't perform well. Polyethylene, the material used in bread wrappers, fails the test. Waxed paper and cellophane are other popular wraps that don't measure up. Each of these materials is too porous.

### Proper Packaging Materials for Freezing

*We can divide packaging materials for freezing fish into those that do and don't work. Those that do work when used correctly include polyvinylidene chloride cling wraps, aluminum foil, Tupperware-type containers, polyester freezer bags and freezer wrapping paper.*

*Polyethylene plastic bags and wax papers don't work because they are porous and don't lock water vapor in and oxygen out.*

Aluminum foil works, though you must use it carefully, for aluminum foil punctures easily. It's best used as a final wrap following cling wrap.

Polyvinylidene chloride, the material used for the cling wraps, such as Saran Wrap, is a good barrier and clings to fish to eliminate air pockets. It's probably the best initial wrap. We often wrap fish in cling wrap, making sure to remove the air from the wrap, then follow with another layer of cling wrap, and finally a layer of wax-coated freezer wrap.

Bags sold as "freezer bags" are good too, especially as outer bags. These polyester bags form barriers against the transmission of air or moisture. They're harder to conform to the shape of your fillets, so air pockets are more likely to result. To minimize that, plunge the filled bags in water to force out air. Seal the bags under water. Leaving a little water in the bag is better than leaving air.

Finally, wax-coated freezer wrap is fairly good at keeping oxygen and water vapor from passing through. This material is difficult to make airtight and waterproof, so it's often used as a final wrap after initial wrap(s) with cling wrap. Write the date frozen, fish type, size, and anything else you want on the outside of the package.

## FREEZING IN WATER

Commercial freezers often glaze fish with a coating of ice to protect flavor and table quality. Your freezer can't be set low enough. But you can seal your catfish in water.

### Freezing Catfish

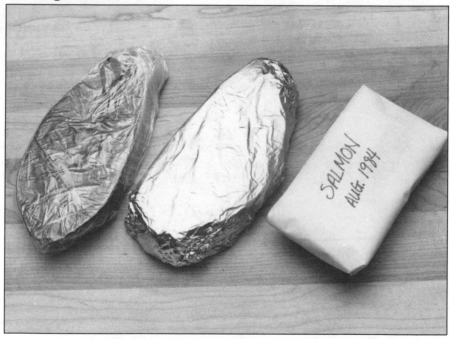

*One of the best ways to freeze fish is to tightly wrap it in cling wrap or aluminum foil. A secondary wrapping in freezer paper is advisable. Write the contents and the date frozen on the package.*

Pack the catfish tightly in plastic containers (such as Tupperware) and fill the containers almost to the brim with water. Use enough water to cover the fish, but don't leave large spaces for water, because the water (1) draws nutrients from the fish and causes the fish to freeze too slowly; and (2) crushes the fish when

*Put fish into a polyester freezer bag and submerge the bag in a sink full of water to squeeze out the air, or add a small amount of water to the bag to help force the air out. Seal the bag.*

the water freezes. Pack the container with as much fish as possible, minimizing empty spaces. Then seal remaining spaces with water. If fish portions protrude from the ice after freezing, add a little more water and refreeze.

## FREEZING TIPS

- Divide your fish into serving-size portions so you don't have thawed fish left over.
- The faster fish freezes the better. Place packages in the coldest part of your freezer. Don't overload the freezer. Keep it at 0°F, if possible.
- Thawing fish at room temperature lets some parts deteriorate while others thaw. Thaw frozen fish in the refrigerator, allowing 24 hours for a 1-pound package. If you don't have that much time, place frozen fish in cold water until it's thawed, but keep it in the vapor-proof wrapping.
- If you refreeze thawed fish, expect a big loss in table quality. Freezing breaks cell walls, the reason frozen fish is less firm than fresh fish. The flesh turns to mush when refrozen.
- Because the fat content of catfish is low, they hold their flavor well when frozen for as long as 6 months. Be sure to remove the fatty areas and package the fish properly, however!

When you keep a catfish, you owe the fish and yourself the care needed to prepare and store it properly. Respect catfish and appreciate the delicious meals they provide.

# COOKBOOKING THE CATCH

In-Fisherman soon will release the first of a series of cookbooks that takes fish conservation to it's logical conclusion: Fish that are caught and kept and cared for and cleaned properly should finally be properly cooked. While you're awaiting this comprehensive coverage that will teach you how to cook like a pro, we offer a few cookbooks to help you now.

*The Catfish Cookbook* (Barry Fast with Dorothy Woods)—Everything you want to know and more than 100 ways to prepare America's favorite fish. It's the only catfish-only cookbook we've found. A good one that's priced right.

Globe Pequot Press, 10 Cenlar Drive, Chester, CT 06412—soft cover $8.95 plus $2.00 shipping.

*Cleaning and Cooking Fish* (Sylvia Bashline)—The finest how-to fish cookbook to date. Written especially for the freshwater fisherman. Thorough, yet easy to read and understand; elegant but not stuffy. Wonderful photography. Plenty of recipes adaptable to catfish.

The Hunting and Fishing Library, Publication Arts, Inc., 5700 Green Circle Drive, Minnetonka, MN 55343—hardcover $17.95; softcover $12.95.

*Complete Fish and Game Cookbook of North America* (Francis MacIlquham)—Many good cookbooks, and this is one of them, teaches fundamental game- and fish-cooking skills. Comprehensive. Francis, bless her, is no fish snob; there are carp recipes, too, plus plenty of recipes adaptable to catfish.

Winchester Press, 220 Old New Brunswick Road, Piscataway, NJ 08854— hardcover $29.95.

*The Complete Fish Cookbook* (Dan and Inez Morris)—Another good teacher;

maybe the best. Comprehensive. More fish recipes than any book we've used. Fun reading, too.

Stoeger Sportsman's Library, 55 Ruta Court, South Hackensack, NJ 07606—softcover $9.95.

*L.L. Bean Game and Fish Cookbook* (Angus Cameron and Judith Jones)—A favorite. Comprehensive. Plenty of recipes adaptable to catfish.

L.L. Bean, Inc., Freeport, Maine 04033—hardcover $21.95.

Good cookbooks are comfortable companions you know and trust. Experiment with basic cooking methods. Expand on approaches you like. Learn to pan-fry or sauté, stir-fry, oven-fry and deep-fry, for example. Do casseroles, bisques, soups and chowders. Experiment with pickling. And why not try smoking catfish? Learn to cook over a wood fire, with a charcoal or gas grill, and with a microwave.

Learn to do basic sauces, a simple task that highlights many main-course dishes. Concentrate on main-course catfish dishes if you're a beginner. Learn dishes that complement main-course dishes, too. Hushpuppies traditionally complement fried catfish, but continue to experiment and expand your horizons.

Once you're comfortable with foundation skills, take control. Have fun. Enjoy yourself. Catfish are as nutritious and delicious as they are fun to catch, clean and cook. And they deserve your best catching, cleaning, and cooking.

All I want is your personal guarantee that the catfish was not caught just downstream from Cleveland.

## Chapter 13

# CATFISH CONSERVATION

## Sustaining Fine Fishing For The Future

You're in catfish country, just leaving the river or sitting in a restaurant or buying bait. The discussion will turn to how many, how big and where and when. Times were when we told people how many and how big. But you can only be thought a liar so often before catching on.

Truth can be painful. Too often the listeners have been fishing a stretch of river for 30 years, never catching more than a couple decent cats on an outing and never catching anything above 8 pounds. Now this ragtag bunch of semi-intelligent-looking yahoos (us) comes along and *says* they caught 50 catfish to 12 pounds from that river stretch that morning, their first morning ever on the river. Sure.

But it's true. Fine populations of catfish remain around the country, often in heavily fished territory, because most catfishermen fish so ineffectively. We often make tremendous catches because many untouched fish remain and because we fish efficiently.

*The world's a little better place when people are catching fish and having fun. But how many fish must we catch and keep to have fun. This is an earlyday catch from the Selkirk, Manitoba portion of the Red River, when regulations still allowed the harvest of many big fish. This 100-pound string of 5 fish, wasn't even an average big catch.*

The catfishing world today is much like the bass world or walleye world years ago when Al and Ron Lindner did their "magic act." They knew that without the aid of depthfinders and other equipment and particularly advanced fishing information, local anglers fishing the same old spots with the same old tackle in the same old way were overlooking tremendous groups of fish. Rockpiles, points, and weededges in almost every local lake held lots of fish because they weren't being fished effectively.

The boys would come to town, outfish local experts 10 to 1 and attribute their success to the lures they were hocking. The lures were but a tiny part of the story. Their fishing system was the key. Their system, of course, was to become the basis for today's "In-Fisherman system," a system that has for years taught millions of North Americans how to catch bass, walleyes, and other fish. We've applied the system to the catfishing world.

Life is some deal, though. If we do this book right so everyone understands, there will be a problem. If everyone who reads this book learns to do everything right, if everyone fishes in the right spot, with the right bait, at the right time. If everyone fishes where everyone else fishes, how everyone else fishes, when everyone else fishes, there won't be any catfish there.

Why teach others to catch more catfish? Because advances in catfishing will happen without us. It will take longer to happen without a book like this, but change is inevitable. In the meantime, too many people aren't catching fish and having fun. The world's a little better place when people are catching fish. We mean to help. Besides, we find that by telling folks the truth about fishing and helping them catch more fish, they more quickly discover the importance of conserving fish populations.

## Down Fishing

We use the term "down fishing" or "fished down," to refer to fish populations adversely affected by fishing pressure. Entire populations can be fished down (almost the entire catfish population removed from a farm pond or a hole on a river during a a low-water period) or portions of populations (most of the big fish removed). Fishing down doesn't mean fished out, but refers to such a reduction in fish numbers that the quality of fishing suffers. While man has always had the ability to fish populations down with commercial gear, only during the past two decades of increasing sophistication in tackle and technique have anglers been able to systematically adversely affect the quality of fishing by removing too many fish.

The point again is that catfish today are in much the same position as the largemouth bass 15 years ago. In the early 1970s, a handful of anglers could catch bass efficiently. Most bass anglers used hit-and-miss tactics, just as most of today's cat anglers do. Many anglers and biologists believed it's impossible to hurt a fish population with hook and line.

They were wrong. Sophisticated fishing pressure can hurt fish populations if that pressure isn't tempered with conservation. Big fish are particularly

*Snag fishermen (1961) with a catch of flatheads from an unchannelized portion of the Missouri River. Times were when such catches probably had little impact on fishing. With the rising popularity of catfishing, and as catfishermen become more skillful and efficient, voluntary and mandatory catch limits will become even more necessary.*

vulnerable to fishing pressure because there usually aren't many of them. Once they're removed, it may take decades to replace them. Fishing a fish population without big fish is like seeing a Star Trek movie without Captain Kirk or Spock. The supporting cast is fine, but there's something missing—part of the excitement.

Again, most catfishermen fish so ineffectively that they don't think catfish populations can be fished down. We'd also suggest, however, that some fishery scientists may believe the same thing. Yet, we see the potential for down fishing populations all the time.

Chapter 11 highlights a common experience for us. In that chapter, Toad Smith and Doug Stange caught 50 or 60 mature (2- to 8-pound) channel cats in a 6-hour afternoon outing. Their success was due to their efficient fishing system. They recognize and understand river structural elements and how catfish relate to them. With the water down, they found mature catfish confined to cover in the deepest holes. Having refined the pattern, they made the most of it by moving quickly from hole to hole, catching fish until the fishing slowed, and then moving on. All but two of the fish they caught were immediately released.

Chapter 11 didn't mention that to prove a point they fished the same river stretch the next day. Conditions were the same, except they guessed they'd sore-mouthed a good portion of the cats in that stretch. If their guess was right, even though conditions were the same, fishing would drastically decline.

They caught only a dozen fish in 5 hours of fishing the same spots. We see that all the time. In some conditions, particularly when water levels are down and active prespawn fish are confined to easily defined areas, it's possible to catch a huge portion of the adult population of catfish in a river. If they had kept every fish they caught, fishing quality would have been affected.

The day is coming soon when many more catfishermen will have the ability to consistently make outstanding catches. The question is whether managers and catfishermen will apply the lessons learned with other fish before similar damage is done to catfish populations.

We need to particularly protect large catfish. Big cats are long lived—20, 30, 40 years. They're rare and wonderful animals, predators that have beaten tremendous odds to survive long enough to become so large. Countless thousands of channel cats hatch to produce just one of those trophy cats that catfish anglers dream about. Reduced to fillets, they're worth perhaps $2 a pound. In the water, they're worth millions as they continue to fuel the imaginations of countless fishermen.

We were lucky to have fished the now-famous Selkirk, Manitoba portion of the Red River for about 5 years before many fishermen knew about it. For those of you not familiar with the fishery, we have called it the most unique fishery we have ever seen—a tremendous population of old and huge channel catfish gathered in a short section of river below the Selkirk dam, the last dam on the Red River before it enters Lake Winnipeg. Even today, it's easier to catch an 18-pound channel cat there than it is a 10-pounder. Twenty- to 25-pounders are almost a daily occurrence, instead of a lifetime quest.

Imagine your wildest fishing dream: wall-to-wall 12-pound walleyes, 25-pound pike, 2-pound crappies, 6-pound smallmouths, 10-pound

*The Selkirk, Manitoba portion of the Red River where 20s are easier to come by than 10s.*

largemouths. That was Selkirk for channel cats in 1983. The channel catfish limit was 8 per person, and with three people in the boat, it was literally possible to sink a small boat with your catch. Catfish were protected only by their lowly status in the eyes of Manitobans, spoiled by easy access to tremendous fishing for the more highly acclaimed walleye, and by ineffectiveness of seasoned catfishermen, usually from the U.S., who came to fish for catfish. It took stringers made from 3/8-inch chain to hold a limit of cats.

The Selkirk fishery remains a unique fishery because fishery managers acted in time. They reduced the bag limit and initiated a size limit that allows one trophy catfish over 30 inches per year. Even that, however, may not be enough to protect this national treasure, still the most unique catfishery we've seen. Certainly, however, without limits, which became necessary with TV publicity and the resulting fishing pressure the fishery received beginning about 1985, the fishery would not have remained healthy.

## Selective Harvest

Catch-and-release fishing is and will remain a vital factor affecting the quality of fishing in many and eventually most environments. We have seen ill effects of overharvest as well as positive effects of release fishing. Release fishing can be a unique act of conservation that helps maintain good-quality fishing for some fish species in some environments.

But like you, we have roots. We owe our fishing lives to grandparents, parents, other family members and friends. The people who started us fishing usually fished simply. They also didn't fish as often as we do now, and eating the fish

# In-Fisherman®

they caught was almost always an important and natural conclusion to an outing.

Harvest, whether resulting from hunting, fishing, or trapping; from berry, asparagus, or mushroom picking; or from tapping maple trees; is a North American tradition. It's a sensible tradition that provides food and recreation from renewable resources. As important as it is to release some fish, we believe it is equally important to maintain a tradition of harvesting some fish, for they are nutritious, delicious and, if harvested wisely, renewable. We believe the In-Fisherman policy of "selective harvest" is a sensible approach.

Selective harvest isn't total catch and release, but neither is it total harvest. We base our approach on relative numbers and size of fish. Top predators like pike, muskies, walleyes, bass, and catfish usually are the largest, yet least numerous species. Panfish like bluegills, perch, bullheads, and crappies are smaller and more numerous than top predators.

Generally speaking then, larger predators (catfish) are more vulnerable and therefore the best candidates for release. As far-fetched as it seems today, perhaps the day will come when catfishermen fishing a body of water with catfish and bluegills and bullheads will release most of the catfish to be caught again, and spend an hour catching bluegills and bullheads if they want fish to eat.

And if you want to eat catfish? Smaller fish of a species are almost always more numerous than larger fish. As we have said, the odds of an individual catfish getting large are slight. Release large fish (capture the moment with a photo) to sustain good fishing; keep the more numerous and more easily replaced small catfish.

By keeping smaller fish you may be doing yourself a favor on another count.

Unfortunately, too many rivers remain a dumping ground for wastes that may contaminate fish. The longer a predator lives, the more small fish it ingests, and the more contaminants it accumulates in its body. Since catfish are long lived, big fish are the least safe to eat. Some states caution against eating big catfish. Others would if they had the time and money required to do appropriate testing. Chapter 12 discusses reducing contaminants in fish you keep by following proper cleaning and cooking procedures. The first step in contaminant reduction, however, is to keep only smaller fish for the table.

## Releasing Catfish

Catfish are deceptively hardy. They can live for hours in a wet burlap sack during cool weather, but you can't abuse a catfish and expect it to survive after you release it.

As with all fish you intend to release, fight the fish with firm pressure to tire it as quickly as practical. When the cat can be handled, grab small fish firmly behind the head. Once large fish are tired, they can be cradled in your hands or held firmly by their lower jaw while they're in the water. A cotton glove reduces wear and tear on your thumb as well as the catfish.

Release catfish as quickly as possible. If you wish to keep a fish momentarily for a photo, hold the fish in a soft-cotton small-mesh keep net. Wazp Brand Products sells such nets. Nets and weigh

*Many nets are hard on the sensitive skin of catfish.*

*Grip small cats firmly behind the gills.*

*Cradle big cats.*

sacks are pictured in Chapter 8.

A catfish's smooth skin is particularly injury prone. Don't net fish with nylon nets with knots at the joints of the mesh. Scrapes and scratches cause infections that may kill catfish after you release them. Use small-mesh nets made from soft cotton. Once again, Europeans, particularly the English and Dutch, who have seriously practiced catch and release for decades, are ahead of us. You could be stoned for carrying a cheap nylon landing net in those countries. Wazp Brand Products also carries a European landing net. We also use the fish cradles made by That Sports Company (Box 756, Walker, MN 56484). They make handling big fish easy.

### Habitat

Fishing pressure may become a problem for the future of catfishing. Destruction of habitat already is. Habitat, defined as the special place where an organism (living thing) lives, remains the basic key to an abundance of any kind of wildlife, including channel catfish.

Throughout North America, marshes continue to be drained, rivers and streams channelized, sewage improperly treated and potent chemicals dumped. Catfish don't live in marshes, but marshes provide spawning habitat for some

---

*Like winds and sunsets, wild things were taken for granted until progress began to do away with them. Now we face the questions whether a still higher "standard of living" is worth its cost in things natural, wild and free.*

—ALDO LEOPOLD

---

catfish populations as well spawning habitat for the forage catfish utilize. Marshes also serve as holding areas for run-off, purifying water before it moves downstream to rivers. Marshes also reduce erosion by storing water, preventing it from running off land at breakneck speed. Channelized waters are little more than ditches, with water running too swiftly through them, too swiftly for fish.

Once, a new river, lake, or forest awaited us over the next hill. Those times are past. What we will have is what we can protect or reclaim. Protecting what exists is easier than reclaiming what has been destroyed. What's good for catfishing will continue to be good for North America. Consider economics. One in four Americans fish. Anglers in some states spend nearly a billion dollars a year on fishing-related recreation that has a significant impact on local, state and national economies.

Consider something so esoteric as national security. National security has meaning only when we have something we don't want to give up. Fishing may not be more important than family and friends, but it has an impact on the family and often determines friends. Fishing is important to our lifestyle. Remove fishing as a recreational pursuit and life in America wouldn't be nearly as good.

It's time to band together to protect remaining resources, reclaim those we can, and preach that habitat is the key to sustaining our catfishing future.

# STATUS OF ALTERATIONS ON MISSOURI'S MAJOR STREAMS (1983)

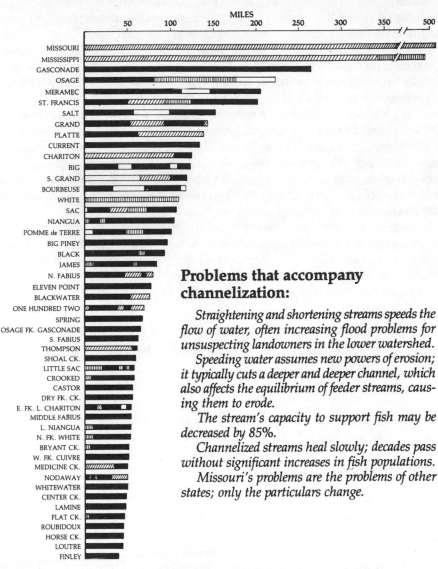

CHANNELIZED
IMPOUNDED
TO BE IMPOUNDED
NO ALTERATIONS

MILES

## Problems that accompany channelization:

*Straightening and shortening streams speeds the flow of water, often increasing flood problems for unsuspecting landowners in the lower watershed.*

*Speeding water assumes new powers of erosion; it typically cuts a deeper and deeper channel, which also affects the equilibrium of feeder streams, causing them to erode.*

*The stream's capacity to support fish may be decreased by 85%.*

*Channelized streams heal slowly; decades pass without significant increases in fish populations.*

*Missouri's problems are the problems of other states; only the particulars change.*

## Catfishery Research

The first fishermen to pay much attention to catfish were commercial fishermen who harvested major U.S. rivers before the turn of the 20th century. Little restriction has been placed on such fisheries, although size limits and restrictions on mesh sizes of nets have been adopted in some areas. Catfish populations have been resilient and catch rates remain economically attractive to netters. But the size of catfish caught in many commercial fisheries shows typical symptoms of overharvest or down fishing—small average size and few old fish.

Despite their commercial importance, relatively little attention has been paid to catfish population dynamics—vital statistics such as growth rate, natural mortality, fishing mortality, fecundity (egg production), and recruitment (number of young fish reaching catchable size). In many areas, catch reports for all species are lumped under the generic "catfish." Finer-tuned assessment techniques, common for trout, salmon, bass and walleye are needed.

In smaller waters where commercial catfishing isn't allowed or feasible, recreational catfishing has been wide open. No size or creel limits exist in many areas. Catfish are unregulated as "commercial species" in some states. Cats have been protected only by inefficient angling tactics that prevail.

Yet as we've noted, catfish are among the most popular fish groups for anglers. Cats are riding a new wave of angling enthusiasm. We've recently seen notices of big-money cat tournaments. To say there's inconsistency here is a gross understatement. It's up to us, the catfish anglers of the world, to ensure that fisheries management agencies do their utmost to maintain good fishing for all catfish species. This isn't an easy task because of the catfish's varied role in the fisheries scene.

In addition to their popular commercial and recreational status, channel cats are the center of a growing aquaculture industry. Their efficient conversion of food into flesh and the high densities at which they can be raised make them attractive to "farmers." Our growing health consciousness and recognition of fish as a prime protein source mean expanded opportunities for growers.

---

*A man has made a start on discovering the meaning of life when he plants shade trees under which he knows full well he will never sit.*

ELTON TRUEBLOOD

---

Yet unlike chickens and hogs, cats also exist as wild animals—populations that must be protected. Because escape of fish from hatcheries and farms is inevitable, and mixing with wild stocks often occurs, genetic tampering—hybridizing species, selective breeding and gene manipulation—must be most carefully controlled. We recommend that fisheries management agencies retain regulatory authority while working with agriculture departments to maximize benefits to farmers and consumers *and* fully protect wild stocks. Regulation by state fisheries agencies of dealers who sell fish to pond owners or lake associations should continue, too.

Catch-out or fee ponds are another facet of catfishing. They are unique in the fishing world and most resemble "U-Pick-M" berry patches. The seller (pond owner) seeks to sell product (catfish) as quickly as possible to consumers (anglers) while also providing recreation. No need for restrictions, except for assuring that genetically maladapted or diseased fish can't escape to mix with wild fish. Receipts should be issued to anglers so law enforcement personnel can tell they aren't wild fish.

Private ponds provide another important source of catfishing. Pond owners should establish their own harvest and stocking schemes after consultation with fisheries management or state extension agencies.

Intensively managed public fishing lakes are often stocked with catfish that may or not reproduce. Fisheries agencies should establish regulations to match angler sentiments, catfish growth and mortality rates, and management philosophy.

Our wild catfish fisheries deserve our close attention and careful management. The sport of catfishing includes unique traditions. Groping (noodling) is unique to catfishing, as is limblining, trotlining and jug fishing. Some of these are basically commercial methods that have a recreational component. We don't recommend banning them outright. But limits must be set that provide for continued health of populations and good fishing. The great importance of sportfishing to our nation's economy demands attention, too, when resources are to be allocated.

High size limits, slot limits and other "quality" regulations that work for bass, trout, and other species in some situations may also be needed for catfish populations. Steve Quinn's studies of flatheads in Georgia's Flint River showed a voluntary release rate less than 2%. Anglers released 25% to 50% of bass caught in adjacent reservoirs. Catfish's food value may be their downfall; release may be required through regulation. In some regions, catfish populations are underfished. Information and education efforts by state and municipal organizations

*Whether river, reservoir, or farm pond, fine quality catfish habitat provides the potential for fine catfish populations.*

might enhance fishing opportunities.

Research on aspects of catfish biology is needed. Several states are conducting large-scale catfish investigations. Some agencies have begun the huge task of studying large-river ecology. Catfish are important pieces in a large puzzle that must be viewed in its entirety to be understood. Since large river systems flow through many states, federal and state cooperation and coordination is needed.

Habitat is critical for catfish, as for all wildlife. Rivers have been badly misused, and it's a long process to correct past errors. But farmland use practices, navigation needs, power and flood-control manipulation need to be reassessed to assure the best possible habitat for cats and other fish and wildlife. Numerous pollution problems and loss of wetlands directly affect catfishing, too, and deserve our concerted efforts. Facing and solving these problems is the long-range challenge.

Zacker concluding his conversation with Doug Stange:

"Danged wonderful, powerful fish," he said as he eased back on the bench. "Say, Mr. Scientist, you know how old those fish are?"

"Experts say the biggest ones may live 40 or 50 years, maybe more," Doug answered.

"Eighty years. Now that's a lot of livin'," he said, pondering his life and the lives of big cats.

"Times is rough and times is good, but fishin' times is good times. Love that danged river. Love them danged cats."

"They're still there?" Doug asked, searching for something to say.

"They are. Danged right. But there's sure fewer big blues and mud cats. Too many dams. Too much river crap (pollution). Some cases, though, folks these days just don't know how to fish cats. There's still plenty fish, 'specially forks."

"So, I've still got time to catch a 30-pound channel cat?" Doug asked.

"Catch a 40 or 50 if you want," he said. "Big cats is easy; simplest thing in the world. Course the size of the fish changes with the water. But you find big-fish water, fish it the right time with good bait 'n you'll catch terrible fish. Danged right!"

# GLOSSARY

## Definition of Select Terms

**Adaptation:** Feature that enables an animal to survive.

**Adapted:** Capable of thriving in a habitat.

**Adipose Fin:** Small fatty fin on back of some fish species, between the dorsal and caudal fins.

**Albino:** Unpigmented animal.

**Algae:** Simple plant organisms.

**Anal Fin:** Fin located on the ventral side of most fish between the urogenital pore and caudal fin.

**Angler:** Person using pole or rod-and-reel to catch fish.

**Aquaculture:** Commercial production of fish for food.

**Backwater:** Shallow area off a river.

**Baitfish:** Small fish often eaten by predators.

**Bar:** Long ridge in a body of water.

**Barbels:** Soft projections for taste or smell on jaws of fish.

**Bell Sinker:** Pear-shaped sinker with brass swivel eye on top.

**Bite Indicator:** Mechanism that allows angler to detect strikes on rod in rod holder.

## CHANNEL CATFISH ANATOMY

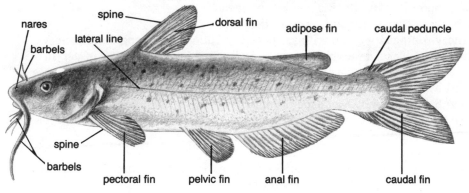

nares, barbels, spine, lateral line, dorsal fin, adipose fin, caudal peduncle, spine, barbels, pectoral fin, pelvic fin, anal fin, caudal fin

**Carrion:** Dead animal matter.

**Catfish Farming:** Commercial catfish aquaculture.

**Caudal Fin:** Fish's tail.

**Caudal Peduncle:** Narrow portion of a fish's body in front of caudal fin.

**Chemical:** Combination of molecules.

**Chum:** Place food items in an area to attract fish.

**Clicker:** Mechanism on larger free-spool reels that makes clicking sound when line is pulled from reel.

**Clutch:** Mass of eggs.

**Commercial Fishing:** Catching fish to sell.

**Community:** Group of interacting organisms within an area.

**Contaminant:** Toxic substance in the environment.

**Crankbait:** Lipped diving lure.

**Crustacean:** Hard-shelled typically aquatic invertebrate.

**Current:** Water moving in one direction.

**Cut Bait:** Fish cut into pieces for bait.

**Dam:** Manmade barrier to water flow.

**Debris:** Natural or manmade objects in water.

**Dike:** Embankment to alter river flow.

**Dip Bait:** Liquid concoction of sticky consistency that adheres to plastic or sponge baits.

**Dissolved Oxygen:** Oxygen molecules dispersed in water.

**Dough Bait:** Pliable flavored bait.

**Drainage:** The area drained by a river and its tributaries.

**Eddy:** Area of slack water or reversed current in a stream or river.

**Egg Sinker:** Tapered, oblong sinker with a hole from end to end.

**Euro-style:** Similar to fishing tackle designed in Europe, especially floats, rods, rigs.

**Extirpated:** Eliminated from former habitat.

**Farm Pond:** Small manmade body of water.

**Fecundity:** Number of eggs produced by a female in one season.

**Feeder Creek:** Tributary to a stream.

**Feeding Strategy:** Set of behaviors used for capturing and metabolizing prey.

**Fertility:** Degree of productivity of plants and animals.

**Fingerling:** Juvenile fish, usually from 1 to 3 inches long.

**Fished Down:** Fish population adversely affected by fishing pressure.

**Fisherman:** Person catching fish by any means.

**Fishery:** Group of fish that support fishing.

**Fishery Biologist:** Person who studies interaction of fishermen and fishery.

**Flat:** Area of lake, reservoir or river characterized by little change in depth.

**Flipping Stick:** Heavy action fishing rod, 7 to 8 feet long, designed for bass fishing.

**Float:** Buoyant device for suspending bait.

**Float Stop:** Adjustable rubber bead or thread set on line above float to determine fishing depth.

**Forage:** Something eaten; the act of eating.

**Front:** Weather system that causes changes in temperature, cloud cover, precipitation, wind and barometric pressure.

**Fry:** Recently hatched fish; cooking method using oil.

**Gamefish:** Fish species pursued by anglers.

**Gigging:** Spearing fish.

**Gradient:** Degree of slope in a stream or riverbed.

**Graph:** Sonar unit that draws marks on paper indicating subsurface objects.

**Habitat:** Set of environmental conditions.

**Hole:** Deep section of a stream or river.

**Hushpuppy:** Deep-fried ball of cornmeal.

**Hybrid:** Offspring of two species or subspecies.

**Ictalurid:** Member of the family Ictaluridae.

**Ictaluridae:** Family of North American freshwater catfish.

**Impoundment:** Body of water formed by damming running water.

**Invertebrate:** Animal without a backbone.

**Jug Line:** Single fishing line suspended below a plastic jug or other large float.

**Keep Sack:** Long, usually cylindrical net of fine mesh to keep baits or caught fish alive.

**Lake:** Confined area where water accumulates naturally.

**Larva:** Immature form of an insect.

**Lateral Line:** Sensory system of fish for detecting low-frequency vibrations in water.

**Ledge:** Sharp contour break in a river or reservoir.

**Limbline:** Single fishing line tied to limb or other shoreline object.

**Location:** Where fish position themselves in response to the environment.

**Management:** Manipulation of biological systems to produce a fishery goal.

**Melanophore:** Skin cell capable of changing color.

**Mending:** Technique used in drifting flies and baits in current; involves flipping floating line back upstream to maintain true drift.

**Migration:** Directed movement by large number of animals of one species.

**Molt:** Shed skin or exoskeleton.

**Mottled:** Blotchy coloring.

**Nares:** Nostrils of fish or other aquatic vertebrates.

**Nymph:** Larval form of an insect.

**Noodling:** Reaching into crevices to catch fish by hand.

**Olfaction:** Sense of smell.

**Omnivore:** Organism that eats a wide variety of items.

**Opportunistic:** Feeding strategy in which items are eaten according to availability.

**Otolith:** Ear bone of fish.

**Oxbow:** Bow-shaped body of water in former river channel.

**Panfish:** Group of about 30 species of small warmwater sportfish, not including bullheads or other catfish.

**Paste:** Pliable prepared bait that can be molded onto a hook or squirted into a bait holder.

**Pay Pond:** Pond where anglers pay by the pound for fish caught.

**Pectoral Fin:** Paired fin usually located on fish's side behind the head.

**Pelvic Fin:** Paired fin usually located on lower body.

**pH:** Measure of hydrogen ion concentration.

**Photoperiod:** Interval during a day when sunlight is present.

**Phytoplankton:** Tiny plants suspended in water.

**Pitch:** Frequency of sound waves.

**Point:** Projection of land into a body of water.

**Pollution:** Material generated by human activity that negatively affects the environment.

**Pond:** Small natural or manmade body of water.

**Pool:** Deep section of a stream or river.

**Population:** Group of animals of the same species within a geographical area that freely interbreed.

**Postspawn:** Period immediately after spawning; In-Fisherman Calendar Period between Spawn and Presummer.

**Predator:** Fish that often feed on other fish.

**Presentation:** Combination of bait or lure, rig, tackle and technique used to catch fish.

**Prespawn:** Period prior to spawning; In-Fisherman Calendar Period between Winter and Spawn.

**Prey:** Fish that are often eaten by other fish species.

**Quick-Strike Rig:** European-style system for hooking live or dead baits; includes 2 hooks rigged in tandem and allows hooks to be set immediately following strike.

**Radio Tag:** Device attached to an animal to indicate its location by emitting high-frequency radio signals.

**Range:** Area over which a species is distributed.

**Ray:** Bony segment supporting a fin.

**Reservoir:** Large manmade body of water.

**Recruitment:** Process by which fish hatch and grow to catchable size.

**Resting Spot:** Location used by fish not actively feeding.

**Riffle:** Shallow, fast-flowing section of a stream or river.

**Rig:** Arrangement of components for bait fishing, including hooks, leader, sinker, swivel, beads.

**Riprap:** Broken rocks placed along a bank.

**Run:** Straight, moderate-depth section of a stream or river with little depth change.

**Salinity:** Concentration of salts in a liquid.

**Sedentary:** Residing within a restricted area.

**Selective Harvest:** Deciding to release or harvest fish, based on species, size and relative abundance.

**Sensory Organ:** Biological system involved in sight, hearing, taste, smell, touch or lateral line sense.

**Serration:** Toothlike projection.

**Set Rig:** Rig cast or drifted into position on the bottom to await a strike.

**Shot:** Small, round sinkers pinched onto fishing line.

**Silt:** Fine sediment on bottom of body of water.

**Sinkers:** Shaped pieces of lead used to sink bait or lures.

**Slip Float:** Float with hole from top to bottom to slide freely on line.

**Slip Sinker:** Sinker with hole through it to to slide freely on line.

**Slough:** Cove or backwater on a reservoir or river.

**Snag:** Brush or tree in a stream or river.

**Solitary:** Occupying habitat without close association to other animals.

**Sour Bait:** Whole fish or pieces cut from decaying fish.

**Spawn:** Reproduction of fish; In-Fisherman Calendar Period associated with that activity.

**Species:** Group of potentially interbreeding organisms.

**Spine:** Stiff, sharp segment of fin.

**Sportfish:** Fish species pursued by anglers.

**Steelhead:** Rainbow trout that inhabit an ocean or large lake and enter rivers to spawn.

**Stock:** Place fish in a body of water; population of animals.

**Stress:** State of physiological imbalance caused by disturbing environmental factors.

**Substrate:** Type of bottom in a body of water.

**Tailwater:** Area immediately downstream of a dam.

**Temperature Tolerant:** Able to function in a wide range of temperatures.

**Terminal Tackle:** Components of bait-fishing system including hooks, sinkers, swivels, leaders.

**Test Curve:** European system for rating rod power, based on weight required to bend rod into a parabolic right angle.

**Thermal Effluent:** Hot water discharged from a power plant.

**Thermocline:** Layer of water with abrupt change in temperature, occurring between warm surface layer (epilimnion) and cold bottom layer (hypolimnion).

**Tracking:** Following radio-tagged or sonic-tagged animals.

**Tributary:** Stream or river that flows into a larger river.

**Trotline:** Unattended line with multiple hooks.

**Turbid:** Murky water, discolored by suspended sediment.

**Turbulence:** Water disturbed by strong currents.

**Waterdog:** Immature salamander possessing external gills.

**Watershed:** Area around a pond, lake or reservoir that brings runoff to it.

**Weberian Ossicles:** Bony process between skull and gas bladder of minnows and catfish.

**Weed:** Aquatic plant.

**Wetland:** Area covered by water at least part of each year.

**Wing Dam:** Manmade earth, wood, or rock ridge to deflect current.

**Zooplankton:** Tiny animals suspended in water.

## IN-FISHERMAN MASTERPIECE SERIES

The sixth book in the IN-FISHERMAN Masterpiece series, **CHANNEL CATFISH FEVER** analyzes one of America's best-loved, but most frequently overlooked gamefish.

Look for these books in the In-Fisherman Masterpiece series:

- **WALLEYE WISDOM:** A Handbook of Strategies.
- **BASS:** A Handbook of Strategies.
- **PIKE:** A Handbook of Strategies.
- **SMALLMOUTH BASS:** A Handbook of Strategies.
- **CRAPPIE WISDOM:** A Handbook of Strategies.

Each masterpiece book represents the collaborative effort of fishing experts—more than a regional perspective or the opinion of one good angler. Each masterpiece book is species specific, but teems with information applicable around the country and to most fishing situations.

**CHANNEL CATFISH FEVER,** like the other books in the series, combines material that originally appeared in *In-Fisherman* magazine with material that appears for the first time in print.

# the In-Fisherman®
## COMMUNICATIONS NETWORK

The In-Fisherman Masterpiece Series including *Channel Catfish Fever*, is but a part of the In-Fisherman Communications Network, a multifaceted, multimedia organization, teaching

**In-the Fisherman® MASTERPIECE BOOK SERIES**

how to catch fish while striving to maintain a healthy fishing resource for future generations.

The In-Fisherman Communications Network began in 1975 with *In-Fisherman* magazine, which continues as the core of our communications network.

**In-the Fisherman®**

Publishing the latest, most comprehensive information about fish, their world, and how to catch them, *In-Fisherman* magazine targets anglers' needs for practical, innovative, and fascinating information.

In addition to *In-Fisherman* magazine and the *Masterpiece Book Series*, the In-Fisherman Communications Network publishes the *In-Fisherman Library Series*, featuring how-to information from individual angling authorities; the *Walleye*

**In-the Fisherman® LIBRARY SERIES**

*Guide* magazine, and *Walleye In-Sider* newsletter North America's #1 source for walleye information; and *Angling Adventures*, a quarterly fishing-travel magazine.

**Walleye** In-Fisherman **GUIDE**

**In-the Fisherman Walleye In-Sider**

**In-Fisherman Angling Adventures TRAVEL GUIDE**

But that's only print media. In addition, we air *In-Fisherman TV Specials*, hailed as the fastest-moving fishing show on television; and *In-Fisherman Radio*, playing to 1,000 affiliates nationwide. *In-Fisherman Videos* present a treasury of angling wisdom on a variety of fish species and

**In-the Fisherman® Television Specials**

**In-Fisherman® Radio**

**In-Fisherman® Video**

fishing situations. *In-Fisherman Product Line* features sportswear and outdoor

**Staff Stuff**

**In-Fisher Kids™**

gear custom-designed by fisherman for fisherman. *Camp Fish*, is a unique educational and recreational facility offering programs for anglers of all ages; while In-*FisherKIDS* is a club for kids, complete with a quarterly newsletter teaching fishing fun.

For information on any area of the In-Fisherman Communications Network, write In-Fisherman, P.O. Box 999, Brainerd, MN 56401 or call 218/829-1648.

TOLLEFSON

I thank Thee, Lord, for these hands of mine
    that can lift a rod and reel,
For the solitude on the river bank
    as I fix myself a meal.

Thank you for each starry night
    that I have pitched a tent,
Where catfish ran, a full moon rose,
    for all these times you've sent.

I thank Thee, Father, for these eyes of mine,
    that's caught a sunset's gold,
These memories I will treasure
    when I take to growing old.

You've protected me when the tide was high,
    and the strong winds began to rise,
And guided my rig to a harbor safe,
    beneath dark, violent skies.

You've taught me, God, through the great
outdoors,
    to see that life is fair.
So I thank Thee, Father, on bended knee,
    as I send this "Angler's Prayer."

                      Sandy Carroll